P9-DWJ-505

DISHING UP® MARYLAND

DISHING UP® MARYLAND

150 Recipes from the Alleghenies to the Chesapeake Bay

LUCIE L. SNODGRASS

Photography by Edwin Remsberg

Foreword by John Shields

Storey Publishing

The mission of Storey Publishing is to serve our customers by
publishing practical information that encourages
personal independence in harmony with the environment.

Edited by Margaret Sutherland and Shauna Toh
Art direction and book design by Jessica Armstrong, based on a
    design by Tom Morgan of Blue Design
Text production by Liseann Karandisecky and Jessica Armstrong

Photography by © Edwin Remsberg
Map, pages 14–15, by © David Cain

Indexed by Christine R. Lindemer, Boston Road Communications

© 2010 by Lucie L. Snodgrass

All rights reserved. No part of this book may be reproduced without
written permission from the publisher, except by a reviewer who
may quote brief passages or reproduce illustrations in a review with
appropriate credits; nor may any part of this book be reproduced,
stored in a retrieval system, or transmitted in any form or by any
means — electronic, mechanical, photocopying, recording, or other
— without written permission from the publisher.

    The information in this book is true and complete to the best of
our knowledge. All recommendations are made without guarantee on
the part of the author or Storey Publishing. The author and publisher
disclaim any liability in connection with the use of this information.

    Storey books are available for special premium and promotional
uses and for customized editions. For further information, please call
1-800-793-9396.

Storey Publishing
210 MASS MoCA Way
North Adams, MA 01247
www.storey.com

Printed in China by R.R. Donnelley
10 9 8 7 6 5

Library of Congress Cataloging-in-Publication Data

Snodgrass, Lucie L.
Dishing up Maryland / by Lucie L. Snodgrass.
    p. cm.
Includes index.
ISBN 978–1–60342–527–8 (pbk. : alk. paper)
1. Cookery, American. 2. Cookery—Maryland.
3. Cookery (Natural foods) 4. Natural foods—Maryland.
I. Title.
TX715.S672 2010
641.59752—dc22
                                        2009052449

To the farmers and watermen of Maryland,
especially my beloved Edmund, and to
my cherished sister, Alexandra, my lifelong
favorite cooking partner

CONTENTS

ACKNOWLEDGMENTS

The idea for this book was in my head for years, but a chance conversation with Mark Powell in the marketing department at the Maryland Department of Agriculture (MDA) rekindled my desire to write it, for which I owe him a debt of gratitude. Subsequently, he and his colleague Karen Fedor sat down with me to share their thoughts and suggestions, which were enormously helpful. Others at MDA to whom I'm grateful are Agriculture Secretary Buddy Hance; my friend Sue DuPont, who always had the statistic I was looking for; and Noreen Eberly of the Office of Maryland Seafood and Aquaculture. All of them embraced this book's vision and its potential to bring positive attention to our farmers and watermen.

Thanks are also due to Pam Art, Margaret Sutherland, Jessica Richard, Amy Greeman, and the rest of the wonderful team at Storey Publishing. I feel privileged to be associated with a publishing house that so thoroughly shares my values.

Thank you to Edwin Remsberg for agreeing to work with me on this book, and for his stunning photographs, which are the visual counterparts to the stories and recipes shared herein.

Thank you to the dozens of farmers, watermen, and chefs who I interviewed throughout Maryland in the course of this book, many of whom shared their recipes as well as their stories. I regret that I was not able to include all of them. I am especially grateful to Holly Foster, who sent me home with delicious Chapel's Country Creamery cheeses; Leo Shinholt for his sublime S & S Maple Camp syrup; everyone at FireFly Farms for the wonderful goat cheeses and a delectable lunch; Scott Fritze at Marvesta Shrimp for those sweet and succulent decapods; my wonderful sister-in-law Eleanor Van Dyke and her husband, Roger, for all their support, never-ending help setting up interviews, finding the perfect location for our Eastern Shore shoot, for the crabs, the rockfish, the expert oyster shucking, the recipes, and just for being who they are; the Balderstons of Colora Orchards for keeping me in apples; Claudia Nami and Susan Lewis for their exquisite Dragonfly Farms

vinegars; Brett Grohsgal for his delicious greens and buttery turnips; Christine Bergmark for her help in southern Maryland and for what she does to preserve farming there; everyone at Roseda Beef, especially Mike Brannon, who sent me home with recipes and all sorts of wonderful cuts to experiment with, and Meghan Norville, who connected me with them; the incomparable Spiliadis family, owners of The Black Olive, especially chef and matriarch Pauline; John Shields, an inspiration and the true champion of Chesapeake cooking; Michele and Jimmy Hayden for taking me with them oystering on their boat; Keith Elliot for letting us use his beautiful dock; and the whole crazy crew of Emory Knoll Farms, who sampled just about every dish that I made — tough as it was, someone had to do the job and they selflessly stepped up to it time and again. My appreciation and admiration also go to the many chefs across Maryland — only a handful of whom are featured in the book — who are committed to cooking seasonally and buying locally. You are leading us by example.

Heartfelt thanks to all my friends and family who encouraged and supported me throughout the process of researching and writing this book, especially my men: Ed, Tim, and Graham, the fifth and sixth generations, respectively, on Emory Knoll Farms. Without my husband, I would never have become a farmer's wife living on a farm, or thought to have written this book, and for those and many, many other reasons, I will always love him. My sister, Alexandra, was, as she has been throughout our lives, a source of great encouragement to me, serving as my sounding board, idea generator, recipe tester, artistic stylist, and cooking companion. Her love and help have made this book better in every way.

Finally, I am thankful to my Ohma, long gone, whose orchard and vegetable garden have been my lifelong inspirations, and I am grateful to the people, she among them, who early in my life instilled in me a love of fresh ingredients and good cooking: my mother and father, Hedy Hauser, Vreni Senft, and my Tante Neck, whose apron I still wear.

Foreword *by John Shields*

I need no convincing in regard to the unique and wonderful flavors from the State of Maryland. It's where I was born and raised. Sometimes referred to as "America in Miniature," Maryland gently dips down from the beautiful mountains along the Appalachian Trail, through emerald mountain valleys and hollers, eventually spreading its watery fingers of tributaries, rivers, and streams into the Chesapeake Bay. When folks from elsewhere hear the state's name mentioned, the Chesapeake Bay immediately comes to mind. Maryland is home to the major share of the Chesapeake waters and traditionally that means seafood — and lots of it.

My family home is in the Baltimore region where I grew up on the delicious products from local farms and local watermen. I began cooking by my grandmother Gertie's side. I remember being a small boy and sharing Gertie's excitement for each approaching season and the treasures it promised for the table. We would marvel at the first asparagus of the spring, breathe in the fragrance of ripe Eastern Shore melons, and laugh at the antics of blue crabs as they escaped from overflowing bushel baskets. When my grandmother prepared the food, be it vine-ripened tomatoes or fresh-from-the-Bay rockfish, I was always aware of the quiet reverence she felt for these prized gifts.

Fortunately for me, we had relatives living on the tranquil banks of Maryland's Eastern Shore. Summer meant trips to the shore, and I grew up eating freshly harvested and skillfully shucked oysters and perfectly baked rockfish larded with smoky bacon. Captain John Smith who sailed into the Chesapeake in 1608 best sums up the preparation techniques of Maryland cuisine. He wrote in the ship's log that "the fish were so thick that we attempted to catch them with frying pans." In the years that followed, the Chesapeake was aptly referred to by H. L. Mencken as "a giant protein factory."

The seafood industry in Maryland defined the tastes and dishes that the rest of the world came to savor and recognize as Maryland cuisine. During the infancy of the United States, Annapolis was for a time the capital of the young nation. Dignitaries from around the globe came to the center of government, and the dining experiences they had were, simply put, Maryland fare. It was the beginning of what the world was to regard as American cuisine. Reading cookbooks from that era in United States history is like reading a Maryland cookbook.

Maryland cuisine is one of the oldest and simplest of North America's regional cuisines. It has certain traits that shape its preparation, flavor, and presentation. The Chesapeake Bay's abundant shellfish are prepared in ways that preserve their delicate flavor. The classic crab cake calls for lumps of blue crab, lightly bound and spiced, to produce a scrumptious mound of crab that can be fried or lightly broiled. The legendary Chesapeake oysters are served au natural on the half shell or are bathed in hot milk enriched with butter in a sublimely elegant stew. Pots of manninose or soft shell clams are carefully cooked until their fragile shells open and release their briny juice, producing delicious dipping broth. In Maryland kitchens, ancestral crab pots hold steaming baskets of lively jumbo blue crabs for boisterous family crab feasts. All manner of fish, fowl, and game are featured in a tremendous number of one-pot meals.

As demonstrated in this wonderful collection of Maryland recipes — some traditional and others newly crafted — the region offers a spectacular array of food choices beyond the well-known seafood dishes. This diversity should come as no surprise to anyone acquainted with the geography of our region. In the cooler climate of western Maryland, maple trees are tapped for sap that's then boiled down to amber maple syrup. It's a notable local product that satisfies a sweet tooth and adds rich flavor to local recipes. The rolling hills and flatlands are home to vegetable farms and acre upon acre of fruit orchards, providing delicious filling for pies, chutneys, and jams. The Eastern Shore has traditionally been the "central valley" of the East Coast — and still lives up to its reputation as a seemingly endless source of vegetables. After a vacation in Ocean City, the trip back to our urban and suburban homes is not complete without a stop at one of the many roadside stands along the way. Sweet summer corn; ruby-red, vine-ripened tomatoes; and heavy, sweet melons are a must — culinary trophies from our holiday.

This book is written from the perspective of someone who knows, lives, and breathes this land. Lucie Snodgrass, besides being a phenomenal writer, is the wife of a Maryland farmer. The reader feels as if he or she is tagging along with Lucie as she takes us on a seasonal, culinary tour through the state. To be sure, there are a goodly number of crab and traditional seafood recipes. But as Lucie illustrates in her recipe selections, the foods and newly created recipes of today are the traditions of tomorrow. She has coaxed handed-down recipes, revered and preserved for years, out of farmers whose families have tilled the same land for generations. Lucie gives the reader a sense of hope and excitement by introducing us to a new generation of dedicated farmers and producers of local artisanal food products. Their newly imagined recipes are included here, too. Feelings of discouragement regarding the plight of small independent family farms is lifted away by the recipes and stories of these new farmers, determined to care for the precious farmlands and open space of Maryland. They will be the stewards of the land for the coming generations.

Farm to table is a new (old) concept that is growing in popularity around the country. As Lucie walks us through the new and ever-growing collection of regional farmers' markets, she offers fresh recipes that pay homage to the wonderful flavors of the seasonal foods offered by local farmers. It is fitting that the recipes we encounter in this book are organized by season. Lucie lives her life on a beautiful family farm and witnesses firsthand the miracle of food each season brings. She sees the shoots of plants as they emerge in the spring. As the humid summer air bathes the vegetables and fruit trees, Lucie watches as these living plants come to maturity. The fall is harvesttime, ablaze with color and bounty, not only enjoyed fresh from the field and vine but also put up and preserved for the coming season. Winter is a time for rest and renewal. The land lies quiet, regenerating itself for a new season of life to come.

Dishing Up Maryland is a culinary love story told by Lucie Snodgrass and the many farmers and food crafters from around the state. She reinstills in us a sense of pride for the wonderful state of Maryland, where generation upon generation has sustained itself. Lucie calls us to be mindful of the way we live; how we shop and eat is crucial to the health of Maryland's waters and fields. It is our health. It is a quality of health that nourishes the natural world, our bodies, and our communities. I invite you to listen to the culinary tales told through the recipes that Lucie presents and to take a bit of time in your own kitchen — dishing up a taste of Maryland.

Introduction

When I moved to Maryland nearly thirty years ago, I first settled near Upper Marlboro, then a predominantly rural town at the northern end of a southern county. I worked in Washington but lived out in the country, surrounded by old family farms with weathered barns full of hand-bundled sheaves of aromatic, drying tobacco. Produce stands with homemade cashboxes abounded, piled high with ripe vegetables, and pick-your-own farms flourished, starting the season with strawberries in May and ending with pumpkins and kale in late October. In summer, roadside vendors with refrigerated trucks sold cheap crabs and fresh rockfish, and church suppers were so plentiful and affordable that you had your choice of fried chicken or barbequed pork almost every night of the week. When the weather cooled, there was even heartier fare: bull and oyster roasts, collards and sweet potato pie, St. Mary's stuffed ham and — for the adventurous — muskrat stew out on the Shore. Food-wise, it was a little like having a Southern mother and a New England father, and I loved it.

Maryland has changed a lot in that time, not always for the better. The vaunted Chesapeake Bay is in trouble, her waters overfished and polluted, and farmland here, as almost everywhere in America, is disappearing at a frightening rate. But there is some hopeful news, too. The number of farms in Maryland is actually climbing, according to the most recent census taken: a sign that there is a renewed interest in agriculture — and from some promising new quarters. Some of the farmers that I interviewed for this book are relatively new to the field and have gone into it because of their commitment to growing local, healthful food in a sustainable way. Even among conventional farmers, there seems to be less of a reliance on heavy pesticides for growing foods — although still far too much to be good for us — and

Maryland has seen an upswing in organic farming, with more than 140 certified organic farms currently in the state.

In the Chesapeake Bay watershed, new steps are being taken to stop pollution from going into the bay in the first place, and farmers are playing a positive, often unnoticed role in that effort. Additionally, Maryland has imposed sensible limits on female blue crab harvests, so that the state's signature crustacean finally has a chance to rebound in a meaningful way. And oyster-restoration efforts, including aquaculture, hold promise for Maryland's ailing oyster population, which a combination of disease, pollution, and overharvesting very nearly wiped out. All of these

steps and more need to be taken to protect our natural resources — and the jobs that depend on them — for future generations.

The positive changes we're seeing are a result of the late-dawning realization that ensuring a safe, local, and sustainable food supply should be among our top priorities. In Maryland, as elsewhere, that recognition has come in part thanks to the sometimes provocative leadership of people in and outside of agriculture — individuals like Alice Waters, Joel Salatin, Michael Pollan, and Barbara Kingsolver, to name a few, and here in Maryland, local farmers like Drew and Joan Norman and Jack and Becky Gurley, who were years ahead of others in their thinking and actions.

And, while it's highly unlikely that we'll ever fully return to the model of the diversified, self-sustaining family farm, it's encouraging to see that many are doing just that. Traveling across Maryland for this book, I was struck by the extraordinary diversity of edible offerings in our state, from traditional favorites like wild-caught seafood and game to farmed oysters, shrimp, and tilapia, to bison, heirloom poultry, and farmstead cheeses to grapes, figs, and an incredible variety of salads and greens. There are also more farmers' markets than ever before — nearly 100 across the state, including a number of year-round markets — with unusual and heirloom offerings that were unimaginable even five years ago. And growing numbers of consumers are buying shares in Community Supported Agriculture (CSA), an upfront investment that helps farmers pay their bills at a time of year when cash flow is slowest. Schools and large institutions, too, are embracing buying fresh, local, unprocessed foods, finally grasping that the cheapest solution is often not the best solution — especially when it comes to addressing the epidemic of childhood and adult obesity afflicting our nation. And even Maryland's governor's mansion has a vegetable garden out front — a clear signal that the politics of food and farming have taken on a new, heightened significance.

My hopes in writing this book are threefold: first, to spotlight the farmers and watermen who work so hard to produce and harvest the food that we eat. Without them, Maryland would be lost. Second, I want to draw attention to the fact that there *is* so much local food available — much more than I think most of us realize. (Kudos to the Maryland Department of Agriculture for the good job they do promoting Maryland agriculture through its Maryland's Best program and website.) And third, I hope to give people a guide — in this case a cookbook — and some inspiration to help them shop, cook, and eat more locally and seasonally. The stakes are so high and our collective health depends on it, but most of us are not making public policy on a grand scale and so assume we can't do anything at all. Nonsense. What we buy, what we cook, and what we eat all have an impact — positive and negative — on what and how things are grown and offered in the marketplace. It doesn't mean that we shouldn't ever eat bananas or

grapefruits, just to cite two things that aren't grown or produced in this region. It does mean that if we regularly make more thoughtful and sustainable food choices, they will not only support local farmers and watermen, but they'll begin to impact bigger issues, like the amount of nonrenewable resources dedicated to producing and transporting food, say, or the amount of subsidized, cheap, processed food that floods our markets and makes our children fat, or fair wages. The less we rely on out-of-season food grown thousands of miles away under conditions that we don't control or necessarily support, the better off I believe we'll all be.

I hope that *Dishing Up Maryland* inspires you not just to eat and cook more locally and seasonally, but to go out and plant your own garden if you can. Or, if not that, then to try to freeze or can as many seasonal foods as possible to enjoy for the rest of the year. It's much easier to do than you may think.

Dishing It Up

This book is organized by season, beginning with spring. Each chapter — through pictures, as well as words — showcases some of the wonderful offerings available in Maryland at that time of year, and every recipe incorporates at least one main local ingredient around which it's built. Obviously, the book is able to focus on only a few of the thousands of farmers, watermen, and chefs who are a part of the local foods movement in Maryland. Still, although the recipes only rarely specify using a named product or "farm-fresh eggs" or a specific local butter, the assumption is that whenever possible, you will try to use ingredients that are local to your area. (For help with finding local ingredients in Maryland, go to the resource list on page 276.) And by all means, use the recipes as jumping-off points if you like, rather than as strict formulas. Many of the recipes work equally well if you substitute a different vegetable, fruit, cheese, or even meat, and I encourage you to play with them and do just that. Half of the fun of cooking is coming up with new recipes and variations on old favorites.

I do hope that you'll also get out and explore Maryland, even if you live here and think you know the state well. Go to Smith Island and meet the incredible people there. Explore St. Mary's City. Go shopping at a farmers' market in Baltimore. Or visit the fall festival in Oakland. You get the idea. Maryland is a beautiful and diverse state, with incredible natural resources, terrific food, and wonderful people.

Happy cooking, happy travels, and bon appétit!

A portion of the proceeds from this book will be donated to the Maryland's Best marketing program.

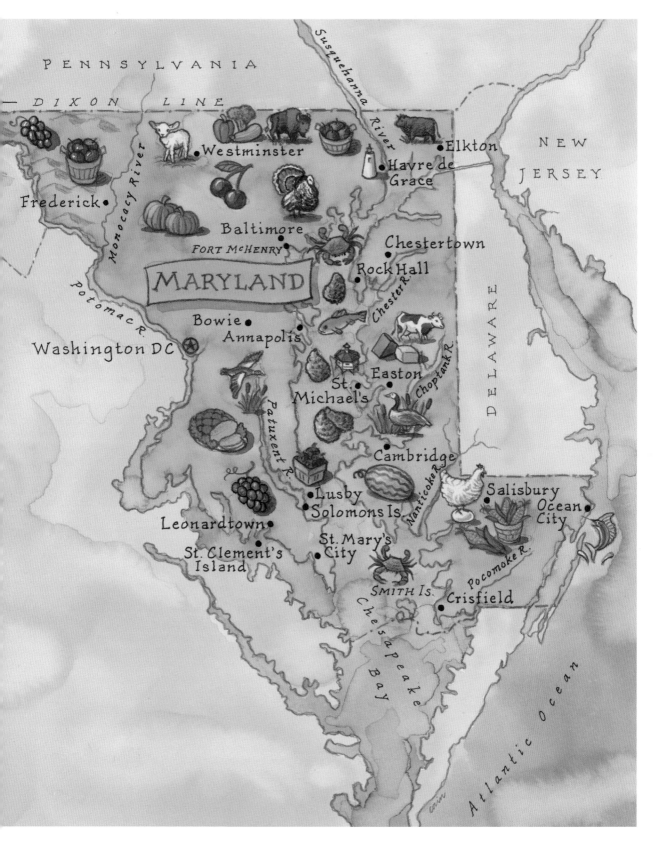

PENNSYLVANIA

— DIXON LINE —

Susquehanna River

NEW JERSEY

Frederick

Monocacy River

Westminster

Elkton

Havre de Grace

Baltimore

FORT McHENRY

Chestertown

Rock Hall

MARYLAND

Chester R.

Potomac R.

Bowie

Annapolis

DELAWARE

Washington DC

Easton

Choptank R.

St. Michael's

Cambridge

Patuxent R.

Nanticoke R.

Salisbury

Ocean City

Lusby

Solomons Is.

Leonardtown

St. Mary's City

Pocomoke R.

St. Clement's Island

SMITH IS.

Crisfield

Chesapeake Bay

Atlantic Ocean

1 Spring

In the spring, Maryland changes out of her black and gray attire and dresses in bright colors, from the clouds of pink peach blossoms to the blankets of green pastures. It's asparagus on the Shore, wild morels in western Maryland, bluebells on the banks of the Susquehanna, and white lambs, yellow chicks, pink piglets, and brown and black calves everywhere. It's the start of baseball season at Camden Yards, the return of the blue crabs, and the reopening of farmers' markets. It's white-water rafting on the Youghiogheny River, fishing on the Potomac, and the running of the Preakness. It's the Flower Mart, maritime festivals, soft-shell crabs, strawberry-rhubarb pie, and pasta primavera with baby peas.

Asparagus Salad with Spring Onions and Orange-Lemon Dressing

Asparagus appears in Maryland farmers' markets around the middle of April, about the same time that spring onions are ready to be pulled. This quintessentially spring salad combines two of the season's best early tastes.

2 pounds asparagus, trimmed

2 oranges

2 tablespoons lemon juice

2 spring onions, finely chopped

2 shallots, peeled and minced

¼ cup olive oil

2 tablespoons white wine vinegar

½ teaspoon salt

¼ teaspoon freshly ground black pepper

6–8 SERVINGS

1. Bring a large saucepan of water to a boil. Steam the asparagus in a steamer over the boiling water for 5 minutes, and then remove immediately and plunge the asparagus into a bowl of ice water. Drain the asparagus, pat dry, transfer to a serving dish, and refrigerate.

2. Bring a small saucepan of water to a boil. Use a zester to remove the zest from the oranges in long, thin strips. Boil the zest for 2 minutes, and then drain it and plunge it into cold water. Drain the zest, and then plunge into cold water again. Finally, drain the zest and pat dry. This process will remove much of the bitterness.

3. Juice the zested oranges. Combine ½ cup orange juice with the lemon juice, onions, shallots, and orange zest. Whisk in the olive oil and vinegar; season with the salt and pepper. Let the dressing stand for 15 minutes to allow the flavors mingle.

4. Remove the asparagus from the refrigerator and pour the dressing over the dish. Serve immediately.

Tom and Lisa Godfrey

GODFREY'S FARM
Queen Anne's County

Tom Godfrey grew up with asparagus in his blood. His grandparents Robert and Hazel Godfrey farmed asparagus and other vegetables in Mt. Laurel, New Jersey, in the 1930s, and Tom's parents, George and Mary Godfrey, moved to Maryland's Eastern Shore in 1952 to start their own asparagus farm. By the late 1960s, they were harvesting 150 acres of asparagus each year, selling much of it to Green Giant's packing plant in Woodside, Delaware. When that plant closed in the 1970s, the Godfreys began selling the green spears locally, a tradition that Tom and his wife, Lisa, have continued. The young couple diversified the crops with blueberries, cherries, peaches, and melons, but it's still their sweet, delicious asparagus that distinguishes them from other farmers on the Eastern Shore. Come April, the spears start pushing their way up from the sandy soil of Queen Anne's County, and customers flock to the farm for Jersey Knight, Jersey Supreme, and Jersey Giant asparagus. "Older people want fat stalks and younger people want the thin ones, but they all taste delicious," Lisa Godfrey says with a smile. "The important factors are freshness and how you store and cook the asparagus."

Three-Beet Salad with Dill and Feta

Among the dozens of certified organic vegetables that Jack and Becky Gurley grow on their five-acre Calvert's Gift Farm (page 106) are Chioggia and golden beets, in addition to some red and some white varieties. You can also make this salad with just golden and white beets, leaving people to guess what's in it.

3 small to medium Chioggia beets

3 small to medium golden beets

3 small to medium red beets

2 teaspoons red wine vinegar

¼ teaspoon Dijon mustard

¼ teaspoon salt

4 teaspoons extra-virgin olive oil

2 ounces feta cheese, crumbled

2 teaspoons chopped fresh dill

2 teaspoons chopped fresh parsley

6 SERVINGS

1. Scrub the beets under running water to remove any dirt, and cut off the tops. Put the beets in a large saucepan, cover with water, and boil them until tender, about 25 minutes. Drain the beets and run under cold water. Set the beets aside until they are cool enough to handle, and then use your fingers or a paring knife to remove and discard the skins. Quarter and then slice the beets, dropping the pieces into a serving bowl.

2. Combine the vinegar, mustard, and salt in a small dish; whisk until the salt dissolves. Whisk in the olive oil until blended, and then pour the dressing over the beets. Sprinkle the feta, dill, and parsley over the salad. Toss the beet salad and cover. Let stand for 2 hours, tossing occasionally, before serving.

FireFly Farms
Garrett County

American cheesemaking has come far in the past two decades. Not so long ago, most high-quality handmade cheeses came from Europe. But Americans now are spoiled for choices produced Stateside, including in unlikely places like western Maryland. Mike Koch and Pablo Solanet started FireFly Farms in the Allegheny Plateau region in 2002, and the cheesemaking operation has grown from a basement shelf in their home to a thriving stand-alone facility with modern pasteurization equipment and a state-of-the-art aging cave.

What hasn't changed, however, is the care lavished upon the thousand or so gallons of goat's milk that comes through FireFly's doors each week. Cheesemakers Matt Cedro and Dan Porter get their milk supply from local Nubian and Saanen herds. They pasteurize the milk, and cool and culture it. The cultured milk sets into a Jell-O–like consistency, and then they cut it and stir it to separate the solid curds from the liquid whey. They press the curds by hand into specially shaped molds, and then ripen the cheeses: turning, washing, and aging them according to different specifications (one variety receives a beer wash, Cedro says with obvious pleasure).

The resulting eight varieties of cheese range from the soft, delectably mild Allegheny Chèvre, to the richly veined, sharp Mountain Top Bleu, to their most aged and sophisticated cheeses: the Bella Vita, Black and Blue, and Cabra La Mancha. Professional chefs and home cooks alike delight in the superb creaminess and flavor of the award-winning FireFly chèvres.

FireFly Farms
Allegheny Chevre

Chèvre Croquettes on Spring Field Greens

This salad is perfect as an appetizer or as a stand-alone lunch with freshly baked bread.

6 SERVINGS

6 ounces (1 log) FireFly Farms' Allegheny Chèvre, or other mild goat cheese

2 tablespoons chopped fresh thyme

Salt and freshly ground black pepper

2 eggs, lightly beaten

1½ cups breadcrumbs or cornmeal

2 medium beets

½ red bell pepper, finely diced

½ yellow bell pepper, finely diced

½ orange bell pepper, finely diced

3 medium shallots, peeled and finely diced

2 tablespoons finely chopped fresh basil

¼ cup olive oil

¼ cup red wine vinegar

1 tablespoon Dijon mustard

8 cups mixed spring salad greens or baby arugula

2 cups vegetable or canola oil

1. Combine the chèvre and thyme in a small bowl and season with salt and pepper to taste. Form six small medallions with the chèvre mixture, using your hands. Dip each of the medallions in the beaten egg, and then coat each one with breadcrumbs and set aside in the refrigerator.

2. Scrub the beets under running water to remove any dirt, and cut off the tops. Put the beets in a large saucepan, cover with water, and boil them until tender, about 25 minutes. Drain the beets and run under cold water. Set the beets aside until they are cool enough to handle, and then use your fingers or a paring knife to remove and discard the skins. Cut the beets into even dice.

3. Combine the bell peppers, shallots, and basil, season with salt and pepper to taste, and toss the mixture together well.

4. Whisk together the olive oil, vinegar, and mustard in a small bowl. Dress the salad greens to taste, and then use some of the remaining vinaigrette to dress the diced pepper mixture. You will have leftover dressing.

5. Prepare the plates by putting a base of the dressed greens on each, and then topping with a spoonful of the diced beets.

6. Remove the breaded cheese croquettes from the refrigerator. Heat the vegetable oil in a large saucepan or skillet. Make sure that the oil is hot before carefully adding the croquettes. The oil should cover the croquettes. Fry the croquettes for 2 to 3 minutes, until golden brown, and then remove from the oil with a slotted spoon or spatula and place on top of the diced beets. Top each croquette with a spoonful of the pepper mixture and serve immediately.

Cream of Asparagus Soup with Rice

The rice in this recipe thickens the soup beautifully and eliminates the need for cream.

2 pounds asparagus

2 tablespoons butter

1 small onion, peeled and chopped

2 garlic cloves, peeled and minced

4 cups Chicken Stock (page 26) or Vegetable Stock (page 27)

½ teaspoon salt

½ teaspoon freshly ground black pepper

⅓ cup white rice

2 cups milk

2 tablespoons chopped fresh parsley

Crème fraîche (optional)

1. Rinse the asparagus well and pat dry. Snap off and discard the tough ends. Cut each of the asparagus spears into three pieces. Place a dozen tips in a small dish and set aside.

2. Melt the butter in a large saucepan over medium heat. Add the onion and garlic, and sauté, stirring constantly, until soft, about 5 minutes. Add the asparagus pieces and cook and stir for 2 minutes. Add the stock, salt, pepper, and rice; cover, reduce the heat, and simmer for 30 minutes. Remove from the heat.

3. Steam the reserved asparagus tips in a steamer for 3 minutes. Plunge them in ice water, drain, pat dry, and then slice each tip in half lengthwise.

4. Purée the soup using a handheld immersion blender, gradually adding the milk until all of it is blended into the soup. Return the soup to the stove and heat it through. Garnish each serving with the asparagus tips, chopped parsley, and a dollop of crème fraîche, if desired.

ASPARAGUS

Asparagus can grow up to 10 inches a day in warm weather, and spears should be harvested every day — they become tough if left to grow too long. Unfortunately, store-bought asparagus is often woody, but if you get fresh-cut asparagus from a farm or market, you can take measures to preserve its tenderness. After the spears are cut, they should be eaten as soon as possible — ideally, within a day, because the accelerated fiber development that takes place during the first 24 hours after harvest will cause woodiness. The higher the temperature, the faster the fiber formation occurs and the tougher the stalk, so you can substantially slow this toughening by putting the asparagus into the refrigerator as quickly as possible after harvest. Also, store asparagus in a moist environment because water loss also increases fiber growth. Place the stalks in a jar of water, wrap them in plastic, or place the stalk ends on a moisture-containing pad — any of those steps will retard fiber development and result in a more tender stalk.

Chicken Stock

Chicken stock is used in countless dishes, from soups to risottos to sauces. You can quadruple this recipe if you regularly use a lot of stock or want to freeze some. Adjust the salt and pepper to your own taste. This recipe calls for chicken bones only. You can boil a whole chicken if you prefer, removing the meat later for a separate use. If you desire a darker, richer-tasting stock, roast the chicken bones first for 30 minutes in a 450°F oven.

4 pounds chicken bones

2 carrots, peeled and thinly sliced

2 large onions, peeled and chopped

2 leeks, white parts only, chopped

2 celery stalks, chopped

1 bay leaf

2 garlic cloves, peeled

2 whole cloves

4 sprigs fresh parsley

2 sprigs fresh thyme

2 sprigs fresh tarragon

2 teaspoons salt

1 teaspoon freshly ground black pepper

MAKES 3 QUARTS

1. Put 4 quarts of water in a large stockpot. Add the chicken bones and bring to a boil over high heat, removing any scum that forms. Add the carrots, onions, leeks, celery, bay leaf, garlic, cloves, parsley, thyme, tarragon, salt, and pepper. Reduce the heat, cover, and simmer the stock for 2 hours.

2. Strain the stock and chill it in the refrigerator for 4 hours. Discard any solidified fat.

Vegetable Stock

Vegetable stock is even more versatile than chicken or fish or beef stock, and the added advantage is that vegetarians will enjoy it, too. This recipe can be tripled, and it freezes beautifully.

½ cup olive oil
4 onions, peeled and chopped
4 parsnips, peeled and chopped
4 carrots, peeled and chopped
4 white turnips, peeled and quartered
3 celery stalks, chopped
4 sprigs fresh parsley
2 sprigs fresh thyme
1 bay leaf
2 teaspoons salt
1 teaspoon freshly ground black pepper
½ teaspoon cayenne pepper

MAKES 4 QUARTS

1. Heat the olive oil in a large stockpot. Add the onions and sauté over medium heat until they are soft but not brown. Add 4 quarts of water, along with the parsnips, carrots, turnips, celery, parsley, thyme, bay leaf, salt, pepper, and cayenne, and bring to a boil. Reduce the heat, cover, and simmer the stock for 1 to 2 hours.

2. Strain the stock. Add additional salt and pepper to taste.

Recipe from ONE STRAW FARM

Sweet and Savory Beet Soup with Orange Juice and Yogurt

This soup is unusual and delicious, especially served with Two-Cheese Popovers (page 179).

6 SERVINGS

- 3 large beets, scrubbed
- 2 cups orange juice
- 5 cups Chicken Stock (page 26) or Vegetable Stock (page 27)
- 1 large onion, peeled and chopped
- ½ teaspoon salt
- ¼ teaspoon freshly ground black pepper
- ⅔ cup plain yogurt

1. Combine the beets, orange juice, stock, onion, salt, and pepper in a large saucepan, and bring to a boil over high heat. Reduce the heat, cover, and simmer until the beets are soft, about 1 hour. Remove from the heat.

2. Remove the beets and peel them under cold water. Quarter the beets, transfer them to a blender with the liquid from the saucepan, and purée thoroughly. Stir in the yogurt. Serve hot or cold.

Cream of Spinach Soup with Toasted Sesame Seeds

Toasted sesame seeds lend a delicate nuttiness to this creamy soup.

4–6 SERVINGS

- 2 pounds fresh spinach
- ½ cup (1 stick) butter
- ½ cup all-purpose flour
- 3 cups Chicken Stock (page 26) or Vegetable Stock (page 27)
- 2 cups half-and-half
- 1 teaspoon salt
- ¼ teaspoon nutmeg
- ¼ teaspoon dried thyme
- ¼ cup sesame seeds, toasted

1. Put 2 cups of water in a saucepan and bring to a boil. In batches, place the spinach in a steamer over the water, steam for 2 minutes, and then transfer the spinach to a bowl. Purée all the spinach and the steaming water in a blender or food processor.

2. Melt the butter in a large stockpot over low heat, and then whisk in the flour, cooking and stirring until the mixture is smooth and bubbling. Whisk in the stock and the half-and-half, and cook over very low heat until the liquid is thickened. Add the puréed spinach, salt, nutmeg, and thyme, and stir until thoroughly combined. Remove the soup from the heat and serve immediately, garnishing with the sesame seeds.

Recipe from THE MARYLAND SEAFOOD AND AQUACULTURE PROGRAM OF THE MARYLAND DEPARTMENT OF AGRICULTURE

Solomons Island Clam Chowder

While visiting Calvert County, be sure to eat some standout locally made chowder at favorite spots, including The Captain's Table, Bilvil's, Trader's, and all three Stoney's locations.

6 SERVINGS

12 chowder-size hard clams purchased in the shell and shucked, or 1 (12-ounce) can chowder-size hard clams

3 large potatoes, scrubbed and diced

2 medium onions, peeled and finely chopped

3 carrots, peeled and finely chopped

2 green bell peppers, finely chopped

3 strips bacon, cooked crisp and chopped

4 tablespoons butter

Salt and freshly ground black pepper

1. Drain the clams, reserving the liquid (strain if necessary). Finely chop the clams and set aside in the refrigerator.

2. Combine the potatoes, onions, carrots, green peppers, and bacon in a large saucepan. Add 3 cups of water and bring to a boil over high heat. Reduce the heat, cover, and simmer for 40 minutes.

3. Add enough water to the reserved clam liquid to bring the volume to 2 cups. Add the clam liquid to the soup, and simmer 15 minutes longer. Stir in the butter and salt and pepper to taste. Serve immediately.

SOLOMONS ISLAND

Solomons Island in southern Calvert County sits in a breathtaking spot where the Patuxent River meets the Chesapeake Bay. Settled in colonial times, when it was first known as Bourne's Island, it was subsequently named for Isaac Solomon, a nineteenth-century businessman from Baltimore who built the island's first oyster cannery. Long an important seafood capital, it was also a highly regarded boat-building center renowned for its schooners, sloops, bugeyes, and later skipjacks.

It's home to the fine Calvert Marine Museum and nearby Patuxent Naval Air Station, universally called Pax River. Solomons Island today supports a thriving recreational boating center and remains a working fishing harbor as well. Commercial watermen still haul in the clams, which make delicious chowder, as well as oysters, crabs, and other seafood. Somewhat overlooked in favor of Eastern Shore vacation areas, Solomons is a delightful weekend getaway destination on the Bay.

Arugula Pesto

This pesto is nice in the early spring, before basil is available locally. The arugula version is also spicier and nuttier than traditional pesto. Serve as an appetizer with crackers, or add to pasta.

MAKES 2 CUPS

1⅓ cups arugula

⅓ cup fresh parsley

⅓ cup fresh spinach

2 tablespoons walnuts or pine nuts, toasted

2 large garlic cloves, peeled

1 teaspoon salt

3 tablespoons olive oil

2 tablespoons freshly grated Parmesan cheese

Blend together the arugula, parsley, spinach, nuts, garlic, and salt in a food processor. Add the olive oil and Parmesan and blend again. Use immediately or transfer to a storage container and refrigerate with a layer of olive oil covering the pesto to help preserve its freshness and color. It will keep this way for several months. Warm the pesto for about 20 seconds in the microwave before using to bring out the flavor.

Oven-roasted Asparagus with Toasted Almonds

The asparagus is roasted in this perfect brunch dish to sweeten and mellow its delicate taste.

8 SERVINGS

3 pounds asparagus

2 tablespoons olive oil

3 garlic cloves, peeled and minced

¾ teaspoon salt

½ teaspoon freshly ground black pepper

½ cup slivered almonds, toasted

1. Preheat the oven to 425°F and lightly grease a baking sheet. Snap off and discard the tough ends of the asparagus. Rinse the asparagus and pat dry.

2. Place the asparagus on the baking sheet. Drizzle evenly with the olive oil, and then sprinkle the garlic, salt, and pepper over the asparagus.

3. Roast for 10 minutes or to desired tenderness. Transfer the asparagus to a serving dish and sprinkle with the almonds. Serve hot or at room temperature.

Spring Greens Nests with Fontina Cheese

The slight bitterness of the season's first greens plays off the cheese's creaminess. Forage for your own greens to make the dish truly unique.

2 pounds arugula, borage, chicory, dandelions, or mustard greens (or any combination of these), tough stems removed

2 tablespoons olive oil

2 garlic cloves, peeled and minced

Cayenne pepper

Salt and freshly ground black pepper

2 ounces Fontina cheese, shredded (½ cup)

6 SERVINGS

1. Preheat the oven to 350°F. Steam the greens in batches over simmering water for 2 minutes, or until wilted. Rinse them briefly in cold water and squeeze out the excess water.

2. Heat the olive oil in a large skillet. Add the garlic and sauté over low heat for about 2 minutes, until golden. Add the greens, a pinch of cayenne (or more if you like), and salt and pepper to taste, and cook and stir for 2 minutes longer. Remove from the heat, and let the greens cool to room temperature.

3. Divide the greens into six equal portions and shape each into a ball. Place the balls in a baking dish and use your thumb to make an indentation in the center of each ball, forming a little nest. Fill the indentations with the grated cheese. Transfer the baking sheet to the oven and bake the nests for 5 minutes, until the cheese is melted.

Recipe from FIREFLY FARMS

Wild Mushroom Tartlettes with Goat Cheese and Bacon

This warm and rustic appetizer can be made with any mixture of flavorful mushrooms, but if wild morels are available, use them.

3 slices country bacon or pancetta, diced

½ cup diced shallots

2 tablespoons olive oil

1½ cups diced wild mushrooms

½ cup red wine

½ cup dried cherries or currants

2 tablespoons balsamic vinegar

2 tablespoons orange or currant marmalade

2 teaspoons minced fresh thyme

Salt and freshly ground black pepper

1 package frozen phyllo dough, thawed

2 tablespoons butter, melted

8 ounces (1 round) Merry Goat Round cheese or other mild, soft, surface-ripened cheese (such as Brie or Camembert)

6 SERVINGS

1. Preheat the oven to 400°F. Cook the bacon in a medium skillet over medium-high heat until crispy. Add the shallots and olive oil and sauté until the shallots are translucent and golden. Add the mushrooms and sauté until they are just beginning to soften, about 2 minutes.

2. Add the wine and stir well. Add the dried cherries, vinegar, marmalade, thyme, and salt and pepper to taste. Stir to combine and reduce the heat to medium. Continue cooking until the wine has fully evaporated. Remove from the heat and allow the mixture to cool.

3. Grease a 12-cup muffin pan. Cut the phyllo dough into 8-inch squares. On a clean work surface, lay one sheet of phyllo and brush it with melted butter. Layer another sheet on top and brush it with butter. Continue stacking until you have assembled six layers of phyllo sheets. Press the stack of layered phyllo sheets into a cup of the muffin pan so that the phyllo lines the cup and creates a small basket. Repeat until you have created 12 individual phyllo baskets.

4. Slice the cheese into thin wedges. Place two wedges in the bottom of each phyllo basket. Top each with a spoonful of the mushroom mixture. Bake the tartlettes for 30 minutes, until the phyllo is golden brown. Remove and serve immediately.

MICHELE & JIMMY HAYDEN
Dorchester County

The January sun is barely rising over Dorchester County when Michele and Jimmy Hayden arrive at the Wingate (pronounced "Wing it") marina, where they keep their fishing boat, the *Michele Dawn*. A small convoy of men in pickup trucks is there already, huddled at the docks, windows down, engines and mouths running. Watermen all, they stare curiously at a visitor, wave laconically at the Haydens, and then finish their coffee before they park their trucks. Each heads to his own boat, alone. The Haydens walk side by side to theirs. Onboard, Jimmy unties the boat and pulls it away from the dock, while Michele lights the small Coleman stove that is their sole source of heat onboard and warms her hands.

The Haydens are an oddity. While watermen's wives have traditionally helped their husbands repair crab pots or keep the books, it's still rare to see a woman — and a young one at that, eyes made up and dressed in a hoodie over several layers of clothing — dredging for oysters or hauling in trotlines, as the 31-year-old Michele does. Other watermen's wives may work full time at jobs that provide health benefits and a steady paycheck, but Michele wanted to work with Jimmy on the boat. They are together all day, every day their boat is in the water. While it might not suit every couple, it suits the Haydens just fine.

On this day so cold that a handkerchief layer of ice covers the Honga River, the Haydens will haul home only four bushels of oysters, partly due to engine trouble that forces them in early and will take Jimmy a week to repair, but mostly because the oysters just aren't there. Despite working nonstop — dumping the mechanical dredge's contents every five minutes or so, quickly but carefully culling the oysters with their gloved hands — two bushels an hour is all they're averaging. At $22 a bushel, this yield will not pay enough even to cover the cost of the diesel fuel they're using.

But despite hard days like this, the young couple — she smart as a whip and outgoing, he much quieter and reserved — say they weren't raised to be quitters: "Nothing good comes easy — so we work hard." Back in October when the season opened, Jimmy said they were pulling in eight bushels an hour, easily making the twelve bushels apiece that their licenses allowed. The oysters, Michele and Jimmy agreed, were the best they'd seen in years, fat and healthy, with no signs of disease. Despite the scant load today, they insist that Chesapeake Bay restoration efforts are working.

In a good year the Haydens bring in about $65,000, enough after all the bait, fuel, and other bills are paid to live modestly in their small, tidy house just a block from the water. Occasionally they get a financial boost when the state selects them to help with oyster-bar cleaning, and Michele supplements their income by designing and selling her own jewelry. It's a challenging life in many respects, made harder by their lack of pension plans, health insurance, and the fragile health of the Chesapeake Bay. But they're passionate in defense of what they do and why. "There is so much history

Jimmy Hayden

behind the tradition — we want to keep that alive," Michele says. And Jimmy, who started out working for a waterman neighbor at the age of eight, says he cherishes the lifestyle and the freedom to be his own boss and go where he thinks the crabs are swimming, the fish are schooling, and the oysters are bedding. They bring home the bounty of the waters and share it with others. To them, nothing is better than that.

Fried Oysters

March is the last of the "R" months, when oyster season is still open. Michele Hayden fixes these whenever she's not too tired and there are enough oysters left over from a day of fishing.

2–3 SERVINGS

- 1 cup vegetable oil
- 1 cup all-purpose flour
- ⅓ cup Old Bay or other seafood seasoning
- ¼ cup onion powder
- 1 dozen oysters, shucked
- Cocktail sauce or prepared horseradish (optional)

1. Heat the oil to 325°F in a large skillet. Mix together the flour, Old Bay, and onion powder in a medium bowl. Drain the oysters in a colander and pat them with a paper towel until they are still slightly damp, but not wet.

2. One by one, dredge the oysters in the flour mixture until they are thoroughly coated. Drop the dredged oysters into the skillet and fry them for 1 to 2 minutes, until they are golden brown. Repeat until all of the oysters are fried. Remove them from the pan and drain on a paper towel. Serve with cocktail sauce or horseradish, if desired.

MARVESTA SHRIMP FARMS
Dorchester County

The story of Marvesta Shrimp Farms (from the Latin "Mar," meaning sea, and "Vesta," the Roman god of home and hearth) and its three young owners, Scott Fritze, Guy Furman, and Andy Hanzlik, reads like the premise for a TV sitcom. A young engineer doing his master's thesis in biological engineering at Cornell builds a model for a hypothetical shrimp farm. He pitches the idea to two other bright 22-year-olds, who decide to join him and turn down offers for well-paying jobs in investment banking and venture capital, much to the dismay of their parents. Essentially penniless, the three plunge in with optimism, conviction, and a complete lack of experience in aquaculture or business. They soldier on through epic early disasters, including the untimely death of hundreds of thousands of shrimp. Eventually, they learn every facet of the business through trial and error (and a lot of support from their parents and the economic development team in their county). They finally have a few shrimp to sell, and once they do, the decapods practically sell themselves. Top chefs across Maryland and Washington DC begin featuring the sweet-tasting, organic shrimp on their menus. The three young entrepreneurs are still doing all of the work themselves, including feeding, netting, boxing, and delivering the shrimp — and the growing demand becomes hard to meet. Eventually, they build more tanks, expand their production capacity to 200,000 pounds of shrimp annually, and even hire an employee.

Most shrimp farms in other parts of the world raise the shrimp outdoors, destroying the environment and relying heavily on chemicals, antibiotics, and hormones. Marvesta doesn't do any of those things. Instead they grow the shrimp indoors in tanks of recirculating salt water with a specific salinity mix and temperature. And they aren't resting on their shrimp shells. They currently buy baby shrimp from a Florida hatchery but want to start hatching their own shrimp. They'd also like to create more local jobs so that watermen and others who have fallen on tough economic times can participate in a new type of seafood industry in Maryland. And they'd like to replicate their model in other places, so they can supply shrimp all over the country without having to ship it so far. "Aquaculture is the last frontier," Fritze says. "Producing our food in a responsible way is something for Maryland to be proud of."

Shrimp Pâté with Crostini

Quick and easy, this appetizer has a delicious bite to it. It's equally delicious served as a dip for fresh vegetables.

6 SERVINGS

1 pound Marvesta or other fresh jumbo shrimp, heads on, in the shell

4 tablespoons butter, softened

2 ounces cream cheese, softened

¼ cup mayonnaise

Cayenne pepper

Juice of 1 lime

2 garlic cloves, peeled and minced

2 tablespoons chopped fresh dill

½ teaspoon salt

½ teaspoon Old Bay or other seafood seasoning

¼ teaspoon Tabasco sauce

1 baguette

2 tablespoons olive oil

1. Bring to a boil in a large saucepan enough water to boil or steam the shrimp; cook them for 2 to 3 minutes. Remove shrimp from the water with a slotted spoon and immediately plunge them into ice water to stop the cooking. Pat the shrimp dry, remove the shells and heads, and devein them. Transfer the shrimp to the bowl of a food processor or blender.

2. Add the butter, cream cheese, mayonnaise, a pinch of cayenne, lime juice, garlic, dill, salt, Old Bay, and Tabasco to the shrimp and pulse the food processor several times, until the shrimp has been chopped into fine pieces. Do not overprocess. Transfer the mixture to a serving dish and chill for at least 1 hour.

3. Preheat the oven to 350°F. Slice the baguette into 1-inch-thick slices. Lay the slices on a baking sheet and brush them with half of the olive oil. Bake in the oven for 5 minutes. Turn the slices over and brush them with the remaining olive oil. Bake for 5 minutes longer. Remove the bread from the oven and let cool slightly. Serve the bread alongside the pâté.

Eggs Florentine

Fresh, local spinach and farm eggs from free-range chickens make this brunch staple something truly special.

½ cup white vinegar

8 eggs

3 egg yolks

1 cup (2 sticks) butter, melted

2 teaspoons lemon juice

Cayenne pepper

Salt

1 tablespoon vegetable oil

¼ cup diced onion

1 garlic clove, peeled and minced

4 cups fresh spinach leaves, washed and coarsely chopped

4 English muffins

4 SERVINGS

1. Poach the eggs: Fill a large, shallow saucepan with water to 1 inch below the rim. Add the vinegar and bring to a boil, and then reduce the heat to maintain a low boil. Crack an egg into the water. Cook the egg for 3 to 5 minutes; remove it with a slotted spoon and set aside on a plate. Continue cooking the rest of the eggs in batches, keeping the cooking liquid at a simmer and adding the cooked eggs to the plate.

2. Make the hollandaise sauce: Fill a saucepan with a couple of inches of water. Bring the water to a low boil. Combine the egg yolks and 1 teaspoon of water in a small metal mixing bowl that will fit snugly on top of the saucepan without touching the water. Whip the egg yolk mixture until creamy, and then place the mixing bowl over the boiling water in the saucepan. Continue to whip for 2 to 4 minutes, until the yolks are light and very fluffy or begin to ribbon. (Be very careful not to overcook, or you will have scrambled eggs.) Remove the yolks from the heat and cradle the mixing bowl on a damp kitchen towel, which will help reduce spinning. Continue to whip the eggs and slowly ladle in the melted butter. The mixture should thicken as you add the butter. If it gets too thick (close to a mayonnaise consistency), add 1 teaspoon lemon juice very slowly until the sauce thins, and then continue again with the butter. If it thickens too much a second time, add a sprinkle of warm water. When all the butter is incorporated, add a pinch of cayenne and a pinch of salt. If you haven't added the lemon juice yet, add it now, and stir to combine. Set aside.

3. Heat the oil in a large skillet. Add the onion and sauté over medium heat until soft. Remove the onions from the skillet and set aside. Heat the skillet again and add the garlic and spinach. With tongs or a wooden spoon, turn the spinach quickly around the skillet until it is just wilted and very slightly cooked. Mix in the onions, and then remove the mixture from the heat and set aside, spreading the spinach mixture out in the pan to cool slightly.

4. Split the English muffins and toast the muffin halves in an oven or toaster oven. Reheat the eggs in simmering water for 1 minute. Place two muffin halves on each of four dishes. Top each muffin half with a mound of the spinach mixture, making a little indentation in the middle of each mound. Remove one egg at a time from the water, using a slotted spoon and carefully draining each egg, and nestle it on a spinach mound. Top each muffin with 2 tablespoons of hollandaise sauce. Serve immediately.

Asparagus Frittata

This is the perfect brunch dish. It's easy to make and the creamy goat cheese complements the asparagus beautifully.

¼ cup extra-virgin olive oil

1 small onion, peeled and finely chopped

2 scallions, finely chopped

2 garlic cloves, peeled and minced

⅓ cup sliced fresh mushrooms

⅓ cup grape tomatoes, halved

2 tablespoons chopped fresh parsley

2 tablespoons chopped fresh dill

2 cups asparagus pieces, cut into 1-inch lengths

5 eggs

1 tablespoon half-and-half

½ teaspoon salt

¼ teaspoon freshly ground black pepper

2 ounces fresh goat cheese, crumbled

1. Preheat the broiler. Heat the olive oil in a medium cast iron skillet. Add the onion, scallions, and garlic; sauté for 3 minutes over medium-high heat. Add the mushrooms, tomatoes, parsley, dill, and asparagus, and continue to cook, stirring occasionally, for 2 minutes longer. Remove from the heat.

2. Whisk together the eggs, half-and-half, salt, and pepper in a small bowl until the eggs are light and frothy. Pour the egg mixture over the vegetables in the skillet. Sprinkle the goat cheese over the eggs and cook over low heat until the eggs are set, about 8 minutes. Remove the skillet from the stove and put it under the broiler for 3 minutes, until the cheese is bubbling and the frittata is firm.

Spinach Cheddar Soufflé

Spring's first tender spinach leaves are the stars in this easy soufflé. You can use any hard cheese to vary the flavor.

1 tablespoon olive oil

1 pound fresh spinach leaves, washed and chopped

1 garlic clove, peeled and minced

4 tablespoons butter

¼ cup all-purpose flour

1½ cups half-and-half

1 teaspoon salt

¼ teaspoon white pepper

¼ teaspoon freshly grated nutmeg

4 ounces cheddar cheese, shredded (1 cup)

3 eggs, separated

¼ teaspoon cream of tartar

1. Heat the oil in a large skillet. Add the spinach and garlic and cook over medium-high heat, stirring occasionally, for 5 minutes. Drain the spinach mixture and set aside.

2. Preheat the oven to 375°F. Butter a 2-quart soufflé dish. Melt the butter in a medium saucepan over low heat, and then whisk in the flour, cooking and stirring until the mixture is smooth and bubbling. Gradually add the half-and-half and continue to cook and stir over low heat until the mixture thickens. Stir in the salt, pepper, nutmeg, and cheese. Continue to cook and stir over low heat until the cheese has melted. Remove the cheese sauce from the heat, and stir in the egg yolks, then the spinach.

3. Beat the egg whites and cream of tartar in a large bowl with a mixer at high speed, until they form stiff peaks. Fold one-third of the egg whites into the spinach-cheese sauce, then gently fold in the remaining egg whites. Pour the mixture into the soufflé dish. Bake for 50 minutes, until a knife inserted into the center of the soufflé comes out clean. Serve immediately.

Pasta Primavera with Baby Vegetables and Fresh Herbs

Baby spring vegetables are like movie trailers for summer's coming attractions. Combine them in this rich, colorful dish that celebrates spring.

½ cup shelled fresh peas

½ cup baby carrots, peeled, sliced lengthwise and halved

½ cup sliced baby yellow squash

½ cup sliced baby zucchini

2 tablespoons butter

1 tablespoon all-purpose flour

1 cup half-and-half

¾ cup freshly grated Parmesan cheese

½ teaspoon salt

½ teaspoon freshly ground black pepper

1 pound fresh fettuccine

3 tablespoons finely chopped fresh basil

1 tablespoon finely chopped fresh chives

1. Bring a large saucepan of water to a boil. Steam the peas, carrots, squash, and zucchini on a steamer rack set over the boiling water for 4 minutes. Remove the vegetables from the steamer and set them aside. Bring a large pot of salted water to a boil for the pasta.

2. Melt the butter in a large skillet over low heat, and then whisk in the flour, cooking and stirring until the mixture is smooth and bubbling. Add the half-and-half slowly, continuing to cook and stir until the sauce is smooth and thick. Add ½ cup of the Parmesan, the steamed vegetables, and the salt and pepper, and heat through.

3. Add the fettucine to the boiling water and cook for 3 minutes. Drain the pasta and transfer it to a large serving bowl. Top the pasta with the creamy vegetable sauce, basil, and chives, tossing until well mixed. Sprinkle with the remaining Parmesan and serve.

MARYLAND WINES

Most people don't know that Maryland's history as a wine-producing state goes back a long way. John Adlum of Swan Harbor Farm in present-day Harford County was Maryland's first maker, cultivating a vineyard on the banks of the Chesapeake in the late 1790s and early 1800s. Adlum was also friends with Thomas Jefferson and is reputed to have given some of his vines to the third president for the vineyard at Monticello. In modern times, Maryland's wine industry dates back to 1945, when Boordy Vineyards in Hydes began producing fine wines on 230 acres in the Long Green Valley section of Baltimore County. Today Maryland has a total of 34 wineries spread throughout every region of the state, producing 300 different wines, selling more than 1.3 million bottles in 2008, and winning many international and national awards of excellence. They all are open to and welcome visitors. Boordy, which also hosts a summer farmers' market and a wonderful concert series, lists ports and some terrific sparkling wines among its offerings, while Fiore Winery, set on rolling hillsides about 20 miles to Boordy's northeast, is famous for

its award-winning Chambourcin that winemaker Mike Fiore, a native of Italy, considers his pride and joy.

Whether you're looking for a deep, soulful red or a playful white, Maryland has wines to please every palate. Newer vineyards are cropping up in southern Maryland and on the Eastern Shore, where the sandy soils and mild climate mimic conditions on New York's Long Island. In western Maryland, Deep Creek Cellars — at 2,100 feet, the state's highest vineyard — takes advantage of its cool nights to produce fruity European-style wines that are perfect for summer evenings under the stars. And Maryland already has five established wine trails in the state, including one in historic Frederick County, where Civil War battlefields and historic homes dot the landscape, and another, the Mason-Dixon trail, straddling the Pennsylvania-Maryland border. Wine tastings are an integral part of the experience, which is why three new trails, the Patuxent, the Piedmont, and the Cheseapeake, are adding even more diversions to a day in the Maryland countryside.

BLACK ANKLE VINEYARDS
Frederick County

Sarah O'Herron, a winemaker who with her husband, Ed Boyce, owns Black Ankle Vineyards in Mt. Airy, is among the new generation of Maryland vintners who have started wineries as second or third careers. As part of their research, O'Herron and Boyce spent 18 months traveling in Europe and the United States to learn everything they could about making wine, and O'Herron undertook three internships, including one each in Bordeaux and California, before they even bought the land on which Black Ankle Vineyards now rests. Black Ankle employs biodynamic principles on its vineyard, utilizing as much compost as possible, keeping pesticide use to a bare minimum, and trying as much as possible to work with the rhythms of the moon, and with a strong emphasis on biodiversity. The beautiful building that holds their wine cellar and tasting room is a straw bale building with many environmentally beneficial features, such as a green roof. As is true across Maryland's wineries, O'Herron is fastidious about her winemaking, lavishing extraordinary care on the grapes to produce a memorable wine made in harmony with nature. Her efforts were rewarded when Black Ankle's lush, intensely dark Crumbling Rock 2006, a Cabernet Franc, Cabernet Sauvignon, Merlot, and Petit Verdot blend, won the Governor's Cup, the state's highest award for winemaking, in 2008 and again in 2009. It's just one of the many excellent choices wine aficionados can now enjoy among Maryland vintages.

Sarah O'Herron

Recipe from BLACK ANKLE VINEYARDS

Risotto with Fresh Greens and Basil

Sarah O'Herron's sister developed this recipe to showcase Black Ankle's Grüner Veltliner wine. The fruity taste of the Veltliner is delicious with the cooked greens in this creamy risotto.

1 pound fresh greens, such as spinach, Swiss chard, or kale

1 teaspoon salt

4–5 cups Chicken Stock (page 26) or Vegetable Stock (page 27)

5 tablespoons unsalted butter

1 small onion, peeled and finely chopped

2 cups Arborio rice

1 cup Black Ankle Grüner Veltliner or other dry white wine

10–15 fresh basil leaves, torn into small pieces

1 cup freshly grated Parmesan cheese

6 SERVINGS

1. Remove the stems from the greens. Bring 1 cup of water to a boil in a large saucepan and add ¼ teaspoon of the salt. Add the greens and cook until wilted. Drain the greens well and chop finely. Set aside.

2. Heat the broth in a saucepan over medium heat. Keep it warm over low heat.

3. Melt 4 tablespoons of the butter in a large saucepan over medium heat. Add the onion and sauté until soft, about 4 minutes. Add the rice and stir to coat thoroughly.

4. Add the wine and cook, stirring frequently, until all of the wine has been absorbed by the rice. Add 1 cup of stock and cook, stirring frequently, until it has been absorbed by the rice. Continue to cook and stir, adding stock as needed, until all of the stock has been used and the rice is tender but still firm to the bite.

5. Stir in the greens and basil, and mix well. Season with the remaining ¾ teaspoon salt, and then stir in the remaining 1 tablespoon butter and ⅓ cup of the Parmesan. Serve immediately, passing the remaining Parmesan at the table.

Chicken Pot Pie with Spring Peas and Carrots

Fresh peas are such a rarity these days that you have to take advantage of them when they're available. Some of the best I've ever had came from the Musachio Produce Farm in Ridgely, out in Caroline County. Michael and Anne Musachio, who have run their 24-acre fruit and vegetable farm since 1979, pride themselves not just on their freshly shelled peas and lima beans, but on the array of unusual fruits and vegetables they grow, including fava beans, Muscatine grapes, Brussels sprouts, and an heirloom Victoria rhubarb that Michael grew from seed. "Customers buy them because they're nostalgic about some of the things I grow. They've had them at their grandparents' house or at their parents', and I like to please them," Michael says. This buttery pot pie gets its sweetness from the peas and baby carrots.

- 2 (10-inch) piecrusts (1 recipe Basic Piecrust, page 76), chilled
- 3 cups cooked chicken, cut into 1-inch cubes
- 2 cups fresh peas
- 1 cup frozen corn
- 2 celery stalks, chopped
- 2 medium potatoes, peeled and cut into 1-inch cubes
- 1 bunch baby carrots or 2 medium carrots, sliced into 1-inch rounds (about 1½ cups)
- 3 tablespoons butter
- ¼ cup finely chopped onion
- 3 tablespoons all-purpose flour
- 1½ cups half-and-half
- 1 cup Chicken Stock (page 26) or Vegetable Stock (page 27)
- ½ cup dry white wine
- 2 tablespoons chopped fresh parsley
- ½ teaspoon dried thyme
- 1 teaspoon salt
- ¼ teaspoon freshly ground black pepper
- Milk

8 SERVINGS

1. Preheat the oven to 375°F. Roll out one piecrust into a 14-inch circle. Fit the crust into a 3-quart deep-dish casserole and set aside. Combine the chicken, peas, corn, celery, potatoes, and carrots in a large bowl; set aside.

2. Melt the butter in a medium saucepan over low heat. Add the onion and sauté for 2 to 3 minutes, until the onion is translucent. Whisk in the flour and cook over medium heat, stirring constantly until the mixture is smooth and bubbling. Whisk in the half-and-half, chicken stock, wine, parsley, thyme, salt, and pepper. Continue cooking, stirring occasionally, until the sauce thickens, 3 to 5 minutes. Pour the hot sauce over the chicken mixture and toss to combine. Transfer the filling to the prepared casserole.

3. Roll the second piecrust into a 10-inch circle. Place on top of the casserole and seal the edges. Make several slits in the top crust, and lightly brush it with milk. Bake for 55 to 60 minutes, until golden brown. Serve immediately.

Grilled Chicken on Microgreens and Mâche with Carrot-Ginger Soy Sauce

Spring brings a dazzling array of salad greens, including mâche, spinach, arugula, peppery microgreens, and more, many of them grown by Cinda Sebastian of Gardener's Gourmet in Westminster. Since 1979, Gardener's Gourmet has grown edible heirlooms, baby varieties, and unusual vegetables and herbs on 40 acres of preserved land, including in 7,000 square feet of greenhouse space. Whenever possible, Sebastian grows her vegetables using organic seeds and with little or no pesticides.

6 boneless, skinless chicken breast halves

½ cup plus 2 tablespoons soy sauce

2 carrots, peeled and cut into 1-inch chunks

¼ cup chopped fresh gingerroot

¼ cup chopped shallots

¼ cup rice vinegar

½ cup peanut oil

¼ teaspoon salt

¼ teaspoon freshly ground black pepper

6 cups microgreens and mâche, washed and torn

¼ cup salted peanuts, chopped

6 Servings

1. Place the chicken breasts in a shallow dish and pour the ½ cup soy sauce over them. Marinate in the refrigerator for 1 hour, turning the chicken pieces once.

2. Make the dressing: Combine the 2 tablespoons soy sauce, carrots, ginger, shallots, vinegar, oil, salt, and pepper in a blender or food processor and blend until smooth. Add 2 to 4 tablespoons water to thin the dressing, as desired.

3. Prepare a gas or charcoal grill for grilling. Remove the chicken breasts from the marinade and grill them over medium heat for 12 to 14 minutes, until the juices run clear. Turn the chicken frequently so that it doesn't burn. Remove the chicken from the heat and slice into strips.

4. Put the greens in a large salad bowl and top with the chicken strips. Pour the dressing over the salad and toss thoroughly. Top with the chopped peanuts.

Curried Chicken with Tropical Fruits and Coconut Sauce

Exotic tastes are married with spring colors in this exquisitely flavored curry dish from my sister, Alexandra Lehmann, a great home cook. Use local, free-range chickens for the best flavor.

6 SERVINGS

- 2 large boneless, skinless chicken breast halves (about 1 pound)
- 1 celery stalk, diced
- 1 carrot, peeled and diced
- 2 sprigs fresh parsley
- 5 black peppercorns
- 1 small onion, peeled and halved
- 4 tablespoons butter
- 3 tablespoons all-purpose flour
- 2 tablespoons hot curry powder (without added salt or garlic)
- ¾ cup coconut milk
- ½ teaspoon salt
- ¼ cup crème fraîche
- ⅓ cup grated unsweetened coconut, fresh or dried
- 1 banana, sliced
- 1 fresh pineapple, peeled, cored, and cut into 1-inch chunks
- 3 cups cooked Basmati rice (kept warm)

1. Wash the chicken breasts and place them in a medium saucepan with 2 cups of water, the celery, carrot, parsley, and peppercorns. Bring to a gentle simmer and poach for 10 minutes. Remove the pan from the heat and let the chicken sit 10 minutes longer in the pan. Remove the chicken from the broth and transfer it to a plate to cool, reserving the broth.

2. Strain the reserved broth into a large measuring cup. Press down on the vegetables to remove all the juices. Add water to bring the volume of broth to 2 cups.

3. Melt 2 tablespoons of the butter in a large skillet over medium heat. Whisk in the flour, cooking and stirring until the mixture is smooth, bubbling, and just golden, about 2 minutes. Add the curry powder and stir until fragrant, about 1 minute. Whisking constantly, add the reserved broth, coconut milk, and salt. Simmer, whisking occasionally, for about 5 minutes, until the sauce is thick and creamy. While the sauce is simmering, shred or cut the chicken into bite-size pieces.

4. Add the crème fraîche and grated coconut to the curry sauce. Stir thoroughly, then add the chicken and simmer another 5 minutes.

5. Melt the remaining 2 tablespoons butter in a medium skillet over medium heat. Add the banana and fry for 3 minutes, until golden. Add the pineapple and sauté for 2 minutes longer. Remove the fruit from the heat.

6. Remove the chicken curry from the heat and transfer it to a serving dish. Mound the rice on a separate serving platter and arrange the fruit around it. Serve immediately.

Cantler's Riverside Inn
Anne Arundel County

Five generations of Cantlers had fished the waters of the Chesapeake Bay, many of them living on the same claw of the Broadneck Peninsula that juts into Annapolis's Mill Creek, when Jimmy Cantler decided to open a seafood restaurant on the point in 1974. There was never any doubt, then, who would supply most of the local seafood: his brothers and cousins. Thirty years later, in what is becoming less and less common, Cantlers, now including the sixth generation, still leave the docks before dawn in search of the crabs, oysters, rockfish, clams, and perch that feed the hungry bodies congregating at Cantler's all summer long.

The crowds begin to swell in May when the soft-shell crabs are fresh out of the shedding tank behind the restaurant and the weather is warm enough for a cold beer on the outdoor deck. Cantler's is a crab shack in the very best Maryland sense of the word. It's real and unpretentious, has no dress code, makes everyone from watermen to international celebrities feel welcome, uses only the finest brown paper for the tablecloths, and serves the freshest local seafood, simply. You sit elbow to elbow at long tables with people you don't know, and by the time you've all picked your way through a bushel of crabs and squirted each other with crab juice, you feel like old friends and walk out back to the washbasin together. It's the kind of place that always smells of beer and fish, where everyone has to stand in line for a spot on the deck and then walk four blocks to get back to their cars, and no one minds a bit.

Crabs are the house specialty, a must-order. Of course, as Dan Donnelly, Cantler's business partner and the restaurant's manager, readily concedes, not all of the crabs they serve are Maryland crabs anymore, because the demand outstrips the supply and people want to eat crabs year-round. But the rockfish, the oysters, the clams, and the perch are all local, and are served in season only, so don't look for oysters in June. When Cantler's has to buy crabs, they buy American crabs, unlike many other restaurants that opt for cheaper foreign crabs. When they have to supplement their own crabs, they pay a premium to buy local crabs from Hooper's Island, home to some of Maryland's oldest picking houses. "We've always tried to stay true to who we are," Donnelly says, "and if it's not broke, don't try to fix it."

Recipe from CANTLER'S RIVERSIDE INN

Pan-fried Maryland Soft-Shell Crabs with Lemon, Capers, and Herbs

Soft-shell crabs are most often served pan-fried between two slices of bread, but this slightly more sophisticated version is wonderful. The pan sauce is tart and powerfully flavored; you need only about one tablespoon per serving.

4 SERVINGS

- 8 medium-to-large soft-shell crabs
- 1 cup all-purpose flour
- 10 tablespoons butter
- 1 teaspoon lemon juice
- 1 teaspoon sherry vinegar
- 1 teaspoon drained tiny capers, chopped
- 1 tablespoon minced fresh parsley leaves
- 1 teaspoon minced fresh tarragon leaves
- 1 scallion, white and tender green parts, minced
  Freshly ground black pepper

1. Clean the crabs and pat them dry with paper towels. Dredge the crabs in the flour and shake off excess.

2. Heat two large skillets over medium-high heat until very hot, about 3 minutes. Add 4 tablespoons of butter to each skillet, swirling to keep the butter from burning as it melts. When the foam subsides, turn the heat to high and add four crabs, skin down, to each skillet.

3. Cover each skillet with a splatter screen and cook the crabs, adjusting the heat as necessary to keep the butter from burning, until they turn reddish brown, about 5 minutes. Turn the crabs with a spatula or tongs and cook until the second side is browned, about 5 minutes longer. Turn off the heat, remove the crabs from the skillets, and drain them on a paper towel–lined plate.

4. Make the sauce: Pour off the frying fat from one of the skillets while it is still warm. Add the remaining 2 tablespoons butter, the lemon juice, vinegar, capers, parsley, tarragon, scallion, and pepper to the skillet. Swirl the skillet to melt the butter.

5. Arrange two crabs on each of four plates. Spoon about 1 tablespoon of sauce over each pair of crabs and serve immediately.

SOFT-SHELL CRABS

Soft-shells are a true spring delicacy in Maryland, but they're served all summer, too. A soft-shell crab is nothing more than a hard-shell crab that has molted, or shed, its shell. In the course of its roughly three-year life cycle, a blue crab will shed its shell up to 23 times, something it must do to continue growing and, for female crabs, to mate. Shedding season is from May to September. After a crab molts, for about four days only a paper-thin husk remains before the new shell starts growing. At that phase, the crabs can be eaten whole. Experienced crabbers can tell when a crab is about to turn into a "peeler," and they'll move it to a shedding tank. As soon as the crab has molted, it's taken out of the water to stop the hardening process, and the crab is graded, packed, and shipped.

Soft-shells are sold fresh or frozen but should be dressed when they're alive. To dress a soft-shell, cut off the face behind the eyes with a pair of scissors. Next, remove the apron of the crab, which is on the underside, and take out all the spongy parts found beneath it: the gills, stomach, and the intestines. Finally, rinse the crab thoroughly and then drain and dry it. If you are freezing the raw soft-shells, you should wrap them individually, first in plastic wrap and then in aluminum foil. They can then be frozen as is, or you can put them in freezer bags or plastic containers. Stored properly, they'll keep for six months. You can also freeze cooked soft-shells using the same wrapping system, but the cooked crabs should be eaten sooner — ideally within two to three months. To thaw soft-shells, place them in the refrigerator.

Recipe from JOHN SHIELDS

Chesapeake Oyster Stew

This rich-tasting stew comes from renowned Baltimore chef, author, and television-series host John Shields. Long before most chefs and food writers were even thinking about local foods, John was helping to define what Chesapeake cuisine is. Schooled first and foremost by his grandmother Gertrude Cleary — the name behind his two restaurants: Gertie's Chesapeake Bay Café in Berkeley, California, and Gertrude's in Baltimore — John grew up with a deep reverence for seasonal and local foods, from blue crabs to oysters and everything in between. Called the "Culinary Ambassador of the Bay" by many, Shields has spent decades celebrating the people and foods of the Chesapeake region and teaching others about their uniqueness. He champions the unsung local farmers, watermen, and old-fashioned cooks, saying that without them, there would be no Chesapeake cuisine left.

½ pound slab bacon
1 cup finely minced onion
1 cup finely minced celery
2 quarts half-and-half
1 quart shucked oysters, with liquor
3 tablespoons all-purpose flour
Salt and white pepper
Cayenne pepper
1 teaspoon Old Bay or other seafood seasoning
2 tablespoons Worcestershire sauce
1 tablespoon butter

8–10 SERVINGS

1. Chill the bacon in the freezer for 20 minutes, and then slice it into thin strips. Fry the bacon in a large saucepan until crisp. Remove the cooked bacon to paper towels to drain, leaving the bacon drippings in the pan. Add the onion and celery and cook in the bacon fat, stirring occasionally, until they are very soft, 4 to 5 minutes. Set aside.

2. Heat the half-and-half in a medium saucepan over medium heat, stirring, until quite hot but not boiling. Heat the oysters and their liquor in a separate medium saucepan, until the oysters' edges begin to curl. Immediately drain the liquor into the hot half-and-half. Cover the oysters and set aside.

3. Add the flour to the onion mixture; cook and stir over low heat for 2 minutes. Whisk in the hot half-and-half mixture and cook over medium heat, stirring constantly, until slightly thickened, about 5 minutes. Season lightly with salt, white pepper, and cayenne. Add the seafood seasoning and the Worcestershire. The stew should be very savory but not salty.

4. Pour the stew into a soup tureen, add the oysters, and stir. Drop the butter into the center and sprinkle with cayenne. Ladle the stew into bowls and crumble the reserved bacon over the top.

Recipe adapted from **GERTRUDE'S**

Rockfish Imperial

This is one of the signature recipes at Gertrude's in Baltimore. When not used as a topping, the crab mixture is a dish on its own and can be baked in a buttered casserole dish in a 350°F oven for 20 to 25 minutes. Serve it with new potatoes or rice and a salad.

6 SERVINGS

- 4 tablespoons butter
- 2 tablespoons diced green bell pepper
- 2 tablespoons diced red bell pepper or pimiento
- ½ cup chopped mushrooms
- 1 cup mayonnaise
- 1 tablespoon Dijon mustard
- 1 tablespoon Worcestershire sauce
- 1 teaspoon capers, drained and chopped
- 1 teaspoon Old Bay or other seafood seasoning
- ¼ teaspoon Tabasco sauce
- ¼ teaspoon freshly ground black pepper
- 1 pound jumbo or lump crabmeat, picked over for shells
- 6 (6–7 ounce) rockfish fillets, skin removed
  Salt and freshly ground black pepper
  Olive oil
- 1 egg, beaten
- 1 tablespoon chopped fresh parsley
  Paprika

1. Preheat the oven to 350°F. Melt the butter in a medium skillet over medium-high heat. Add the bell peppers and mushrooms and sauté until soft. Set aside.

2. Combine ¾ cup of the mayonnaise, the mustard, Worcestershire, capers, Old Bay, Tabasco, and pepper in a medium bowl and mix well. Add the cooked bell peppers and mushrooms. Add the crabmeat and toss gently. Refrigerate until ready to use.

3. Season both sides of the rockfish fillets with salt and pepper. Heat a large ovenproof skillet until it is very hot and lightly coat the bottom with olive oil. Place the fillets flesh side down in the skillet and sear for 1 minute over medium heat. Turn the fish over and sear the other side for 1 minute. Remove the skillet from the heat and turn over the fish once again. Distribute the crabmeat mixture evenly over the fillets.

4. Transfer the skillet to the preheated oven and bake for 18 to 20 minutes. Meanwhile, make the imperial topping: Combine the egg, the remaining ¼ cup mayonnaise, the parsley, and a pinch of paprika in a small bowl and mix well.

5. Remove the skillet from the oven and top the crabmeat mixture with the imperial topping. Increase the oven temperature to 400°F. Return the skillet to the oven and bake the fillets for 3 to 5 minutes longer, until lightly browned. Remove the rockfish from the oven and serve immediately.

BROME HOWARD INN
St. Mary's County

In 1840, a certain Dr. Brome Howard built his bride a classic plantation house with a glorious view on the banks of the St. Mary's River. But 150 years later, when modern technology revealed that the house had been built on top of the first permanent settlement in the state, the state of Maryland, which owned the house, decided to move it to a similar location in St. Mary's City, about a mile away. Michael and Lisa Kelley were visiting the area from the Washington DC suburbs, saw the historic house, heard that the state was trying to figure out what to do with it at its new location, and spontaneously decided to put in a bid to run it as a bed-and-breakfast with a restaurant. Michael's background as an executive in the food-service industry helped convince the state to award the Kelleys the contract.

The personable new innkeepers maintained the original charm of the building and accented it with a tasteful mix of antiques and modern amenities. And now, more than a dozen years later, the intimate but grand four-bedroom inn is a showpiece, consistently rated one of Maryland's best. The gracious white house with its spacious veranda sits on 30 acres of land and still enjoys a stunning view of the river. A day at the inn begins with a sumptuous breakfast cooked by Michael with fresh local eggs and produce in season. At day's end, another fine meal awaits, often showcasing seafood that's been caught that morning by a waterman down the road.

Michael and Lisa Kelley

Recipe from THE BROME HOWARD INN

Grilled Confetti Rockfish

It's hard to surpass the sweet, delicate flavor of fresh, wild rockfish, also known as striped bass. It's a fish that wants little, if any, additional seasoning. In this recipe, a simple confetti salsa and a bed of couscous combine to dress up this elegant entrée.

1½–2 **pounds rockfish fillets, skin-on**

2 **tablespoons olive oil**

¼ **cup finely diced carrot**

¼ **cup finely diced red bell pepper**

¼ **cup finely diced onion**

½ **cup finely diced tomato**

¼ **cup finely diced cucumber**

2 **tablespoons finely chopped cilantro**

1 **tablespoon lime juice**

½ **teaspoon salt**

¼ **teaspoon freshly ground black pepper**

3 **cups cooked couscous, kept warm**

Lemon or lime slices

4 SERVINGS

1. Prepare a gas or charcoal grill for grilling. Clean the rockfish by trimming away any belly fat and fins. Score the skin two to three times in opposite directions to just below the surface of the skin, using a sharp knife and being careful not to cut too deeply (this prevents curling of the fillet during cooking). If necessary, cut the fillets into more manageable sizes.

2. Make the confetti salsa: Heat 1 tablespoon of the olive oil in a medium skillet. Add the carrot, red pepper, and onion, and sauté over medium-high heat for 2 minutes, until the vegetables begin to soften. Remove from the heat and stir in the tomato, cucumber, cilantro, and lime juice.

3. Brush the rockfish fillets on both sides with the remaining tablespoon olive oil. Sprinkle the fish with the salt and pepper and place the pieces skin side up on the grill. Grill the rockfish for 2 to 3 minutes on each side, being careful not to overcook.

4. Mound the couscous evenly on four plates, or on one large platter if serving family-style. Lay the fish over the couscous. Spoon the salsa over the fish. Garnish with lemon or lime slices.

Boneless Spring Lamb Roast

Maryland still has many farms that raise succulent spring lambs, including Zekiah Farms in Charles County, Jehovah Jireh Farm in Washington County, Bietschehof Farm in Garrett County, and Greene's Lamb Farm in Baltimore County. Most of these farms sell their meats locally, although some will ship, as well. Scented with garlic and Mediterranean seasonings, this roast is delicious with Gratin Dauphinois (page 230).

1 lemon
¾ cup olive oil
10 garlic cloves, peeled
2 teaspoons dried oregano
2 teaspoons dried rosemary leaves
½ teaspoon paprika
½ teaspoon salt
1 (3–3½ pound) boneless leg of lamb
1 tablespoon coarse sea salt
1 teaspoon freshly ground black pepper

6 SERVINGS

1. Zest and juice the lemon. Combine the lemon zest and juice with the olive oil, 3 of the garlic cloves, 1 teaspoon of the oregano, 1 teaspoon of the rosemary, the paprika, and the salt in a blender or food processor and blend until smooth. Place the leg of lamb in a large ziplock bag and add the marinade. Put the ziplock bag into a larger plastic bag or large container to ensure there is no leakage and place it in the refrigerator to marinate overnight, or for at least 4 hours.

2. Remove the lamb from the refrigerator and allow the contents to come to room temperature. Preheat the oven to 450°F. Remove the lamb from the bag and pat dry. Combine the remaining 1 teaspoon oregano and 1 teaspoon rosemary with the sea salt and pepper. Rub this mixture all over the lamb. Cut small incisions into the lamb and insert the remaining 7 garlic cloves into the incisions. Insert a meat thermometer into the roast.

3. Place the lamb on a rack in a roasting pan, fattiest side up. Roast for 15 minutes. Reduce the oven to 325°F and roast an additional 10 to 15 minutes per pound, 30 to 45 minutes, until a meat thermometer reads 140°F for medium rare to 150°F for medium. Remove the lamb from the oven, cover it with foil or a lid, and allow it to rest for 20 minutes. Cut the strings from the lamb and transfer the roast to a serving platter. Cut the lamb into ½-inch-thick slices. Strain the pan drippings and pour them over the lamb.

Recipe from **ROSEDA BEEF**

Flank Steak Salad with Mixed Spring Greens and Ranch Dressing

Maryland is home to Roseda Beef, one of the largest and choicest Angus cattle operations on the East Coast. Mike Brannon, Roseda Beef's director of operations, prepares this signature dish by baking the steak in the oven, instead of grilling it, which is perfect for cool or rainy spring days.

1 (1–1¼ pound) flank steak
1 tablespoon sea salt
1 tablespoon freshly ground black pepper
1 (12-ounce) bottle of honey brown beer or lager
¼ cup finely chopped onion
1 teaspoon olive oil
2 whole heads garlic, loose skin discarded
4 cups mixed spring lettuce
   Ranch Dressing (page 71)

3–4 SERVINGS

1. Pound the steak with a tenderizer or with the edge of a saucer. Mix the salt and pepper together and rub the steak with the mixture.

2. Place the steak in a ziplock bag and pour in enough beer to cover the steak. Add the onion and seal the bag, squeezing out any air. Refrigerate and allow the marinade to permeate the steak for at least 1 hour.

3. Preheat the oven to 450°F. Grease a rimmed baking sheet with the olive oil. Cut the heads of garlic crosswise and place them onto the sheet to hold the steak above the surface of the sheet.

4. Heat a cast iron skillet until it is extremely hot. Remove the steak from the bag and pat dry. Cook the steak in the skillet over high heat for 1 to 2 minutes on each side, until the steak is well seared.

5. Place the steak on top of the garlic and transfer the baking sheet to the oven. Bake for 15 minutes, and then use tongs to check for desired doneness (a rare steak will feel spongy, while a well-done steak will be firm). Remove the steak from the oven, place it on a cutting board, and allow it to rest for 5 minutes before slicing. Arrange the lettuce on a serving platter. Slice the steak against the grain and arrange over the lettuce. Top the steak and salad with ranch dressing.

Ranch Dressing

½ cup buttermilk

¼ cup mayonnaise

¼ cup sour cream

2 tablespoons lemon or lime juice

1 garlic clove, peeled

⅛ teaspoon salt

⅛ teaspoon freshly ground black pepper

1 teaspoon chopped fresh parsley

1 teaspoon snipped fresh chives

MAKES 1 CUP

Combine the buttermilk, mayonnaise, sour cream, lemon juice, garlic, salt, and pepper in a blender or food processor. Briefly blend or pulse until the dressing is well mixed. Stir in the parsley and chives. Refrigerate until needed.

NOTE: The dressing will keep in the refrigerator for at least 1 week and makes a terrific dip for vegetables or tortilla chips, too.

Ricotta Hotcakes with Strawberry Compote

Ethereally light, these hotcakes with cooked strawberries are habit-forming. Other berries or stewed fruits, depending on the season, work well, too.

2–4 SERVINGS

- 2 cups strawberries, hulled and sliced
- ¼ cup sugar
- 2 eggs, separated
- ½ cup ricotta cheese
- ½ cup milk
- ⅓ cup all-purpose flour
- 2 teaspoons baking powder
- 1–2 tablespoons vegetable oil

1. Make the compote: Combine the strawberries, ¼ cup water, and the sugar in a small saucepan. Bring the mixture to a boil and reduce the heat. Simmer until the strawberries are soft and cooked, about 5 minutes. Remove the strawberry compote from the heat and transfer it to a bowl to cool for 10 minutes.

2. Beat the egg whites in a mixing bowl with a whisk or electric mixer at high speed until they form stiff peaks. Set the egg whites aside. Combine the egg yolks, ricotta, and milk in a medium bowl and mix until blended. Add the flour and baking powder. Carefully fold the egg whites into the egg yolk mixture, gently blending them together, but not overmixing.

3. Lightly coat a large skillet with oil and heat until hot but not smoking. Ladle in enough batter for the desired pancake size and fry the hotcakes over medium heat until they are cooked through and golden, about 2 minutes on each side. Serve immediately with the warm strawberry compote.

Rhubarb and Red Currant Fool

I have a soft spot for rhubarb, partly because of my Swiss heritage (rhubarb is as common in Swiss gardens as it is in English ones) and partly because it's the first potentially sweet thing to grow in the garden. And red currants, which ripen in June in Maryland, are simply underappreciated for their taste and for the amount of vitamin C that they pack. I grow both of them in my garden, but they're also readily available at farmers' markets, if not at supermarkets. They're among the fleeting and therefore special tastes of late spring and early summer.

Rhubarb and red currants are sympathetically paired in this dessert, because the sweetness of the whipped cream contrasts beautifully with their tart tastes and pinkish red colors. If you absolutely can't find local red currants, substitute strawberries.

1¼ cups sugar

1½ pounds rhubarb, trimmed, woody fibers removed, and chopped

1 teaspoon lemon zest

1½ pounds red currants, stems removed

1 pint heavy cream

1 teaspoon vanilla extract

Mint leaves

6 SERVINGS

1. Preheat the oven to 375°F. Mix together ½ cup of the sugar, the rhubarb, and the lemon zest in a baking dish. Cover and bake for 45 minutes, until the rhubarb is completely soft. Drain the juice, purée the rhubarb, and transfer the purée to a bowl.

2. Combine the red currants with ½ cup of the remaining sugar in a food processor or blender and purée until smooth.

3. Whip the cream, vanilla, and the remaining ¼ cup sugar in a chilled bowl with an electric mixer. Transfer the whipped cream to a trifle dish and alternate folding in the rhubarb and the red currant purées, deliberately making streaks of color. Garnish with mint.

Strawberry-Rhubarb Pie

Tart yet sweet strawberry-rhubarb pie is a Maryland tradition, marking the start of the fresh fruit pie season. Served warm with Vanilla-Bean Ice Cream (page 77) or whipped cream, it's sure to please. Buy your strawberries locally at places like Shlagel Farms in Waldorf, a former tobacco farm owned and run by Russ and Eileen Shlagel and their five children. It's one of many "pick your own" farms in the state.

2 (10-inch) piecrusts (1 recipe Basic Piecrust, page 76)

4 cups fresh, local strawberries

4 large stalks local rhubarb, trimmed, woody fibers removed, and cut into 1-inch-thick slices (2½ cups)

1½ cups of sugar

3 tablespoons tapioca flour or 2 tablespoons quick-cooking tapioca

2 tablespoons all-purpose flour

1 egg yolk, beaten

1 teaspoon vanilla extract

½ teaspoon cinnamon

⅛ teaspoon nutmeg

1. Preheat the oven to 400°F. Line a 10-inch pie plate with one of the crusts and put the pie plate in the refrigerator, along with the second crust, to chill.

2. Rinse and hull the strawberries, slicing them into a large bowl. Add the rhubarb to the strawberries. Add the sugar, tapioca flour, all-purpose flour, egg yolk, vanilla, cinnamon, and nutmeg to the fruit mixture and toss until blended. Spoon the fruit mixture into the crust-lined pie plate.

3. Cover the pie with the second crust and crimp and seal the edges. Make slits in the piecrust to allow steam to escape from the pie. Bake the pie at 400°F for 15 minutes. Reduce the oven to 375°F and bake for an additional 40 minutes. If necessary, collar the pie with aluminum foil to keep the edge of the crust from getting too brown.

Basic Piecrust

I have been making this crust since I was a little girl, and it's never failed me. It's the same basic crust that my grandmother and millions of other bakers have used for generations. The keys are to use good-quality, cold ingredients.

1 cup (2 sticks) cold butter
2½ cups all-purpose flour
⅛ teaspoon salt
¼ cup ice water

MAKES TWO 10-INCH PIECRUSTS

1. Cut the butter into small pieces and put it in the bowl of a food processor or, if you prefer to make the crust by hand, in a large mixing bowl. Sift together the flour and salt, and then add to the butter.

2. Pulse the mixture in the food processor for about 5 seconds or cut in the butter with a pastry cutter until the mixture is crumbly. Add the ice water a few drops at a time, pulsing or mixing, until the dough holds together but is not sticky.

3. Form the dough into two equal balls and wrap each piece in plastic wrap, flattening the balls. Chill until needed.

PIECRUST VARIATIONS

There are many variations of the Basic Piecrust recipe given above, and they all work well, depending on your need or inclination. If you are using the crusts to bake a dessert, you can add a tablespoon of sugar to the dough to sweeten it. Sometimes I will add a teaspoon of vinegar to the dough, which helps to relax the glutens and keeps the dough from getting tough. If you prefer even richer, sweeter dough, you can also add an egg yolk and another teaspoon of sugar to it. And if you like to use nut flours, which I do, you can substitute ½ cup of almond, hazelnut, or pecan flour for an equal amount of the all-purpose flour. To make nut flours, just grind the nuts in a food processor or blender.

If you prefer the taste and texture of shortening, you can substitute that for the butter, or you can use both butter and shortening in equal proportions. For cherry and blueberry pies, I usually use ½ cup of butter and ½ cup shortening. Many bakers use vegetable oil in their crusts, which I don't care for, but many others love. Experiment a little bit yourself to see what you like best. You may be among the bakers who still swear by lard for the lightest, flakiest crust.

Vanilla-Bean Ice Cream

Vanilla ice cream is the dessert accompaniment of choice to pies and many other baked goods in my household.

1 pint heavy cream
1 cup whole milk
½ cup sugar
⅛ teaspoon salt
2 vanilla beans, split lengthwise
3 eggs

4 SERVINGS

1. Combine the cream, milk, sugar, and salt in a saucepan. Scrape the seeds from the vanilla beans with the tip of a knife and add the seeds and the pods to the cream mixture. Heat the cream mixture over medium heat just to the boiling point. Remove from the heat and remove the bean pods.

2. Whisk the eggs in a large bowl, and then whisk in the hot cream mixture in a slow stream. Pour this custard mixture back into the saucepan and cook over medium-low heat, stirring constantly, until slightly thickened and heated to 170°F on a candy thermometer (do not let the custard boil). Pour the custard through a fine-mesh sieve into a clean metal bowl and let it cool, stirring occasionally. Chill, covered, until cold, at least 3 hours. (See Note.)

3. Freeze the custard in an ice cream maker according to the manufacturer's instructions. Transfer the ice cream to an airtight container and store in the freezer.

NOTE: To cool custard quickly after straining, set the bowl into a larger bowl of ice and cold water and stir until chilled. Custard can be chilled up to 24 hours before freezing.

Strawberry Shortcake with Biscuits

In the South, strawberry shortcake is always made with biscuits rather than sponge cake; in this and many other culinary leanings, Maryland seems to side with the South over the North. I always serve this dessert for Memorial Day, the traditional start of Maryland's strawberry season.

½ cup sugar

2 quarts strawberries, hulled and cut in half

2 cups all-purpose flour

3 teaspoons baking powder

1 teaspoon lemon zest

¼ teaspoon salt

6 tablespoons cold butter, cut into small pieces

1 egg

½ cup half-and-half

1 pint whipping cream

6 SERVINGS

1. Sprinkle 3 tablespoons of the sugar on top of the strawberries and toss. Cover and macerate for 1 hour.

2. Preheat the oven to 425°F. Combine the flour, 3 tablespoons of the remaining sugar, the baking powder, lemon zest, and salt in a large bowl and mix well. Add the butter, cutting it in until the mixture is crumbly.

3. Whisk together the egg and the half-and-half in a small bowl until blended. Add the egg mixture to the flour mixture and stir until moist. Turn out the dough onto a floured surface and knead it three times. Roll out the dough to a ½-inch thickness and, using a biscuit cutter, cut out 6 biscuits. Bake them on an ungreased baking sheet for 10 minutes, until golden brown.

4. Combine the cream and the remaining 2 tablespoons sugar in a chilled bowl. Whip with a whisk or electric mixer until soft peaks form.

5. Split the biscuits and spoon strawberries over them. Top with whipped cream and serve warm.

2 Summer

Maryland summers are spent outdoors: eating crabs, boating on rivers, sitting on stoops, grilling in suburban backyards, and swimming in Ocean City. Summers mean watching the Orioles at Camden Yards, picking blueberries, taking the kids to the county fairs, and kayaking on Deep Creek Lake. They're about sailing the Bay, canoeing at Blackwater, fireworks in Havre de Grace, Artscape in Baltimore, birding on Mt. Savage, and touring St. Mary's City. And with all of that, there is food: spicy and sweet, hot and cold, crab feasts and grilled beef, fried chicken and seafood frys, sugary tea and lemonade, corn and coleslaw, sweet berries, fruit pies and cobblers, and even more.

Cucumber Salad with Dill, Feta, and Red Onion in Tangy Vinaigrette

Crumbly feta gives this salad a nice salty counterpoint to the crisp cucumbers and piquant dressing. This is wonderful served with Southern Fried Chicken (page 110), grilled meats, or just about any other main course.

4 large cucumbers

½ teaspoon salt

1 medium red onion, peeled

½ teaspoon Dijon mustard

2 tablespoons white wine vinegar, preferably balsamic

¼ cup extra-virgin olive oil

¼ teaspoon freshly ground black pepper

2 tablespoons chopped fresh dill

8 ounces feta cheese, crumbled

8 SERVINGS

1. Peel the cucumbers and slice them into ¼-inch-thick rounds. Transfer the cucumbers to a bowl and sprinkle them with ¼ teaspoon of the salt. Let the cucumbers sit for 15 minutes and then squeeze them out and discard the excess water.

2. Quarter the onion and slice the quarters into very thin strips. Add the onion to the cucumbers.

3. Combine the mustard and vinegar in a small bowl, stirring to dissolve the mustard. Add the olive oil and whisk together until smooth. Add the remaining ¼ teaspoon salt and the pepper and pour over the cucumbers. Sprinkle the dill and the feta cheese over the salad and toss well until thoroughly blended. Chill for at least 1 hour before serving.

Cucumber Salad with Asian Dressing

This intriguing variation on classic cucumber salad is rejuvenating on the hottest of summer days.

4–6 SERVINGS

2 large cucumbers

½ teaspoon salt

2 tablespoons sesame seeds

½ cup cider or rice vinegar

1 cup toasted (dark) sesame oil

¼ cup peanut oil

¼ cup light soy sauce or tamari

1 tablespoon peeled and chopped gingerroot

2 garlic cloves, peeled and chopped

¼ onion, peeled and chopped

½ teaspoon dried tarragon

¼ cup packed fresh mint leaves

4 scallions, white and tender green parts, chopped

1 tablespoon honey

1 tablespoon white wine

1 egg

1. Peel and thinly slice the cucumbers and transfer them to a colander in the sink. Sprinkle with ¼ teaspoon of the salt and allow the cucumbers to drain for 30 minutes. Gently press down on the cucumbers to squeeze out any remaining water. Transfer the cucumbers to a medium salad bowl.

2. Make the dressing: Toast the sesame seeds in a skillet over medium heat until golden brown; cool 5 minutes. Blend the remaining ¼ teaspoon salt, the vinegar, sesame oil, peanut oil, soy sauce, ginger, garlic, onion, tarragon, mint, scallions, honey, white wine, and egg in a blender for 30 to 60 seconds, until smooth. You should have about 1½ cups dressing.

3. Pour ⅓ cup of the dressing over the cucumbers and refrigerate the salad for at least 1 hour before serving. Refrigerate the remaining dressing for future use. It will keep for several weeks.

NOTE: If you prefer not to use the raw egg in the dressing, substitute a pasteurized egg product.

Corn and Quinoa Salad with Lemony Mint Dressing

This is a most refreshing and delicious summer salad. If you don't want to roast the corn on the grill, just steam it and cut it from the cob.

4 ears corn in their husks

1 cup quinoa, rinsed well

1 teaspoon salt

4 scallions, white and tender green parts, thinly sliced then chopped

½ cup fresh mint leaves, cut into thin ribbons then chopped

1 tablespoon lemon zest

¼ cup lemon juice

2 tablespoons honey (preferably unfiltered)

¼ cup olive oil

¼ teaspoon freshly ground black pepper

1. Pull the husks of the corn back, but not off. Remove the silk from each ear of corn and then pull the husks back up. Roast the ears of corn over a hot grill for 5 minutes, turning the ears several times so that they roast evenly. Let the corn cool slightly. Shuck the ears and cut the corn from the cobs with a sharp knife. Put the corn into a large bowl.

2. Combine the quinoa with 2 cups water and ½ teaspoon of the salt in a medium saucepan and bring to a boil. Cook for 8 to 10 minutes, until all of the water has been absorbed. Remove from the heat, fluff, and set aside for 5 minutes.

3. Add the scallions and the mint to the roasted corn. Add the quinoa, the remaining ½ teaspoon salt, the lemon zest, lemon juice, honey, olive oil, and pepper, and toss well. Cover and allow the salad to marinate for at least 2 hours before serving.

CORN

Every week without fail from July to September, I buy at least two dozen ears of Quigley Farm corn. Bill Hanna, his daughter Amy, and his son-in-law, Todd Steiner, grow the best corn in the state, and I'm not the only one who thinks so. In 2008 their early, bicolor Temptation corn took first prize at the state fair. I just steam it for 3 minutes, boil a few potatoes from the garden, melt some butter, slice some tomatoes, and call it dinner.

Freezing corn is so simple that everyone should do it if they have enough freezer space. Working with six ears at a time, shuck the corn and steam the ears in batches for 2 minutes over boiling water on a steamer rack. Remove the rack from the pot and immediately put the corn in ice water to stop the cooking. Drain the corn in a colander, shake off any excess moisture, and then cut the kernels from the cobs and transfer them to 1-gallon ziplock bags, making sure to expel as much air as possible, so the bags lie flat. Repeat the process as needed to prepare all the corn. The corn keeps beautifully for six months in the freezer.

Corn Fritters with Sweet and Spicy Dipping Sauce

Sweetly crunchy and suggestively spicy, these are crowd pleasers.

4 SERVINGS

- 1 egg, separated
- 2 cups fresh white and yellow corn kernels
- ¼ cup all-purpose flour
- ¼ cup milk
- 1 tablespoon butter, melted
- 1 teaspoon baking powder
- 1 tablespoon grated onion
- 1 teaspoon salt
- ⅛ teaspoon cayenne pepper
- 2 tablespoons honey mustard
- 1 teaspoon prepared horseradish
- 2 tablespoons chopped fresh parsley
- 1 cup vegetable oil

1. Preheat the oven to 200°F. Beat the egg white in a mixing bowl, with a whisk or with a mixer at high speed, until it forms stiff peaks. Set aside.

2. Mix together the egg yolk, corn, flour, milk, butter, baking powder, onion, salt, and cayenne. Fold the beaten egg white into the mixture and toss until mixed.

3. Make the dipping sauce: Stir the honey mustard, horseradish, and parsley together in a small bowl. Set aside.

4. Heat the oil in a large skillet until it sizzles. Drop the corn batter in the skillet by ¼ cupfuls and fry until golden, turning once, about 4 minutes total. Drain the fritters on a paper towel and keep them warm in the oven. Serve immediately with the dipping sauce.

Corn and Basil Muffins

Two of summer's freshest flavors come together in these savory muffins. Try some of the unusual basil varieties, like Thai or lemon or purple, to vary the taste.

MAKES 12 MUFFINS

- 1¼ cups all-purpose flour
- ¾ cup yellow cornmeal
- 2 tablespoons sugar
- 3 teaspoons baking powder
- ¾ teaspoon salt
- 1 cup milk
- 1 egg, lightly beaten
- ¼ cup vegetable oil
- 1 cup uncooked fresh corn kernels
- 1 tablespoon chopped fresh basil

1. Preheat the oven to 400°F. Grease 12 muffin cups.

2. Mix the flour, cornmeal, sugar, baking powder, and salt in a medium bowl. Add the milk, egg, and oil, and stir until blended. Add the corn and basil and mix until blended.

3. Divide the batter among the muffin cups. Bake for 20 to 25 minutes. Remove the muffins from the oven and allow them to cool for 5 minutes. Turn the muffins out onto a wire rack. Serve warm.

Zucchini Fritters with Thyme

Pepper flakes add some heat to this summer side dish, which uses up some of one of the garden's most prolific vegtables.

- ¾ cup all-purpose flour
- 1 teaspoon baking powder
- 2 eggs, beaten
- ¼ cup milk
- 2 medium zucchini
- 2 tablespoons fresh thyme
- 1 teaspoon hot pepper flakes
- ½ teaspoon salt
- 1 cup vegetable oil

1. Preheat the oven to 200°F. Combine the flour and baking powder in a medium bowl. Make a well in the flour mixture, pour the beaten eggs into the well, and gradually incorporate the dry ingredients into the eggs. Add the milk and stir to make a thick batter.

2. Grate the zucchini and drain it in a paper towel–lined colander for 5 minutes. Add the zucchini, thyme, pepper flakes, and salt to the batter, and mix well.

3. Heat the oil in a large skillet until hot but not smoking. Drop the batter by the tablespoon into the hot oil. Fry for 3 to 4 minutes on each side, until golden brown. Remove the fritters from the oil and drain on a paper towel. Transfer the fritters to the oven to keep them warm. Repeat the process until all of the batter has been used. Serve immediately.

Maple-glazed Carrots with Ginger and Parsley

Fresh carrots are best fixed simply. This glaze of maple syrup, butter, and ginger combines heat with cool flavors. For color interest, try to find the red, purple, or white carrots that have become popular in the past few years.

- 1 pound (about 8 large) carrots, peeled and sliced
- 3 tablespoons butter
- ¼ cup Maryland maple syrup
- ¼ teaspoon salt
- 2 teaspoons freshly grated gingerroot
- 2 tablespoons chopped fresh parsley

Bring 1 cup of water to a simmer in a medium saucepan. Steam the carrots in a steamer over the simmering water for 8 to 10 minutes. Remove the steamer; drain the carrots and discard the water. Melt the butter in the saucepan over medium heat. Add the maple syrup and stir until the glaze thickens, about 1 minute. Add the carrots, the salt, and the ginger, and toss well to mix. Transfer to a serving dish and sprinkle with parsley. Serve immediately.

Summer Succotash with Red Peppers and Parsley

Succotash, from the Narragansett word "msickquatash," meaning boiled corn kernels, is just about the easiest, yet most satisfying, summer vegetable dish there is. I make mine from Silver Queen or bicolored Temptation corn and velvety, fresh local lima beans. The red pepper gives the dish some extra color and crunch.

4 tablespoons butter

1 garlic clove, peeled and minced

1 shallot, peeled and finely chopped

½ cup finely diced red bell pepper

2 cups shelled fresh lima beans

½ teaspoon salt

⅛ teaspoon freshly ground black pepper

4 ears Silver Queen corn, husked and kernels cut from the cob

2 tablespoons chopped fresh parsley

6 SERVINGS

1. Melt 2 tablespoons of the butter in a medium saucepan. Add the garlic, shallot, and bell pepper, and sauté for 3 to 5 minutes. Add the lima beans, salt, pepper, and ¼ cup of water; cover and simmer for 10 minutes.

2. Add the corn kernels and the remaining 2 tablespoons butter and cook for 3 to 5 minutes longer. Stir in the chopped parsley and transfer to a serving dish. Serve immediately.

Joan and Drew Norman

ONE STRAW FARM
Baltimore County

Twenty-five years ago, when newlyweds Joan and Drew Norman started an organic farm in Whitehall, they bucked conventional thinking in production agriculture. Back then, toxic pesticide use was not only ubiquitous, it was largely unchallenged: the more you sprayed and killed, the reasoning went, the easier it would be to grow crops. But Drew, who had studied agriculture at the University of Maryland, where he and Joan met, knew there was a better way to farm than using toxic chemicals. They named One Straw Farm in honor of Japanese farmer Masanobu Fukuoka's revolutionary book, *The One Straw Revolution*, which argued for a sustainable farming model that would prevent most disease and pest damage from ever occurring.

Today One Straw Farm is just one of more than 140 USDA-certified organic farms in Maryland — many of them modeled after the Normans' —

and it's still the largest, with 200 acres in organic production. Many chefs and restaurants have come to rely on One Straw's quality produce, and Joan relates well to all the customers, bantering with her outgoing, wonderfully raucous, sometimes blunt nature, and concocting the recipes that she shares — with wry annotations — on the farm's Web site.

Drew and his longtime crew of largely Mexican workers take tremendous pride in growing more than 80 fruit, vegetable, and herb varieties each year, all sold at Maryland Whole Foods stores, in some local groceries, and at several farmers' markets in the Baltimore area. But by far their biggest enterprise is providing weekly produce shares to more than 1,100 Community Supported Agriculture (CSA) subscribers, such as the Johns Hopkins University School of Public Health (where faculty and staff practice what they teach by eating healthful and local foods) and churches and other community organizations to whom One Straw donates free CSA shares.

Recipe from ONE STRAW FARM

Arugula and Nectarine Salad

Use both white and yellow nectarines to add more color to this refreshing salad.

4–6 SERVINGS

- 3 tablespoons raspberry vinegar
- 1 teaspoon Dijon mustard
- ½ teaspoon salt
- ¼ teaspoon freshly ground black pepper
- ⅛ teaspoon sugar
- 5 tablespoons extra-virgin olive oil
- 2 cups arugula leaves
- 2 cups Bibb or Boston lettuce leaves
- 3 ripe nectarines, peeled and sliced
- ⅓ cup walnut pieces, toasted

1. Make the dressing: Stir together the vinegar and mustard in a small bowl. Add the salt, pepper, and sugar. Whisk in the olive oil.

2. Wash and spin dry the arugula and lettuce. Tear the greens into medium-size pieces and arrange them in a bowl. Pour the dressing over the greens and toss. Top with nectarine slices and walnuts.

Summer Coleslaw

Marylanders live outside during the summer months, enjoying long days and warm (some would say hot and sticky) nights. We love a good summer cookout, and that usually involves a dish of coleslaw. This version is fairly traditional, with green peppers added for color and sour cream for tanginess.

4 SERVINGS

- 3 cups finely shredded cabbage
- 1 cup finely shredded carrots
- ¼ cup finely chopped green bell pepper
- ½ cup Old-Fashioned Boiled Salad Dressing (page 108)
- 2 teaspoons sour cream

1. Combine the cabbage, carrots, and green pepper in a medium bowl.

2. Pour the dressing over the cabbage mixture and toss well. Add the sour cream and mix thoroughly. Refrigerate for at least 30 minutes before serving.

Recipe from ONE STRAW FARM

Fattoush Salad

One of summer's best flavor combinations — tomatoes and cucumbers — marries in this tangy salad with a wonderful crunchy texture. Sumac powder is available at Middle Eastern markets; if you can't find it, leave it out, but it adds to the salad's distinctive taste.

2 medium white or whole-wheat pita bread rounds

6 medium tomatoes, chopped

4 Kirby (pickling) cucumbers or one English cucumber, chopped

4 scallions or 1 small yellow or white onion, peeled and chopped

6 radishes, leaves cut off and sliced

1 cup packed flat-leaf Italian parsley, chopped

½ cup mint leaves, chopped

1 cup purslane, stems removed, leaves chopped (optional)

½ teaspoon salt

2 tablespoons sumac powder

⅓ cup extra-virgin olive oil

2 tablespoons lemon juice

4–6 SERVINGS

1. Preheat the oven to 250°F. Cut open each pita bread into two rounds, transfer to a baking sheet, and toast in the oven 7 to 10 minutes, until golden and crisp. Set aside to cool.

2. Combine the tomato, cucumber, scallions, and radishes in a large salad bowl. Scatter the parsley, mint, and purslane, if desired, on top of the vegetables. Crumble the toasted pita bread on top and sprinkle the salad with salt and sumac powder.

3. Whisk together the olive oil and lemon juice and pour onto the salad. Toss lightly and serve immediately.

Fingerling Potato Salad with Shallots and Dill

Fingerling potatoes are small and buttery and need no peeling. They are absolutely delicious in this fresh-from-the-garden salad.

3 pounds fingerling potatoes, well scrubbed

3 hard-boiled eggs

1½ cups finely chopped celery

2 shallots, peeled and finely chopped

2 kosher dill pickles, finely chopped

1 tablespoon finely chopped fresh dill

1 tablespoon finely chopped fresh parsley

1 teaspoon salt

¼ teaspoon freshly ground black pepper

½ cup mayonnaise

½ cup Old-Fashioned Boiled Salad Dressing (page 108)

8–10 SERVINGS

1. Boil the potatoes in a large saucepan with enough water to cover for about 10 minutes, until tender. Drain and cool. Peel and chop the hard-boiled eggs. Combine them with the celery, shallots, and dill pickles in a large bowl.

2. Slice the potatoes — skin on — and add them to the egg mixture. Stir in the dill, parsley, salt, pepper, mayonnaise, and dressing. Toss well to combine all the ingredients. Allow to marinate for at least 1 hour before serving.

Tomatoes Stuffed with Basil, Breadcrumbs, Mushrooms, and Parmesan

Use heirloom tomatoes like Brandywine to add an even more distinctive taste to this summer classic. Pair them with a garden salad and grilled steak or burgers for a complete meal.

4 large tomatoes
¼ cup olive oil
1 cup sliced local mushrooms
1 small onion, peeled and minced
2 garlic cloves, peeled and minced
3 tablespoons chopped fresh basil
¼ cup white wine
1 tablespoon chopped fresh parsley
1 teaspoon salt
½ teaspoon freshly ground black pepper
½ cup breadcrumbs
¼ cup freshly grated Parmesan cheese

4 SERVINGS

1. Slice off the tops of the tomatoes, keeping the stems intact, and reserve them. Carefully scoop out the insides of the tomatoes, chop the flesh, and set it aside in a small bowl. Invert the tomato shells on paper towels to drain.

2. Preheat the oven to 350°F. Heat the olive oil in a large skillet. Add the mushrooms, onion, and garlic, and sauté for 3 to 5 minutes over medium heat. Add the chopped tomato flesh, basil, wine, parsley, salt, and pepper, and simmer for 3 to 5 minutes longer. Stir in the breadcrumbs and Parmesan. Remove from the heat.

3. Stand the tomatoes up in a baking dish and divide the stuffing evenly among them. Cap them with the reserved tomato tops. Bake for 30 minutes, until the tomatoes are tender. Serve hot or at room temperature.

DRAGONFLY FARMS
Frederick County

Claudia Nami and Susan Lewis have taken literally the old adage that when life hands you lemons you make lemonade. Substitute grapes for lemons, and vinegar for lemonade, and that's their story. Some years ago when the new farmers harvested a surfeit of grapes and couldn't find buyers for them, the two intrepid women decided to make the best of their predicament. Nami, a retired, widowed businesswoman, loved to cook and reasoned that vinegar was something that everyone used. So with the fastidiousness that has come to be the hallmark of Dragonfly Farms, she and Lewis first rigorously educated themselves about winemaking, because, as Nami points out, "You first need to make the wine and then the vinegar." Then they learned how to make vinegar the old-fashioned way, starting with the finished wine, adding a bacterial "mother,"

which looks like a sponge and is akin to a sourdough starter, and allowing it to ferment naturally and slowly. It takes two years "from vine to bottle," and the results are astonishing: deeply flavorful, assertively fruity, complex vinegars that vary in degrees of acidity — the smooth Black Cabernet, the spicy Syrah, the slightly mellower Black Merlot, and the smoky, all–black currant Dragonfly. A little of these concentrated vinegars goes a long way, which is why Nami and Lewis don't blink at selling them for $40 per bottle.

Lewis and Nami do virtually all of the work on the farm themselves, from harvesting the fruits and making the wines and vinegars, to bottling, labeling, packing, and shipping them. Their 100-plus-acre farm is covered with vineyards of Merlot, Cabernet Sauvignon, Gewürztraminer, Syrah, and Chardonnay grapes. Black-currant bushes cling to a steep hill, and rows of perennial flowers stretch to the horizon. In the immaculate shed building that houses the winery and the vinegary, oak casks of wine age on one side, and glass demijohns of various vinegars rest on the other, carefully dated and labeled. Lewis points out new tomato and Gewürztraminer vinegars, awaiting bottling. And Nami recounts with pride that Alice Waters, one of the country's top chefs, recently sampled one of their vinegars and pronounced it "among the very best" she'd ever had. That sentiment is not unusual, and it makes the hard work worth it. "A lot of people remember the taste of our vinegars for a long time," Nami says with satisfaction.

Claudia Nami and Susan Lewis

Black Merlot

100% Estate Produced
Merlot & Black Currant Wine Vinegar

Dragonfly Farms
Mount Airy, Maryland 21771

200 ml (6.76 oz) 6% acetic acid

Dragonfly Gazpacho

Delightfully refreshing, this cold soup fairly bursts with flavor. Use only the ripest and freshest ingredients. Serve it as the first course for an outdoor dinner party.

8 SERVINGS

- 2 pounds tomatoes, diced
- 1 large Vidalia onion, peeled and chopped
- 1 large red onion, peeled and chopped
- 1 large cucumber, peeled and chopped
- 1 large green or red bell pepper, chopped
- 2 scallions, white and tender green parts, chopped
- 4 garlic cloves, peeled and finely chopped
- 2 tablespoons olive oil
- ¼ cup Dragonfly Syrah wine vinegar or any fine red-wine vinegar
- 1 teaspoon hot sauce
- 1 teaspoon salt
- ¼ teaspoon freshly ground black pepper
- ¼ teaspoon freshly ground white pepper
- 1 tablespoon chopped fresh dill
- 1 tablespoon chopped fresh cilantro
- 1 tablespoon chopped fresh parsley

Combine the tomatoes, Vidalia onion, red onion, cucumber, bell pepper, scallions, garlic, olive oil, vinegar, hot sauce, salt, black pepper, white pepper, dill, cilantro, and parsley in a blender. Blend quickly to achieve a smooth consistency. Refrigerate for at least 1 hour before serving. Serve cold.

Pesto Sauce with White Wine

This recipe comes from Brett Grohsgal of Even' Star Organic Farm in southern Maryland. In addition to growing dozens of varieties of greens, including an exotic array of herbs, Brett is also a superb cook who was a professional chef for 18 years. This pesto is wonderful on pasta or new potatoes, or served with chicken or fish.

¾–1 cup extra-virgin olive oil

8 garlic cloves, peeled and coarsely chopped

½ teaspoon salt

¼ teaspoon freshly ground black pepper

¼ cup white wine

¼ cup almonds or pine nuts, toasted and cooled

4 cups basil leaves, preferably Genoa type

¼ cup grated Romano cheese

MAKES 2 CUPS PESTO

1. Heat ¼ cup of the olive oil in a medium skillet. Add the garlic and sauté over low heat for about 2 minutes, until soft and golden.

2. Add the salt, pepper, and wine to the skillet, and simmer until the wine volume has reduced by half. Remove from the heat and let the mixture cool. Transfer the mixture to a food processor and process until the garlic is fully puréed.

3. Add the nuts and process until nearly smooth. Add the basil, and then gradually add an additional ½ cup of olive oil. Process further, until the basil is just barely smooth, with no leaf pieces bigger than ⅛ inch, adding more oil if the surface of the basil appears exposed to air.

4. Add the cheese and process 15 seconds longer. Use immediately or store (see below).

STORING PESTO

The trick to keeping pesto looking and tasting good is to cover it with olive oil. The oil stops oxygen from oxidizing the basil and turning it bitter. If you aren't using the pesto right away, store it in a glass jar with at least ¼ inch of olive oil on top and then refrigerate immediately. It keeps that way for 6 weeks.

Pesto also freezes well covered in ample amounts of olive oil. Stored in jars or in plastic containers, it can keep in the freezer for a year.

Baba Ganoush

When the markets are overflowing with cheap eggplants, this is one of my favorite appetizers. If you don't want to turn on the oven, do as I do and roast them on the gas grill, turning them frequently. Serve this savory spread with soft or toasted pita bread.

3 large globe eggplants
½ cup tahini (sesame paste)
1 teaspoon salt
3 tablespoons lemon juice
3 large garlic cloves, peeled
2 tablespoons olive oil
¼ cup finely chopped
   Italian parsley

6 SERVINGS

1. Preheat the oven to 450°F. Prick the eggplants in several places and place them on a large baking sheet. Bake the eggplants for 30 minutes, until they are very soft. Remove them from the oven and allow them to cool for 15 minutes.

2. Cut the eggplants in half. Discard any water and then scoop out the flesh. Transfer the flesh to a food processor or blender. Add the tahini, salt, lemon juice, garlic, and olive oil. Process until smooth. Transfer to a serving dish and add the parsley, stirring to incorporate it. Serve at room temperature.

Savory Summer Ratatouille with Couscous

Lushly flavorful, this traditional French summer dish uses summer's bounty of tomatoes, zucchini, and eggplants. It's also wonderful with new potatoes or with a little local feta cheese and a loaf of Crusty Whole-Wheat Bread (page 182).

8 SERVINGS

1 large eggplant

2 teaspoons salt

1 tablespoon olive oil

1 medium onion, peeled and chopped

3 garlic cloves, peeled and minced

2 small zucchini, quartered and cut into 1-inch pieces

3 cups diced fresh plum tomatoes

2 teaspoons chopped fresh basil or 1 teaspoon dried basil

1 teaspoon fresh rosemary leaves or ½ teaspoon dried rosemary

1 teaspoon chopped fresh oregano or ½ teaspoon dried oregano

1 teaspoon fresh thyme leaves or ½ teaspoon dried thyme

½ teaspoon freshly ground black pepper

2½ cups Chicken Stock (page 26) or Vegetable Stock (page 27)

1 tablespoon butter

2½ cups couscous, preferably tomato or spinach variety

1. Cut the eggplant into 2-inch cubes and transfer it to a paper towel–lined colander. Sprinkle with 1 teaspoon of the salt and leave it to drain for 30 minutes.

2. Heat the olive oil in a large, deep skillet. Add the onion and garlic, and sauté for 2 to 3 minutes over medium to low heat, until soft. Add the eggplant and stir to distribute the oil, then cover. Reduce the heat to low and simmer for 15 minutes.

3. Add the zucchini, tomatoes, basil, rosemary, oregano, thyme, pepper, and the remaining teaspoon salt. Stir, cover, and simmer for 25 to 30 minutes, until the eggplant and zucchini are tender, but not mushy.

4. Fill a medium saucepan with the stock, add the butter, and bring to a boil. Remove the saucepan from the heat, add the couscous, stir, cover, and set aside for 5 minutes. Fluff with a fork. Serve immediately with the ratatouille.

Fresh Tomato Sauce with Herbs

For tomato sauce, San Marzano, Roma, Amish Paste, and Zapotec tomatoes are all excellent varieties, but I've been known to toss anything that's ripe into my saucepan, including yellow cherry tomatoes. The bottom line is that any really ripe tomato will make a good sauce, but the consistency will vary widely, depending on how "meaty" the tomato is. In season, you might find yourself with an embarrassment of beautiful tomatoes; this recipe can be doubled, tripled, or even multiplied tenfold. If you have the room in your freezer, I recommend freezing individual portions for use later in the year. And you can add to this basic sauce recipe in many ways, including ground beef or chicken, Italian sausage, mushrooms, peppers, parsley, or any other tasty variation your stomach might dream up.

4 pounds tomatoes

3 tablespoons olive oil

1 onion, peeled and chopped

3 garlic cloves, peeled and minced

1 carrot, peeled and diced

3 tablespoons chopped fresh basil

1 tablespoon chopped fresh oregano

1 teaspoon sugar

1 teaspoon salt

½ teaspoon freshly ground black pepper

MAKES 4 CUPS SAUCE

1. Bring a large saucepan of water to a boil. Immerse the tomatoes in the boiling water for 20 seconds, or until the skins burst. Remove the tomatoes with a slotted spoon and allow them to cool slightly, until you are able to handle them. Peel the tomatoes, remove and discard the cores, and finely chop. Set aside.

2. Heat the olive oil in a large skillet. Add the onion and garlic and sauté over medium heat for about 3 minutes. Add the chopped tomatoes and cook and stir for another 5 minutes. Add the carrot, basil, oregano, sugar, salt, and pepper. Stir, reduce the heat to low, cover, and simmer for an hour or longer, until the sauce is reduced by one-third. Adjust seasonings as needed. If desired, purée the sauce in a food processor or blender.

TOMATOES

It's hard to imagine anymore, but 20 years ago the only tomatoes you could buy in most places in this country, even at summer produce stands, were beefsteak and cherry tomatoes. Plant breeders were breeding tomatoes for size and ease of transport and storage, rather than for taste. Literally hundreds of tomato varieties disappeared from nearly everywhere but home gardens, where backyard growers, many of them immigrants, continued growing flavorful, if sometimes ugly, vegetables. Fortunately, heirloom and unusual tomatoes are back, thanks in no small part to organizations like Seed Savers Exchange, which has continually kept seeds readily available to people who want them. Today, it's not at all uncommon to see a dozen varieties of tomatoes at farm stands and markets, from Maryland favorites like Amish Paste and Brandywine to more exotic varieties like Green Zebra and Cherokee.

Three-Bean Salad with Edamame, Chives, and Oregano

This is a tasty remake of the old and tired three-bean salad. With its fresh yellow and green colors and slightly crunchy texture, it's a vast improvement over its ancestor and gets even better after marinating for a few hours.

1 pound fresh green beans, washed and trimmed

1 pound fresh yellow wax beans, washed and trimmed

1 pound fresh edamame in their pods

1 small onion, peeled and grated

¼ cup red wine vinegar

2 teaspoons lemon juice

½ teaspoon Dijon mustard

¼ cup olive oil

2 teaspoons chopped fresh parsley

1 teaspoon finely chopped fresh chives

½ teaspoon chopped fresh oregano

½ teaspoon salt

¼ teaspoon freshly ground black pepper

6 SERVINGS

1. Put a few inches of water in a large saucepan and bring it to a simmer. Steam the green and yellow beans until just tender, about 10 minutes. Add the edamame to the steamer and continue steaming for an additional 3 minutes. Immediately plunge the beans and edamame into ice water to stop the cooking. Drain and cool the beans, remove the edamame from their pods, and then transfer them to a salad bowl.

2. Combine the onion, vinegar, lemon juice, and mustard in a small bowl. Whisk in the olive oil and add the parsley, chives, oregano, salt, and pepper. Pour the dressing over the beans and toss thoroughly. Let stand at room temperature for 30 minutes before serving.

Green Beans with Summer Savory

I grew up eating these beans, and to this day I think they're the tastiest I've ever had. This is the way that they're usually served in Switzerland. Summer savory, not plain savory, is the key to their unusual taste; it can be found in some supermarkets and at some farmers' markets. I grow it fresh and dry it. Don't undercook these beans; they're meant to be quite soft, and they taste even better reheated.

6 SERVINGS

- 2 tablespoons butter
- 1 medium onion, peeled and finely chopped
- 2 pounds fresh green beans, washed and trimmed
- 1½ cups Chicken Stock (page 26 or Vegetable Stock (page 27)
- 2 tablespoons dried summer savory
- 1 teaspoon salt
- ¼ teaspoon freshly ground black pepper

1. Melt the butter in a large saucepan. Add the onion and sauté over low heat until translucent, about 3 minutes.

2. Add the green beans, stock, summer savory, salt, and pepper. Cover and simmer over medium-low heat for 45 minutes, stirring occasionally to turn the beans. Serve warm.

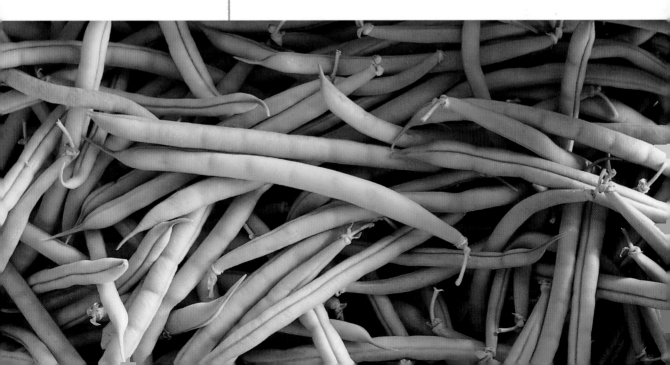

CALVERT'S GIFT FARM
Baltimore County

To the naysayers who think that a family farm can't be profitable anymore, Jack and Becky Gurley beg to differ. When the two trained scientists and environmental consultants made the decision to go into farming 14 years ago, they started out with two acres of land, two bright minds, and one simple business plan: make enough money to do it full time. The Gurleys have done that and more with Calvert's Gift Farm, a modest five-acre, USDA-certified organic produce farm in rural Sparks. Through hard work, an aversion to debt, and the savvy to find their particular niche and stick with it, the Gurleys have built a premium produce operation that the two of them can run almost entirely by themselves. They don't own any big, expensive equipment, incur high labor costs, or generate huge pesticide and fertilizer bills, and the scale of their operation is tailored to what they can personally manage. Becky does all the farmers' markets and runs their 50-family CSA (which has a long waiting list), and Jack is responsible for most of the growing and fieldwork. In turn, they've cultivated an intensely loyal customer base and built a financially profitable business that allows them to take off three months of the year and go with their daughters, Taylor and Emma, on family vacations.

"We grow a lot of things where the yield may not be the best, but they're a premium crop," Becky says, explaining their business strategy. "A lot of farmers wouldn't grow those, because they don't fit in the commercial market." Among those offerings: tender pea shoots for salads and stir-frys, buttery fingerling potatoes, baby white turnips as sweet as honey, exotic green and white zebra tomatoes, and hard-to-find Ronde de Nice squash, kohlrabi, and pencil-thin haricots verts. The diversity of crops also helps ensure against a total crop failure, Becky explains. If one thing does badly, there is always something else that's doing well to balance it out.

Asked why more people, especially young people, don't follow their successful lead, Jack says he ponders that question a lot. In part, it's the work itself. They work from 7 to 5 every day, 7 days a week, for 9 months of the year, and all of their revenue comes in a 6-month period. That requires careful budgeting and the ability to live with delayed gratification. And success doesn't come overnight. "I don't think people have the patience they need. They have expectations that [success] will be immediate, but it's a gradual process," he says, noting that he and Becky worked several jobs simultaneously as they transitioned to farming. The Gurleys also fault the traditional mind-set of many agriculture schools and extension agents, who still think almost exclusively in terms of traditional commodity crops and big farms. "You don't have to be totally out of the box to be an alternative farmer," Jack asserts. "We have a middle-class lifestyle."

To encourage more people to go into farming, the Gurleys are active in a number of sustainable-farming organizations. They also teach interns to run small farms like theirs, and they host a succession of tours for farm organizations and elected officials — even World Bank officials — to promote small-scale, sustainable farming. "We are successful, and our model does work, and yet it doesn't seem as though we're able to get the message across. We need more farmers, so there needs to be more diversity in the education system, giving the message that you can be successful."

Tarragon Chicken Salad with Toasted Hazelnuts

Serve this on a bed of buttery Bibb or Boston lettuce and it's a meal by itself.

4 SERVINGS

- 4 cups cubed cooked chicken
- 1 cup chopped celery
- 1 tablespoon chopped fresh tarragon
- ⅓ cup Old-Fashioned Boiled Salad Dressing (below)
- ⅓ cup sour cream
- 1 tablespoon tarragon vinegar
- 1 teaspoon sea salt
- ¼ teaspoon freshly ground black pepper
- 1 cup chopped hazelnuts, lightly toasted

Combine the chicken, celery, tarragon, dressing, sour cream, vinegar, salt, and pepper in a large bowl, and toss well to mix. Refrigerate for 1 hour. Just before serving, add the hazelnuts and toss the salad again.

Old-Fashioned Boiled Salad Dressing

This dressing is easy to make and is very good for chicken salad, potato salad, and coleslaw, among other things.

MAKES 2 CUPS

- 3 eggs
- 1 cup milk
- 2 tablespoons all-purpose flour
- 2 tablespoons sugar
- 1 teaspoon salt
- 1 teaspoon dry mustard
- 1 teaspoon celery seeds
- ½ teaspoon freshly ground black pepper
- ½ cup hot cider vinegar

Whisk together the eggs and milk in a small saucepan. Add the flour, sugar, salt, mustard, celery seeds, and pepper, and cook over low heat, whisking constantly, until the dressing is smooth and thick. Remove from the heat and whisk in the vinegar. Refrigerate until ready to use. Keeps several weeks in the refrigerator.

CHICKEN

Maryland is famous for its chicken, in large part because chicken-processing giant Perdue is headquartered on the Eastern Shore, and poultry represents by far the biggest sector of farming in the state. Mile after mile of chicken houses dot the Eastern Shore — most of them belonging to independent family farmers who grow for Perdue. A huge poultry festival takes place on the Shore every summer, with the world's largest skillet used to cook up thousands of pounds of fried chicken. Recent years have seen increasing numbers of farmers who raise small flocks of free-range, hormone- and antibiotic-free chickens, which are in huge demand. With diets consisting mostly of insects and grass, they are much more flavorful than those grown under tightly confined conditions where they are fed huge amounts of feed to fatten them quickly. Free-range chickens cost more than the regular store-bought variety, but the difference is worth it in taste. And because a single chicken can often be stretched to make several meals, it's actually still quite economical.

Southern Fried Chicken

Serve with Fingerling Potato Salad (page 93) and Cucumber Salad with Asian Dressing (page 83) for a complete Southern chicken feast.

8 SERVINGS

2 cups buttermilk

¼ cup lemon juice

1 onion, peeled and grated

2 tablespoons Tabasco or hot pepper sauce

1 (3–4 pound) chicken, cut into 8 pieces, rinsed, and patted dry

2 cups all-purpose flour

1 teaspoon salt

¼ teaspoon freshly ground black pepper

¼ teaspoon cayenne pepper

2 cups vegetable shortening or oil

1. Combine the buttermilk, lemon juice, onion, and Tabasco in a rectangular baking dish. Put the chicken pieces in the buttermilk mixture, cover, and refrigerate to marinate for at least 8 hours, turning several times.

2. Remove the chicken from the refrigerator. Combine the flour, salt, black pepper, and cayenne in a large, heavy paper bag, and shake to combine the ingredients. Remove 1 piece of chicken from the marinade, shake off excessive liquid, and then add it to the paper bag. Shake the bag until the chicken is thoroughly coated. Transfer the chicken to a paper towel–lined plate. Repeat the process until all 8 pieces have been coated. Let the chicken sit for 30 minutes to dry.

3. Preheat the oven to 200°F. Heat the shortening in a large cast iron or other heavy skillet until hot but not smoking. Fry chicken 3 to 4 pieces at a time in the skillet over medium-low heat for 10 minutes. Turn the chicken and continue frying until the chicken's juices run clear when pierced, another 10 to 12 minutes for breasts and 8 to 10 minutes for thighs. Remove the chicken from the skillet and transfer it to a paper towel–lined platter. Move the platter to the oven to keep the chicken warm. Repeat the process with the remaining chicken.

Peggy Elliott's Piquant Crab Balls

Peggy and Bill Elliott have been married for 60 years, and he crabbed for that entire time. When they started out, Peggy used to clean all the crab pots by hand, a job she loved and that never diminished her pleasure in cooking and serving crabs. Peggy is a superb cook, one of those old-fashioned wonderful cooks who rarely writes down recipes but never turns out a bad meal. She graciously put pen to paper for this book.

SERVES 6–8

1 pound Maryland jumbo lump crabmeat

1 cup Italian breadcrumbs

1 small onion, peeled and finely minced

1 egg

¼ cup Dijon mustard

2 tablespoons mayonnaise

½ teaspoon salt

½ teaspoon Worcestershire sauce

¼ cup vegetable oil

1. Pick through the crabmeat and remove any shells and cartilage. Set aside.

2. Mix the breadcrumbs, onion, egg, mustard, mayonnaise, salt, and Worcestershire in a large bowl. Add the crabmeat and gently toss until blended. Form into 1-inch balls.

3. Heat the oil in a large skillet until it sizzles but does not smoke. Fry the crab balls until they are browned on all sides, about 5 minutes. Serve immediately.

THE ELLIOTTS
Dorchester County

When Bill Elliott graduated from high school in 1945, World War II had just ended and the engineering school he'd applied to was swamped with returning servicemen. So while he bided his time, Elliott fell back on what he'd been doing since he was five years old: crabbing for his father, himself the son and grandson of a waterman. "By the time they let me in [to engineering school], I'd had two or three good years in a row and that was it," recalls the Dorchester County native. "It was hard work, but I liked the challenge of knowing that I could succeed and no one could take that away from me."

In following the family path as a waterman, Elliott claimed one of Maryland's most longstanding and storied professions. For 60 years, Elliott happily plied the marshy waters of Dorchester County. The Little Choptank River, the Big Choptank, Hutchins Creek — he knew all those waters just like he knew where his own 900-plus crab pots were.

The day started at 4 a.m., and at the end of it, his wife, Peggy, was always there, ready to wash crab pots and to cook something tasty from whatever Elliott had held back from selling to the JM Clayton Company, which was started in 1890 and is the oldest working crab-processing plant in the world. Even in the slack years — and there were a few — the Elliotts always ate well.

When Elliott's son Keith began working with him, the father taught the son the same things his father had taught him: how to set and check the crab pots, run trotlines, tong oysters, fix equipment, maintain the boat. They kept their boat 20 minutes outside of Cambridge, on a piece of marshy land that Bill and Peggy bought in the 1960s, a spot so lovely that before you even set foot on the boat, you've seen more beauty than most people do in a week. Blue-green marsh grasses. A great blue heron. An osprey. Keith learned to dive for oysters and for a few years the men worked together on that, the son in the water in a dry suit, the father on the boat, culling the oysters. It wasn't a job for the lazy.

In the 1940s and 1950s, Elliott recalls, the restrictions on watermen were few, the crabs plentiful, and the oysters healthy. Hauling in a few dozen bushels a day of crabs was a given. It wasn't easy, but if you were willing to work 100 hours a week, as Elliott did most summers, you could not only pay for your equipment and other bills but also have enough left over to put something away every month. Thirty years later, it wasn't nearly as profitable. The oysters they pulled up were more and more "boxes," or empty shells, and the crabs began to dwindle, the result of pollution and overharvesting.

Reluctantly, Bill Elliott finally retired in 2006, and since then, declining health has kept him off his beloved boats and waterways. Keith, however, is still crabbing, although he supplements his income with side jobs, especially in the winter, a common reality for watermen all over Maryland these days. The crabs and oysters are not, father and son agree, what they once were. "There won't be the young people going into this anymore," the father predicts. But Keith is already there. His father gave him the land and some equipment, and now it is the son, and not the father, who brings crabs home for Peggy to cook. Asked why he does it, Keith gives the same reason that every true waterman seems to utter: "It's in my blood." And the father, bent into a perpetual crouch from his decades on the water, lights up and nods in agreement. "I couldn't wait to get out there every day."

Hot and Spicy Crab Dip with Jarlsberg

Marylanders are very particular about their crab dips, since just about everyone has his or her own version. This variation has some nice sharp accents to it.

- 1 pound Maryland backfin crabmeat
- 1 (8-ounce) package cream cheese, softened
- 1 cup sour cream
- 1 teaspoon lemon juice
- 2 garlic cloves, peeled and pressed
- 1½ teaspoons Old Bay or other seafood seasoning
- 1 teaspoon Worcestershire sauce
- ½ teaspoon dry mustard
- 1½ ounces Jarlsberg cheese, shredded (⅓ cup)

1. Preheat the oven to 350°F. Pick through the crabmeat and discard any shell bits and cartilage. Combine the crabmeat, cream cheese, sour cream, lemon juice, garlic, Old Bay, Worcestershire, and mustard, and mix until combined.

2. Spoon the crab mixture into a shallow baking dish. Top with the shredded Jarlsberg and bake for 30 minutes. Serve hot with crackers or bread.

OLD BAY SEASONING

Just as crabs are one of Maryland's most beloved icons, so, too, is Old Bay seasoning. The distinctively spicy, coarsely ground seafood seasoning was sold only in Maryland for many years, where it quickly gained cult status. No crab feast is complete without seafood seasoning to give it zip, and although other brands exist, including Baltimore Spice and J.O. Spice, most Marylanders would rather root for the Yankees than dream of putting anything but Old Bay on their seafood — and many other dishes. Jerk chicken, chili, and even Bloody Marys and scrambled eggs have been known to benefit from the still-secret formula of celery salt, mustard seed, black pepper, bay leaves, cloves, pimiento, ginger, mace, cardamom, cinnamon, and paprika, invented by a German Jewish spice merchant named Gustav Brunn in 1939.

Brunn briefly worked for the McCormick Spice Company before going out on his own and setting up a shop opposite the wholesale fish market in Baltimore. He quickly noticed that crabs were a local obsession, with many housewives making their own "secret" crab seasoning. Brunn tried his own hand at a version that he named Old Bay for a steamship that traveled between Baltimore and Norfolk in the early twentieth century. It enjoyed little success originally, but once a wholesaler finally agreed to sell it at the fish market, its popularity quickly spread.

Celebrating its 70th anniversary in 2009, Old Bay seems to define summer in Maryland, when the crabs are steamed, the beer is cold, and the seasoning stains your fingers and burns your lips. It just doesn't get any better than that.

Kathleen's Crab Salad

My friend Anne Raver's mother, Kathleen Moore Raver, hailed from Denton on the Eastern Shore and was a friend to many crabbers and clammers. Like many women of that era, she was a wonderful cook, accustomed to using the freshest local ingredients. As Anne put it once, "She would never buy a soft-shell crab that wasn't kicking." This is Kathleen's crab salad, which Anne makes as well, and it really relies on the freshness of the crabmeat for its clean, sweet taste. I love it because it's simple, yet sophisticated, and tastes divine. It's perfect with a plate of sliced tomatoes and some corn on the cob.

1 pound jumbo lump crabmeat
2 celery stalks, chopped
½ cup mayonnaise
Juice of one lemon
3 dashes of Worcestershire sauce
3 dashes of Tabasco sauce
½ teaspoon dry mustard
½ teaspoon freshly ground sea salt
¼ teaspoon freshly ground black pepper
2 cups mixed lettuce, washed and dried
Grape or cherry tomatoes (optional)

4–6 SERVINGS

1. Pick through the crabmeat and remove any shell bits and cartilage. Combine the celery, mayonnaise, lemon juice, Worcestershire, Tabasco, mustard, salt, and pepper in a medium bowl, and toss to mix thoroughly. Fold in the crabmeat.

2. Place the mixed lettuce on a serving plate. Mound the crab salad on top of that and garnish with tomatoes, if desired. Serve at room temperature.

Crab Spring Roll with Pink Grapefruit, Avocado, and Toasted Almonds

These delicious spring rolls are one of Chef Salter's signature summer dishes at Sherwood's Landing restaurant. "Brick dough" or "feuillete brick" is a versatile, thin dough that comes in sheets and can be found in some specialty food stores.

½ pound bok choy

4 scallions

4 ounces jumbo lump crabmeat

1½ limes (juice from)

2 slices pickled ginger

1 teaspoon chopped cilantro

Salt and freshly ground black pepper

4 sheets spring roll casing (use either brick dough or good egg roll wrapper)

4 egg yolks, beaten

Vegetable oil

1½ teaspoons sugar

1½ cups pink grapefruit juice

¾ cup grapeseed oil

1 teaspoon clover honey

4 cups mesclun greens, washed and dried

1 pink grapefruit, segmented

1 avocado, peeled and sliced

¼ cup sliced almonds, toasted

4 SERVINGS

1. Bring a medium saucepan of salted water to a boil. Shred the bok choy and blanch it by cooking in the boiling water for 2 to 3 minutes, and then remove to a bowl of ice water to stop the cooking. Slice the scallions and blanch in the boiling water for 30 seconds, and then squeeze out most of the water. Combine bok choy and scallions in a large bowl with the crabmeat, the juice from half a lime, ginger, cilantro, and salt and pepper to taste.

2. Lay out the spring roll casings and spoon the crab filling on one-third of each. Brush the remaining two-thirds of the casing with beaten egg yolk. Roll up the wrapper "egg roll" style. Fill a medium saucepan with 2 inches of vegetable oil, and heat to 350°F.

3. Meanwhile, make the dressing: Melt the sugar in a small stainless steel saucepan over low heat. Add the pink grapefruit juice and cook to reduce the mixture by two-thirds. Whisk in the grapeseed oil, the juice from 1 lime, and the honey. Lightly season with salt and pepper.

4. Deep fry the spring rolls in the vegetable oil for 3 to 4 minutes, until golden.

5. Place one-quarter of the mesclun in the middle of each of four plates. Top each with three pieces of grapefruit and three pieces of avocado. Sprinkle with the toasted almonds and drizzle with the dressing. Cut each spring roll in half on the bias and lay on the salad. Drizzle each plate with additional dressing and serve.

St. Michaels
Talbot County

Named for the Archangel Michael in 1677, St. Michaels sits on the banks of the Miles River in Talbot County, just minutes from the Chesapeake Bay. It has a proud history as a boat-building center, where "bugeye" boats, skipjacks, and log canoes were handcrafted, and as a major oyster- and crab-packing hub in the nineteenth and early twentieth centuries. Perhaps its proudest moment came during the War of 1812, when the townspeople evacuated the town and retreated to a hill to hang lanterns in the trees, drawing the British cannonfire away from the town and leaving it unscathed, but for one house. Today St. Michaels is a preferred weekend destination for many of Washington DC's elites, especially Republicans, and is a popular sailing and boating hub. Tourists are drawn to its superb maritime museum, beautiful preserved houses, fine shops, inns, and restaurants, many of which source foods locally.

Mark Salter is the renowned executive chef of the Sherwood's Landing restaurant at The Inn at Perry Cabin in St. Michaels. This international culinary star has a strong commitment to buying locally, and the restaurant's menu changes across the seasons, showcasing local products where possible.

Eleanor Van Dyke's Crab Cakes

My sister-in-law Eleanor Van Dyke and her husband, Roger, have owned a crab business in Cambridge for decades and know and buy crabs from many of the watermen in Dorchester County. Like everyone, they have seen a huge decline in the crab population at the same time that demand for crabmeat keeps growing. This is a slight variation on Eleanor's delicious crab cakes. Roger has his own version, which some family members prefer, although they never tell Eleanor that.

8 SERVINGS

- 1 pound Maryland jumbo lump crabmeat
- 18 saltine crackers, crushed by hand into tiny pieces
- 1 cup mayonnaise
- 2 tablespoons chopped fresh parsley
- 1 teaspoon Old Bay or seafood seasoning
- 1 teaspoon dry mustard
- ½ teaspoon salt
- ¼ teaspoon freshly ground black pepper

  Tartar Sauce with Dill and Capers (page 123) (optional)

1. Preheat the oven to broil. Pick through the crabmeat and discard any shell bits and cartilage. Combine the crabmeat in a large bowl with the crackers, mayonnaise, parsley, Old Bay, mustard, salt, and pepper, and gently toss until the mixture is well combined. Without handling excessively, form the mixture into 8 crab cakes and place them on an ungreased broiler pan or nonstick baking sheet.

2. Broil the crab cakes for 6 to 8 minutes, turning once, until golden brown on both sides. Serve immediately with tartar sauce, if desired.

Fried Crab Cakes with Dijon Mustard

Crab cakes come in as many sizes and with as many variations as you'd expect from Maryland's favorite food, and you'll taste different versions throughout the Chesapeake region. To some Marylanders, a crab cake is authentic only when it's been fried, but you can decide for yourself. Frying adds a little crunch to them, but they're equally good — and less fattening — broiled (see Eleanor Van Dyke's Crab Cakes, page 120).

8 SERVINGS

1 pound Maryland backfin crabmeat

1 egg

2 slices white bread, crusts removed

⅓ cup mayonnaise

1 tablespoon Worcestershire sauce

1 teaspoon Old Bay or other seafood seasoning

1 teaspoon Dijon mustard

½ teaspoon salt

¼ teaspoon freshly ground black pepper

Vegetable oil

1. Pick through the crabmeat and discard any cartilage and shells. Beat the egg in a medium bowl. Tear the bread into very small pieces and add it to the egg. Add the crabmeat, mayonnaise, Worcestershire, Old Bay, mustard, salt, and pepper, and mix gently.

2. Form into 8 crab cakes. Put 2 inches of vegetable oil in a medium skillet and heat to 350°F. Deep fry the crab cakes 6 to 7 minutes, until golden brown.

Tartar Sauce with Dill and Capers

This quick and easy tartar sauce is a great accompaniment to fried perch, crab cakes, or crab balls.

2 tablespoons white balsamic vinegar

2 teaspoons lemon juice

1 teaspoon Dijon mustard

½ teaspoon salt

½ teaspoon sugar

2 egg yolks

1 cup extra-virgin olive oil

4 teaspoons chopped capers

4 teaspoons sweet pickle relish

2 teaspoons chopped fresh dill

2 teaspoons finely chopped onion

1. Combine the vinegar, lemon juice, mustard, salt, sugar, and egg yolks in a food processor. Turn the food processor on and begin to add the olive oil, a few drops at a time, until the mayonnaise emulsifies and thickens. Stop the motor and transfer the mayonnaise to a small bowl.

2. Add the capers, relish, dill, and onion, stirring to blend. Chill the tartar sauce, covered, for at least 1 hour before serving.

NOTE: If you are concerned about making a raw-egg mayonnaise, begin the recipe with 1 cup good-quality commercial mayonnaise. Stir in the 2 teaspoons lemon juice and the 1 teaspoon Dijon mustard, and then proceed with step 2.

THE BLUE CRAB

Ask a Marylander to name something unequivocally "Maryland," and nine out of ten will pick the blue crab. *Callinectes sapidus*, meaning "beautiful, savory swimmer," is hands down Maryland's most popular Chesapeake Bay resident and an iconic statewide symbol, emblazoned on everything from billboards to license plates. Revered for its sweet taste that goes well with everything from spicy seasonings to heavy cream, crabs are eaten in dozens of forms: steamed, pan-fried, baked, broiled, in soups, crab cakes, dips, and everything else in between. What the lobster is to Maine, the blue crab is to Maryland, and while it's true that blue crabs are found up and down the Atlantic seaboard, 60 percent are found and harvested in the Chesapeake Bay, giving Maryland and Virginia equal bragging rights.

Come Memorial Day, families across the state indulge in their first bushel of crabs for the year. Steamed over a mixture of vinegar and water or beer, with layers of Old Bay or other seafood seasoning between the crabs, they're properly dumped directly onto a newspaper or brown paper "tablecloth" that is rolled up and thrown away at the end of the crab feast. Just as a lobster feast isn't a sitdown fancy dinner, steamed crabs in Maryland are a casual, messy affair. Ideally, you're sitting outside at a picnic table, dressed in old shorts and a T-shirt, with a stack of paper towels at your side and a mallet

or knife at the ready. A hard thump or a quick slice into the steamed crabs, and crab juice sprays onto your neighbor's hair and clothing. This is perfectly acceptable crab-eating etiquette.

For those less familiar with blue crabs, here are a few important things to know about our beautiful swimmers:

Jimmies are male crabs: the heaviest, meatiest, most in-demand crustaceans. They're easily identified by looking at the "apron" that all blue crabs have on their undersides. Jimmies have an inverted T-shaped apron.

Sallies are immature female crabs. Their aprons are triangular, their claws red.

Sooks are mature females, readily identified by the red claw tips and their inverted U- or bell-shaped aprons. Sooks are mostly sold to processing houses to be "picked" for their meat.

Sponge crabs are pregnant females that carry their fertilized eggs under their abdomen. From a distance, the eggs look like sponges. It is illegal to harvest sponge crabs.

Peelers are crabs that are getting ready to molt, or shed their shells, which blue crabs must do periodically in order to keep growing. When a crab is about to peel, it displays a colored line next to its backfin claw. Experienced watermen can tell almost exactly when a crab will molt by looking at the color of the line. A red line classifies the crab as a "rank" peeler, meaning the molt is imminent. Peelers are often kept in "shedding" tanks by watermen who sell them for soft-shell crab-eating.

Soft-shell crabs are a true spring delicacy in Maryland, but they're served all summer. See page 59 for details.

Jumbo lump is the best crabmeat, and it's the most expensive, consisting of big pieces of crab with no shell or cartilage. If you want to make crab cakes that consist only of big chunks of meat, use jumbo lump meat.

Backfin crabmeat is harvested from the backfin section of the crab. It has nice lumps of meat but also some broken body meat. Backfin is also excellent for making crab cakes.

Special meat is meat from the crab's body that isn't in lumps. Special meat is used in all crab dishes, including crab cakes.

Claw meat is just what the name suggests. It is dark and sweet, wonderful for eating as an appetizer, with the shell cracked off; it's also used for soups and other dishes, but not for crab cakes. It's the cheapest crabmeat.

Maryland Steamed Crabs

You can't say you've experienced Maryland until you've picked and eaten steamed crabs. Beer and soda are de rigueur. Additional food is optional, but many people serve crabs with corn on the cob, sliced tomatoes, and fresh melon slices. Others even go so far as to provide coleslaw (try Summer Coleslaw, page 91) and potato salad (try Fingerling Potato Salad with Shallots and Dill, page 93) for people who don't like crabs or who eat only one or two.

½ cup Old Bay or other
   seafood seasoning

½ cup kosher salt

3 cups white vinegar

3 cups beer or water, or
   a mix of the two

3 dozen live crabs
   (see Note)

9–12 SERVINGS,
DEPENDING ON THE SIZE OF THE CRABS

1. Mix the seafood seasoning and salt together in a bowl. Combine the vinegar and beer in a lidded stockpot with a steamer rack.

2. Pile half of the crabs onto the steamer rack and sprinkle them with half of the seasoning mixture. Pile in the remaining crabs and sprinkle on the rest of the seasoning mixture.

3. Close the lid tightly and steam the crabs over high heat for 20 to 30 minutes, until they are bright red. Serve hot or cold.

NOTE: Never cook a crab that is already dead. Bacteria grow very quickly in dead crabs and can make you very sick. Always discard any dead crabs.

Rockfish Kabobs in Classic Greek Marinade

This simple recipe, ideal for a summer barbeque, demonstrates how delicious rockfish tastes when it's properly marinated and grilled. You can also broil the kebabs instead of grilling them. Use the same care to turn them so that they brown evenly and aren't overcooked.

2 SERVINGS

- 2 thick rockfish fillets, cut into 1½- to 2-inch cubes
- 1 red, yellow, or orange bell pepper, cut into 1½- to 2-inch squares
- 2 large red onions, peeled and cut into quarters
- ⅔ cup olive oil
- ⅓ cup lemon juice
- 1 teaspoon sea salt
- ½ teaspoon dried oregano
- ¼ teaspoon freshly ground black pepper

1. Soak four (10-inch) bamboo skewers in water for 1 hour. Remove them from the water, pat them dry, and assemble the kabobs on the skewers, alternating pieces of the fish, pepper, and onion. Place the kabobs into a shallow glass baking dish.

2. Combine the olive oil, lemon juice, salt, oregano, and pepper in a blender and blend at high speed until the mixture emulsifies. Pour the mixture over the kabobs and put them in the refrigerator to marinate for at least 10 to 15 minutes; turn the kabobs over and let them marinate for at least another 10 to 15 minutes.

3. Heat a gas or charcoal grill to high. Remove the kabobs from the marinade and grill them for about 3 minutes on one side. Turn the kabobs and grill for an additional 2 minutes, until the rockfish is cooked through. Serve immediately.

THE BLACK OLIVE
Baltimore

The Spiliadis family never consciously set out to be restaurateurs or owners of one of Baltimore's top-rated restaurants. The busy couple with two sons had very full lives already: Stelios was a social worker and Pauline a librarian. But food and entertaining were always important in their lives, and Pauline, a voracious reader of cookbooks, gradually immersed herself in the cuisine of her husband's native Greece. She began doing some catering out of their home, thinking that she might do that full time when she retired, possibly with her son Dimitri, who also showed a great interest in food.

When Pauline and Stelios saw a dilapidated row house for sale around the corner from their own home in the Fells Point section of Baltimore, their fate was sealed. The Black Olive has had a loyal customer base since the day it opened. Everything is made in-house, from breads to desserts. It also serves only organic produce, wild-caught fish, and locally sourced ingredients of the highest quality whenever possible, from heirloom tomatoes and arugula to crabs and rockfish. The menu changes weekly to reflect what is local and in season. One day it might be a beet salad with local goat cheese; on another, it could be fresh zucchini and carrots. While it's possible to find fish from as far away as Chile and Australia on the restaurant's menu, chances are there will be a Maryland seafood option as well, whether it be oysters, crabs, or something else from the Bay's bounty.

Recipe from THE MARYLAND SEAFOOD AND AQUACULTURE PROGRAM OF THE MARYLAND DEPARTMENT OF AGRICULTURE

Clams Mornay in Puff Pastry

While clams aren't nearly as popular as crabs or oysters in Maryland, they're still one of the Bay's shellfish and are eaten steamed, fried, in soups and chowders, and, of course, raw on the half shell. Clams are especially popular at the beach in Ocean City, where every restaurant offers a wealth of seafood choices and often features clams as part of a raw bar. The Chesapeake Bay is home to both hard-shell clams, including cherrystone, littleneck, and surf clams, and soft-shell, or manninose, clams. Marylanders usually refer to soft-shell clams as "manos" or "steamers" and, in all candor, they've never had the following that they enjoy in New England. Many Marylanders still consider steamers as fish bait, but in recent years, enlightened eaters are discovering just what they've been missing.

3 SERVINGS

6 frozen puff-pastry shells

¾ cup chopped soft-shell clams

¾ cup sliced fresh mushrooms

2 tablespoons white wine

1 tablespoon butter

1 tablespoon all-purpose flour

¼ cup plus 2 tablespoons clam juice

½ teaspoon lemon juice

2 ounces Gruyère cheese, shredded (½ cup)

1½ tablespoons shredded carrot

1½ tablespoons chopped parsley

¼ teaspoon salt

Cayenne pepper

White pepper

1. Bake the puff-pastry shells according to package directions. Remove the center pieces. Set oven to 375°F.

2. Cook and stir the clams, mushrooms, and wine in a large skillet for 3 to 4 minutes. Drain and spoon the mixture into the pastry shells.

3. Melt the butter in a small saucepan over medium heat, then whisk in the flour, cooking and stirring until the mixture is smooth and bubbling. Stir in the clam juice and lemon juice and heat for 4 to 5 minutes. Add the Gruyère, carrot, parsley, salt, a dash of cayenne, and a pinch of white pepper, and mix well. Heat for 2 to 3 minutes, until the cheese is melted.

4. Spoon the hot cheese sauce over the clams and mushrooms. Bake in the oven for 10 minutes. Serve immediately.

Stuffed Eggplants with Ground Lamb and Feta

Spices from the Middle East waft from this succulent main course dish. Try finding some of the unusual heirloom eggplant varieties that are finding their way to farmers' markets: Cambodian Green Giant, Rosa Bianca, Listada de Gandia, and Chinese Round Mauve. Because of their varying sizes, you may need four, instead of two, eggplants.

2 large eggplants

1 pound ground lamb

2 garlic cloves, peeled and minced

¼ cup chopped fresh parsley

3 tablespoons pine nuts

1 tablespoon chopped fresh cilantro

1 tablespoon chopped fresh mint

1 teaspoon ground coriander

½ teaspoon ground cumin

¼ teaspoon cinnamon

1 teaspoon kosher salt

2 cups cooked rice

2 ounces feta cheese, crumbled

4 SERVINGS

1. Preheat the oven to 400°F. Line a baking sheet with parchment paper. Cut the eggplants in half and prick the skins. Place them cut side down on the baking sheet and bake for 25 minutes. Remove the eggplants from the oven and allow them to cool for 5 minutes. Turn the eggplants cut side up and scoop out and reserve most of the flesh, leaving a 1-inch shell. Keep the oven at 400°F.

2. Sauté the lamb, eggplant flesh, and garlic in a large skillet. Add the parsley, pine nuts, cilantro, mint, coriander, cumin, cinnamon, and salt. Continue cooking and stirring until the lamb is cooked through, 5 to 7 minutes. Remove from the heat and add the rice and feta. Mix thoroughly.

3. Mound a quarter of the filling into each eggplant shell. Return the stuffed eggplants to the oven and bake for 15 minutes. Reduce the oven temperature to 350°F and bake for an additional 15 minutes. Serve immediately.

ROSEDA BEEF
Baltimore County

When Ed Burchell retired at the age of 52, wealthy from his share of the sale of a big health care company, he knew he needed to do something other than just play golf. First, he and his wife, Rosemary, acquired two cows. After that Burchell bought a few Black Angus steers to raise for their own consumption. And from there, an idea began to take shape: to raise the finest beef under the best conditions possible and target it to the upper end of the retail market. Burchell's research showed that at least 2 percent of the population was willing to pay top dollar for top quality, and with Maryland in such a prime geographic location, the potential audience was substantial.

Roseda Beef was born from that idea. From the start Burchell was obsessed with the quality of the meat. "We selected the best Angus for positive DNA tenderness markers and started a breeding program that has resulted in 93 percent of our beef being graded as choice or better," he says with pride. Their cattle are primarily hay and silage fed and, unlike most cattle, they are pastured, with plenty of room to graze and round-the-clock access to clean water and shelter. Roseda calves spend two-thirds of their lives eating grass alongside their mothers. They are never fed hormones, and antibiotics are administered rarely and only if an animal is sick. And when they're slaughtered, they're done so under humane guidelines and conditions. Mike Brannon, Roseda's general manager, tracks every possible statistic about their beef, from who the dam and sire are, to weaning weight, hanging weight, and so on.

The company started by selling 56 head of Black Angus cattle in 1999 and progressed to selling more than 2,000 head in 2008, becoming one of the largest Angus operations on the East Coast. In Burchell's own words, he "doesn't like to do things badly," and Roseda's dry-aged beef — richly flavored and marbled, buttery soft, and barely requiring cutting — is the ultimate decadent testament to his drive for quality.

Recipe from ROSEDA BEEF

Grilled Sirloin Tip Roast with Coffee Spice Rub

A ground coffee rub adds an extraordinarily rich, dark flavor to this summer cookout star.

4–6 SERVINGS

¼ cup salt

¼ cup freshly ground
    black pepper

¼ cup paprika

¼ cup very finely ground dark
    roast coffee beans

1 teaspoon garlic powder

1 (2–3 pound) sirloin tip roast

1. Combine the salt, pepper, paprika, ground coffee, and garlic powder in a medium bowl, and mix well. Pat the roast dry and massage the coffee rub into its surface, coating it completely. Transfer the roast to a dish, cover, and refrigerate for at least 2 hours.

2. Preheat a two-burner gas grill on medium for 15 minutes. Shut off one side of the grill and turn the other side to low. Place the roast on whichever side is off. Close the grill's lid and leave the roast on the grill for 2 hours. Or heat the oven to 275°F and roast the meat for 2 hours.

3. After 2 hours, check the internal temperature with a meat thermometer. For rare, cook to 140°F; for medium rare, cook to 145°F; for medium cook to 160°F; for well done, cook to 170°F. Remove the roast from the heat when the internal temperature reaches desired doneness. Set aside to rest for 5 minutes before slicing.

Bell Peppers with Ground Beef and Barley Stuffing

Barley lends whole-grain wholesomeness to this summer classic. Brown rice also works well and has a nice nutty flavor. In fact, many other grains, including quinoa and amaranth, can be substituted with delicious results.

4 SERVINGS

4 green, red, yellow, or orange bell peppers

2 tablespoons olive oil

1 medium onion, peeled and chopped

1 small zucchini, chopped

1 pound ground beef

1 teaspoon chopped fresh basil

½ teaspoon chopped fresh oregano

½ teaspoon chopped fresh marjoram

½ teaspoon salt

¼ teaspoon paprika

1 large tomato, chopped

1 cup cooked barley

½ cup breadcrumbs

3 tablespoons chopped fresh parsley

½ cup grated Pecorino cheese

1. Preheat the oven to 375°F. Wash the peppers, cut off their tops and reserve, and hollow out the insides. If needed, level the bottoms so that the peppers will stand up. Place the peppers in an 8-inch square baking dish. Chop the reserved pepper tops, discarding the stems.

2. Heat the olive oil in a large skillet and add the onion, chopped pepper tops, and zucchini. Sauté the vegetables for 3 to 5 minutes, until tender. Add the ground beef, basil, oregano, marjoram, salt, and paprika, and cook the meat for 5 minutes, until browned. Add the tomato and cook and stir for 2 to 3 minutes. Add the barley, breadcrumbs, parsley, and ¼ cup of the Pecorino. Toss to mix well and remove from the heat.

3. Stuff each pepper with the filling and top with a tablespoon of the remaining Pecorino. Cover the baking dish and bake for 45 minutes. Uncover and bake for 5 additional minutes, until the cheese is melted and brown. Serve immediately or cool to room temperature.

Blueberry Buckwheat Pancakes

Summer-ripened blueberries and nutty, stone-ground buckwheat flour make these hotcakes healthy as well as delicious. Serve them for Sunday brunch with Summer Fruit Salad with Mint (page 155).

MAKES 16 PANCAKES

2 eggs, separated

1½ cups buttermilk

6 tablespoons butter, melted

¾ cup all-purpose flour

¾ cup buckwheat flour

2 tablespoons turbinado sugar

1½ teaspoons baking powder

1 teaspoon baking soda

1 teaspoon salt

1 teaspoon vanilla extract

1½ cups blueberries

Maple syrup

1. Whip the egg whites in a bowl with a whisk or electric mixer until they form medium to stiff peaks. Set aside.

2. Combine the buttermilk and the egg yolks in a separate large bowl and stir until well mixed. Gradually add 4 tablespoons of the butter, the all-purpose and buckwheat flours, sugar, baking powder, baking soda, salt, and vanilla. Gently fold in the egg whites. Gently stir in the blueberries until mixed.

3. Heat a griddle or large skillet and brush with the remaining 2 tablespoons butter. Spoon the batter in quarter cups onto the griddle. Cook the pancakes over medium heat until bubbles form, about 2 minutes. Flip the pancakes and cook for 2 minutes longer, or until golden. Serve with maple syrup.

Spring Valley Farms
Cecil County

Blueberries are in season from late June through the end of July in Maryland, and I pick huge quantities of them to freeze and use year-round, which I heartily recommend. One of my favorite pick-your-own farms is Spring Valley Farms in Conowingo in Cecil County. The town's name means "at the rapids" in Susquehannock, the language of the Native Americans of the same name and after whom the Susquehanna River is named. In 1608 Captain John Smith sailed up from the Chesapeake Bay into the Susquehanna, came up against those rapids, and had to turn around.

Spring Valley Farms, just a few miles up from the river, is owned and run by Dan and Elizabeth Derr, two of the nicest people you'd ever want to meet. Dan prunes and irrigates (but doesn't spray) eight varieties and 3,300 bushes of blueberries, along with sour cherries, white and yellow peaches, and three varieties of blackberries. Elizabeth runs the stand, where customers check in and weigh and pay for their produce, and she cheerfully dispenses advice on recipes and freezing berries.

On weekends, the fields fill with multigenerational families, who often speak foreign languages and come from as far away as Washington and Philadelphia. They laugh, talk, and eat as they fill their buckets with perfectly ripe berries. But if you go during the week, you'll usually have a whole field to yourself, with just the bald eagles that regularly glide above the farm's gently spooling hills to keep you company.

Blueberry Fruit Kuchen

Filled with creamy custard and bursting with flavor, this popular dessert is ideal with an afternoon cup of tea or coffee, which is how it would be served in Germany, where this cake gets its name.

1 cup (2 sticks) cold butter, cut into small pieces

2 cups all-purpose flour

½ teaspoon salt

4 eggs

2 tablespoons half-and-half

3 cups blueberries

1¾ cups sugar

¾ cup milk

1 teaspoon vanilla extract

1 teaspoon cinnamon

12 Servings

1. Preheat the oven to 350°F. In a large bowl, cut ¾ cup (1½ sticks) of the butter into 1½ cups of the flour; mix well until the dough is crumbly. Add the salt, 1 egg, and the half-and-half, and mix until smooth. Pat the dough into a 9- by 13-inch baking dish, covering the bottom and creating a small lip up the sides. Arrange the blueberries on top of the crust.

2. Whisk the remaining 3 eggs until they are frothy. Add 1 cup of the sugar, the milk, and the vanilla; whisk until smooth. Pour the egg mixture over the fruit.

3. Combine the remaining 4 tablespoons butter, ½ cup flour, and ¾ cup sugar, and the cinnamon in a medium bowl; mix together with a fork until crumbly. Sprinkle the topping over the fruit. Bake for 50 minutes, or until the topping is golden brown and the blueberries are bubbling. Cool and serve.

Blackberry-Nectarine Cobbler with Cream-Cheese Crust

Crusty, fruity, and warm to the touch, cobblers are the quintessential summer dessert and a perfect punctuation to a summer crab feast, a day at the beach, or a barbeque with family and friends. Try to find local white nectarines, which are seductively perfumed and astonishingly sweet.

8 SERVINGS

5 cups peeled and sliced white nectarines

3 cups fresh blackberries

1¼ cups sugar

3 tablespoons quick-cooking tapioca

1 teaspoon vanilla extract

1 teaspoon cinnamon

4 ounces cold cream cheese

½ cup (1 stick) cold butter

¾ cup all-purpose flour

1 tablespoon vanilla sugar (see Note)

Milk

Whipped cream or Vanilla-Bean Ice Cream (page 77) (optional)

1. Prepare the fruit filling: Combine the nectarines, blackberries, sugar, tapioca, vanilla, and cinnamon in a large bowl, and mix until well blended. Cover the bowl and set aside for 45 minutes.

2. Prepare the crust dough: Mix the cream cheese and butter in a bowl with an electric mixer. Add the flour and vanilla sugar and mix until well blended, but not too long or the dough will be tough. Form the dough into a ball, wrap it in plastic wrap, and chill for 30 minutes.

3. Preheat the oven to 350°F. Pour the fruit into an 8-inch square baking dish. Roll out the dough and lay it on top of the fruit, crimping the edges. Brush the crust with milk and cut several slits in the top. Place on a baking sheet and bake for 1 hour, until the crust is golden brown. Remove from the oven and cool slightly before serving. Serve warm with whipped cream or ice cream, if desired.

NOTE: Vanilla sugar can be bought in some supermarkets and specialty stores. If you can't find it, combine 2 vanilla beans and 1 cup of sugar in a food processor or blender and pulse until the mixture is very fine and the beans have been pulverized. Store in a jar or canister and use as needed.

Summer Fruit Tart with Cream Filling

This extravagant fruit- and cream-filled dessert is surprisingly easy to prepare and yet never fails to elicit glowing reviews.

4 **eggs**

¾ **cup sugar**

3 **tablespoons butter, melted**

¾ **cup plus 1 tablespoon all-purpose flour**

1 **(8-ounce) package cream cheese, softened**

2 **teaspoons vanilla extract**

1 **cup heavy cream**

2 **pints fresh raspberries**

1 **pint fresh blueberries**

¼ **cup apple juice**

1 **tablespoon cornstarch**

2 **tablespoons corn syrup**

8 SERVINGS

1. Preheat the oven to 375°F. Grease and lightly flour a 12-inch tart pan.

2. Whip together the eggs and ½ cup of the sugar until blended. Bring water to a simmer in the lower half of a double boiler, and then heat the egg mixture in the upper half of the double boiler until just warm. Remove from the heat.

3. Whip the egg mixture with an electric mixer at high speed, until tripled in volume. Fold in the melted butter and the flour. Spread the batter in the tart pan. Bake until golden, 20 to 25 minutes. Transfer the tart pan to a wire rack to cool for 10 minutes. Turn the crust out onto the rack to cool completely.

4. Beat together the cream cheese, vanilla, and ½ cup of the heavy cream until well mixed. Whip the remaining ½ cup heavy cream and the remaining ¼ cup sugar in a separate bowl with an electric mixer until stiff peaks form. Gently fold the whipped cream into the cream cheese mixture. Spread the filling into the center of the cooled crust. Arrange the berries in a decorative pattern on top of the cream filling.

5. Bring the apple juice and a ¼ cup of water to a boil in a small saucepan over medium heat. Pour half of the liquid into a cup, add the cornstarch, and stir to dissolve. Pour the cornstarch mixture back into the saucepan and cook until thickened. Add the corn syrup and bring to a boil. Remove the glaze from the heat and let it cool slightly. Using a pastry brush, spread the glaze over the top of the fruit.

Red Raspberry Ice Cream

Tartly sweet and fruity, this most royal of fruits makes a wonderful ice cream that pleases even the most discriminating palate.

3 cups milk

3 eggs, beaten

2 cups sugar

2 tablespoons all-purpose flour

1 teaspoon salt

5 cups raspberries

1 tablespoon lemon juice

1 quart half-and-half

1 pint heavy cream

MAKES ABOUT 3 QUARTS

1. Mix the milk and eggs together in a large saucepan. Stir together the sugar, flour, and salt in a medium bowl, and then add to the milk mixture. Cook over medium-low heat, stirring constantly, until the mixture thickens to a soft custard. Remove from the heat and chill. Meanwhile, combine the raspberries and lemon juice in a food processor or blender and purée until smooth.

2. Add the half-and-half and heavy cream to the chilled custard. Stir in the puréed raspberries and pour the custard into the bowl of an ice cream maker. Freeze according to the manufacturer's instructions.

Cherry Clafoutis with Ground Almonds

This fragrant, delectable cross between a custard and a cake is simple enough that even beginning cooks, like children, can make a tasty clafoutis. Traditionally, it's served with unpitted sweet cherries, but I prefer sour cherries, and I pit them.

6 SERVINGS

- 3 cups Montmorency, Morello, or other tart cherries
- ½ cup sugar
- ½ cup whole blanched almonds
- ½ cup all-purpose flour
- 2½ cups half-and-half
- 1 teaspoon vanilla
- 4 eggs
- ⅛ teaspoon salt
- 2 tablespoons confectioners' sugar

1. Preheat the oven to 375°F. Pit the cherries if desired. Butter a 9-inch pie plate and line the pie plate with the cherries.

2. Combine the sugar and the almonds in a food processor and pulse until they are finely ground. Add the flour, half-and-half, vanilla, eggs, and salt, and blend thoroughly. Pour the batter over the cherries.

3. Bake for 40 to 45 minutes, until a knife inserted in the center of the custard comes out clean. Cool until warm or room temperature. Just before serving, sift the confectioners' sugar over the top of the clafoutis.

CHERRIES

Cherries thrive in Maryland's hilly counties, from Cecil and Harford counties west. Of all of them, however, Frederick and Washington counties are probably best known for their orchards, many of which are clustered along scenic country roads in and around Smithsburg and Thurmont, home to the presidential retreat, Camp David. At family-run establishments like Catoctin Mt. Orchard, where the Black family has been growing delicious fruits since 1948, they offer both sweet and sour cherries for sale. Because the season for cherries is so short, I usually pick as many of them as I can and freeze some for use out of season.

Mrs. Balderston's Streusel Cream Peach Pie

This festive-looking dessert will be the hit of any summer gathering. Mrs. Balderston has been making it for decades to great acclaim.

8 SERVINGS

1 (9-inch) piecrust or ½ recipe Basic Piecrust (page 76), chilled

8–10 ripe peaches, peeled, halved, and pitted

½ cup sugar

⅛ teaspoon nutmeg

1 egg

2 tablespoons heavy cream

½ cup brown sugar

½ cup all-purpose flour

4 tablespoons butter, cut into tiny pieces

1. Preheat the oven to 425°F. Roll out the piecrust and fit it into a 10-inch pie plate.

2. Line the piecrust with the peach halves, pit side up, in concentric circles. (You will need to lean the peach halves against each other, almost standing them up.) Sprinkle the sugar and the nutmeg over the fruit. Beat the egg and the cream together and pour over the peaches.

3. Mix the brown sugar, flour, and butter in a bowl until crumbly. Crumble the mixture over the peaches. Bake for 35 to 45 minutes, until nicely browned. Cool before serving.

Wine Berry Pavlova

For about two weeks in late July, much of Maryland's countryside is covered with wild wine berries, the fruit of an Asian native introduced to the United States many years ago. They taste like a cross between a red currant and a red raspberry. Wine berries make mouthwatering jams, jellies, and (rumor has it) wine. They are also delicious fresh. Wine berries are just tart enough to be the foil to the chewy sweetness of the meringue in this easy, but sumptuous, dessert named for the legendary Russian ballerina Anna Pavlova. Of course, if you aren't lucky enough to have wine berries growing around you in profusion, as I do, any other berry or tart fruit makes a fine substitute.

8 egg whites
1½ cups plus 1 tablespoon sugar
2 teaspoons white vinegar
1 pint heavy cream
1 teaspoon vanilla extract
2 pints wine berries

8 SERVINGS

1. Preheat the oven to 275°F. Trace an 8-inch circle on a sheet of parchment paper and place the paper on a baking sheet.

2. Prepare the meringue: Whip the egg whites in a large bowl with a whisk or electric mixer until they form soft peaks. Continuing to whip, gradually add the 1½ cups of sugar in small amounts, followed by the vinegar. Continue beating until the egg whites are very thick, stiff, and glossy.

3. Bake the meringue: Spoon the mixture onto the parchment paper, being careful to keep it within the confines of the circle. The top should be slightly concave, the edges higher than the center. Bake in the center of the oven for 1½ hours, until it takes on a pale golden sheen. Cool thoroughly, and then carefully invert it, remove the parchment paper, and transfer the baked meringue to a large serving plate with the concave side once again facing up.

4. Whip the cream, the 1 tablespoon of sugar, and the vanilla in a cold bowl with an electric mixer with chilled beaters. Whip until the cream forms soft, not stiff, peaks. Spread the whipped cream on the meringue, and then immediately cover the whipped cream with the wine berries. Serve immediately.

COLORA ORCHARDS
Cecil County

Though few people know it, the peaches and apples that many Maryland, Pennsylvania, and Delaware grocery stores stock probably were grown in the oldest orchard in Maryland by a man with one of America's most storied pedigrees. Not that Stephen Balderston would tell you himself, but when asked if it's true that he is the great-great-grandson of Betsy Ross of Philadelphia, he smiles and says yes.

Modest as the shy and gracious Balderston is, it's clear that he treasures his family's history, which literally surrounds him. It's not just the handsome 1843 stone house built by his great-great-grandfather, Lloyd Balderston, which now belongs

Stephen Balderston

to Stephen and his family, or the 500 or so acres that make up Colora Orchards today. It's also the hamlet Colora, named for the family's orchard, a name Lloyd Balderston concocted from the Latin "culmen" (peak or height) and "aura" (air or wind). Just up the road lies the picture-perfect 1841 Quaker meetinghouse where five generations of Balderstons, including Betsy Ross's daughter and her granddaughter, Catharine Canby Balderston, are buried. And a mile in the other direction are Stephen's parents, Donald and Jane Balderston, both in their 80s and still helping their son with the orchard. "It's in the genes, I guess," Stephen says one day when I visit, watched over by family photographs and two dogs, Gala and Honey, one named for an apple, the other for a peach. If ever a family cared about history and continuity, it is the Balderstons.

Even the people who work for the family share in the history: Mike Gonzalez, a native of Puerto Rico who manages the farm with Balderston, has been there for 25 years. And many of the packers, local women who work seasonally, started working there even before that; today they work side by side with a crew of Mexicans who also return year after year. It is poignant to hear, then, that Balderston isn't sure what will become of the business when he is no longer able to run it. His two daughters are not interested in taking it on and are pursuing professional careers off the farm, he says, and while he is clearly proud of them, there is an air of sadness about Balderston, as if the responsibility for the farm's future rests heavily on his shoulders.

The 19 peach and 10 apple varieties that Colora grows go mostly wholesale to supermarkets,

but visitors are welcome to buy fruit at the packinghouse, as well. Most locals, though, head straight to Balderston's parents' house. There, in the basement of the cozy stone bungalow that Jane and Donald Balderston built themselves over a half century ago, people select fruit from among a dozen or more wooden crates that the senior Balderstons have laid out. Hand-lettered signs distinguish the different varieties and their cost. There's a scale and a money box, and customers buy what they want on the honor system. If they're in the mood for a visit or need some change, they'll call up the stairs to the house and Jane Balderston, a retired schoolteacher whose love is voice and opera, will come downstairs and chat for a spell. Like everything about Colora, it's an experience not to be missed.

Baked Peaches with Honey and Custard Sauce

Buttery, honeyed peaches are ambrosial with this warm custard sauce. Use local raw honey if you can find it; it is superior in taste and offers many health benefits. Local raw honey is especially good for combatting allergies. Harris Orchard in Anne Arundel County sells its delicious sweetener at farmers' markets throughout the region.

1½ cups heavy cream

4 egg yolks

½ cup sugar

1 tablespoon cornstarch

2 teaspoons vanilla extract

¾ cup raw honey

¼ cup lemon juice

3 tablespoons butter, melted

1 teaspoon cinnamon

6 peaches, peeled, halved, and pitted

6 SERVINGS

1. Preheat the oven to 375°F. Cook the cream in a medium saucepan over medium heat until it just comes to a boil. Remove from the heat.

2. Whisk together the egg yolks in a medium bowl and gradually whisk in the sugar and cornstarch until the mixture is light and creamy. Then gradually whisk the hot cream into the egg mixture. Return the cream mixture to the saucepan, stir in the vanilla, and cook over medium heat, stirring constantly for about 4 minutes, until the mixture thickens. Do not let it boil, or it will curdle. Remove the custard sauce from the heat. Cover to keep warm.

3. Combine the honey, lemon juice, butter, and cinnamon in a small bowl. Place the peach halves in an oiled baking dish, pit side up, and drizzle them with the honey mixture. Cover, and bake for 15 minutes. Uncover the peaches and bake for an additional 15 minutes. Remove from the oven and cool for 15 minutes. Serve warm with the custard sauce.

PEACHES

Peaches are called "chin dribblers" for good reason: there's simply nothing juicier or more delicious than a tree-ripened summer peach. In Maryland, orchards grow dozens of varieties of yellow and white, cling and freestone, and the coolness of our winters combined with really hot summers produces some of the best peaches you'll ever eat. Beginning in early July and continuing until the middle of September, there is a local peach for just about everyone. Among orchards like Lohr's in Harford County, or Ivy Hill in Washington County, or Catoctin Mountain in Frederick County, you'll find a huge variety — Early Red, Garnet Beauty, Loring, White Rose, Blake, Summer Breeze, September Queen, Autumn Prince, or Snowball, the season's last peach — and many of them are available for self-picking, which means they're inexpensive as well as delectable.

One of my favorite things about local peaches is that they're usually superior in smell and taste to varieties sold in supermarkets. Because they're not bred for the ease of transport, perfect looks, and long shelf life that grocery stores require, local peaches are apt to be heirloom or old-fashioned varieties, or feature unusual coloring and richer tastes, though they may only be available for ten days or may bruise easily. Also, local orchards almost always feature "seconds" peaches: slightly bruised but usually perfectly ripe peaches sold at half-price, ideal for same-day pies or jams. At a local orchard just across the border into Pennsylvania, Amish farmers in buggies arrive early to see what the specials of the day are, and then buy bushels of them.

Peaches are low-calorie and vitamin-rich: the perfect summer snack, whether eaten out of hand at the beach, sliced, or dried as fruit leather. Peaches also star in numerous summer drinks, from shakes and daiquiris to Bellinis. They're versatile in baked dishes, and many varieties (such as the Chinese native) are so easy to freeze or can that you can enjoy a taste of summer all year-round.

Spiced Peach Crisp with Oatmeal-Coconut Topping

This is another recipe from my sister, Alexandra. The spicy hint of ginger and toasted coconut topping make it irresistible. I like to use white peaches for this dessert. Try Swann Farms in Calvert County for several delicious varieties.

10 SERVINGS

5 cups peeled and sliced fresh peaches

½ cup granulated sugar

3 tablespoons cornstarch

½ teaspoon almond extract

½ teaspoon ground ginger

¼ teaspoon ground nutmeg

1½ cups old-fashioned (not instant) oats

¾ cup brown sugar

½ cup unsweetened fresh or dried coconut, shredded

⅓ cup all-purpose flour

1 teaspoon cinnamon

½ teaspoon baking powder

½ cup (1 stick) cold butter, cut into small pieces

Whipped cream or Vanilla Bean Ice Cream (page 77) (optional)

1. Preheat the oven to 375°F. Combine the peaches, granulated sugar, cornstarch, almond extract, ginger, and nutmeg in an 8-inch square baking dish or a 10-inch pie plate. Toss to coat the peaches with the sugar and spices.

2. Make the topping: Combine the oats, brown sugar, coconut, flour, cinnamon, and baking powder in a large bowl. Add the butter, using a pastry cutter or knife to cut it into the dry ingredients. Mix until crumbly and the butter pieces are the size of small peas.

3. Sprinkle the topping over the peaches and bake for 45 minutes. Serve warm with a dollop of whipped cream or ice cream, if desired.

Apricot Jam with Rosewater

My sister and I learned to make jams and jellies in our grandmother's kitchen in Switzerland, using berries from her garden and fruits from her neighbors' orchards. Homemade preserves are intensely fruity, not cloyingly sweet and gummy. And you can make quirky combinations that you'll rarely, if ever, find in stores, like rhubarb-peach, or this one, with its taste of rosewater. For the two weeks that apricots are in season in Maryland, I pick and buy as many as I can. Some go right into a tart or pie, others are frozen or dried for later use, and the rest are made into jam.

7 cups finely chopped apricots

2 tablespoons lemon juice

4½ cups sugar

1 package reduced-sugar pectin (I use Sure-Jell For Less or No Sugar Needed Recipes)

½ teaspoon butter

2 teaspoons rosewater

NOTE: Rosewater is used primarily in sweet dishes – especially in Indian desserts – and can be found in Asian markets and specialty stores in the flavorings and extracts section. It's also readily available online or, if you are ambitious and have your own pesticide-free roses, you can make your own. Simply pour 2 cups of boiling water over 1 cup of packed rose petals. Allow the liquid to cool, and then refrigerate overnight. Strain the mixture and discard the rose petals. You'll be left with a delicately colored and wonderfully scented flavoring that will keep for months in the refrigerator.

MAKES 8 CUPS

1. Gather four 1-pint canning jars with bands and new lids. Wash the jars in hot, soapy water and then rinse. Place the jars in a stockpot large enough to hold them, fill the pot halfway with water, and bring the water to a boil over high heat. Add the canning lids to the water and turn off the heat. Leave the jars and lids in the water until you are ready to fill them.

2. Combine the apricots and the lemon juice in a large saucepan. Mix ¼ cup of the sugar and the pectin together in a small bowl. Add to the apricots and toss thoroughly. Cook over high heat, stirring vigorously and constantly, until the mixture reaches a rolling boil. Add the butter and the remaining 4¼ cups sugar. Stirring constantly, return the jam to a rolling boil and cook for exactly 1 minute. Remove from the heat and stir in the rosewater.

3. Remove the jars and lids from the water and shake them off. Ladle the jam into the jars, filling them to within ⅛ inch of the top. Place the lids on the jars and screw the bands onto the jars. Place a rack or towel in the bottom of the pot of hot water. Put the jars on the rack and bring the water to a boil. Boil the jars for 10 minutes. Carefully remove them from the water, and cool. The jam may take a day or two to set. Store in a cool, dark place for up to 1 year.

Will Hales

HALES FARM
Wicomico County

Maryland has a long history of growing watermelons, and its Eastern Shore region is the perfect place to grow them because of the sandy soil, long growing season, and steady, hot temperatures. Will Hales and his father, Donald, tend 400 acres of the seedless sweet melons in Salisbury, something the family has been doing successfully for decades. In 1981 Donald grew the first variety of seedless watermelons in the country for Sun World in Bakersfield, California, a company the family still does business with. Will and Donald largely grow the classic oblong watermelons that most people grew up eating, but they also produce the newer "personal" watermelons, as the five- to seven-pound round fruits are called. From the end of July until the middle of September, the Hales' farm buzzes with well over 80 people who help pick and pack the roughly 2,400,000 pounds of watermelon that the farm produces each year. But despite the labor-intensive nature of the crop, which keeps some farmers from raising them, Will says that growing watermelons is a tradition for his family, something they like doing because it's a fruit that has such happy memories associated with eating it.

Summer Fruit Salad with Mint

This cooling fruit salad is best in the middle of summer when it's so hot that you barely want to eat, much less cook. Vary the ingredients according to what's freshest. If you're lucky, you might even find the local brown Turkish figs that Sand Hill Farm in Caroline County grows and sells.

8 SERVINGS

2 cups watermelon chunks, seeds removed

1 cup sliced white peaches

1 cup sliced yellow peaches

1 cup cantaloupe chunks or other musk melon variety

1 cup honeydew chunks or other pale-fleshed melon variety

1 cup blackberries

1 cup blueberries or raspberries

1 cup strawberries, hulled and cut in half

½ cup honey

¼ cup lemon juice

½ cup fresh mint leaves, cut into fine ribbons

Crème fraîche (optional)

1. Combine the watermelon, the white and yellow peaches, cantaloupe, honeydew, blackberries, blueberries, and strawberries in a large serving bowl, and toss gently.

2. Heat the honey and lemon juice in a small saucepan over low heat until just at the boiling point, stirring to combine well. Remove from the heat and cool.

3. Pour the honey mixture over the fruit and toss to combine. Sprinkle the mint over the fruit salad and toss. Chill or serve immediately, garnishing with crème fraîche, if desired.

Chocolate Mousse with Summer Raspberries

This is the perfect summer dessert for when you've eaten a lot of salad and vegetables and feel virtuous enough to cap it all with something exquisitely rich. The keys to a perfect chocolate mousse are great chocolate (I always use Lindt Excellence), farm-fresh eggs, and fresh heavy cream. Because the mousse is so rich, you need only offer small portions. I like to serve mine in my yellow and green Depression glass tumblers.

20 ounces top-quality bittersweet chocolate

½ cup (1 stick) butter

8 eggs, separated

1 cup superfine sugar

3 tablespoons strong coffee

2 cups whipping cream

2 tablespoons vanilla sugar (see page 141)

1 pint raspberries

10–12 SERVINGS

1. Break the chocolate into small pieces and melt in the top pan of a double boiler over simmering water. Do not stir. Remove the chocolate from the heat and stir in the butter with a wooden spoon until smooth.

2. Whip the egg yolks and sugar with an electric mixer on high until the yolks are pale yellow and thick, 2 to 3 minutes. Stir the coffee into the yolk mixture and then add the chocolate, stirring until smooth. Set aside to cool.

3. Whip the egg whites with an electric mixer on high until they form soft peaks. Set aside.

4. Whip the cream and vanilla sugar with an electric mixer on high until the cream forms soft peaks. Combine the beaten egg whites with the cream and carefully fold them into the cooled chocolate mixture. Pour into a serving dish or dishes and refrigerate for 4 hours. Remove the mousse from the refrigerator and garnish with raspberries.

3 Fall

Fall brings cooler weather, brilliant leaves, and Ravens football. The crabs depart and oyster season arrives. It's duck- and goose- and deer-hunting time, and in the Atlantic, the bluefish are running hard. There are lighthouse tours, haunted hay wagon rides, corn mazes, and wine festivals galore. Weekends mean pumpkins to pick, pies to bake, and skipjacks to race. And once again, it's turkey time.

Apple and Pear Salad with Grilled Chicken and Pecans

Sweet and savory combine in this fall cornucopia salad. Up at Rinehart Orchards in Washington County, they've been offering dozens of varieties of just-picked apples, pears, and other fruits since 1930.

8 cups assorted salad greens, torn into pieces

1 large, ripe pear, cored and sliced

1 tart apple, cored and sliced

3 chicken breast halves, grilled, skinned, and cut into strips

2 tablespoons minced scallions

½ cup pecan halves

1 ounce FireFly goat cheese, crumbled

½ teaspoon good-quality honey mustard

2 tablespoons balsamic vinegar

1 tablespoon orange juice

6 tablespoons olive oil

¼ teaspoon salt

Freshly ground black pepper

4 SERVINGS

1. Line a platter with the salad greens. Top with the pear and apple slices, chicken, scallions, and pecans. Sprinkle the cheese over the salad.

2. Combine the mustard, vinegar, orange juice, olive oil, and salt in medium bowl. Whisk together until smooth and pour over the salad. Finish with pepper to taste.

Carrot and Fennel Slaw with Hazelnut Vinaigrette

Look for locally grown fennel and purple carrots at farmers' markets in Takoma Park and Baltimore, among others. Hints of licorice and hazelnuts blend delightfully well in this crispy salad.

6 SERVINGS

1 pound carrots
2 fennel bulbs
3 tablespoons white balsamic vinegar
½ teaspoon Dijon mustard
1 teaspoon lemon juice
¼ teaspoon salt
7 tablespoons hazelnut oil

1. Peel and trim the ends of the carrots. Trim the woody parts of the fennel bulb and cut the bulbs into quarters. Shred the carrots and the fennel, using a food processor with the shredding attachment or by hand with a grater. Transfer the mixture to a large bowl.

2. Mix the vinegar and mustard in a small bowl until the mustard has almost dissolved. Add the lemon juice and salt, then whisk in the hazelnut oil. Pour the dressing over the carrot mixture, cover, and chill for 2 hours. Let the slaw return to room temperature for serving.

Recipe from CALVERT'S GIFT

Creamy Kohlrabi Slaw

Jack and Becky Gurley in Baltimore County are among the few farmers who still grow kohlrabi. It is a shame that more do not, since this cabbage relative has its own delicious, mild taste.

6 SERVINGS

8 small kohlrabi
1 carrot, grated
½ cup sour cream
½ cup mayonnaise
3 tablespoons milk
2 teaspoons chopped fresh dill
2 teaspoons lemon juice
1 teaspoon lemon zest
1 teaspoon salt
½ teaspoon sugar
¼ teaspoon freshly ground black pepper
Fresh dill sprigs

1. Peel the kohlrabi and cut into thin slices.

2. Combine the kohlrabi, carrot, sour cream, mayonnaise, milk, chopped dill, lemon juice, lemon zest, salt, sugar, and pepper in a medium bowl. Gently toss to mix, cover, and refrigerate at least 1 hour, stirring occasionally. Garnish with dill sprigs.

Pear, Spinach, and Bacon Salad

Red and yellow Bartlett pears, crispy bacon, and dark green spinach echo the changing colors of the fall in this spectacular harvest salad. Catoctin Mountain Orchard up in Frederick County has wonderful pears and also sells fresh pies. Its proprietors, the Black family, won Maryland's Farmer of the Year award in 2007 and were inducted into the Governor's Agriculture Hall of Fame in 2009.

8 cups fresh spinach

1 ripe yellow Bartlett pear, cored and sliced

1 ripe red Bartlett pear, cored, and sliced

4–5 strips bacon, cooked crisp and crumbled

½ cup white mushrooms, sliced

½ cup Blue Cheese Dressing (see below)

6–8 SERVINGS

Arrange the spinach leaves on a serving platter or in a large salad bowl. Layer with the red and yellow pears, bacon, and mushrooms. Top with the dressing. Toss the salad and serve immediately.

Recipe from **DRAGONFLY FARM**

BLUE CHEESE DRESSING

3 tablespoons Dragonfly Cabernet wine vinegar, or other flavorful red-wine vinegar

1 large garlic clove, finely chopped

1 teaspoon dry mustard

½ cup olive oil

5 ounces blue cheese, crumbled (1 cup)

½ cup sour cream

2 tablespoons milk

MAKES 2 CUPS DRESSING

Combine the vinegar, garlic, and mustard in a blender or food processor, and blend to combine. Add the oil in a slow stream and blend to incorporate. Add the blue cheese, sour cream, and milk. Blend dressing until well combined. Refrigerated, this dressing will keep for 2 weeks.

Cream of Broccoli Soup with Parmesan Cheese

Aromatic and filling, this soup hits the spot on a cold fall evening. Broccoli is available at farm stands across the state right up until December.

3   tablespoons butter

4   shallots, peeled and finely chopped

2   garlic cloves, peeled and finely minced

1   bay leaf

6   cups broccoli, cut into small pieces

4   cups Chicken Stock (page 26) or Vegetable Stock (page 27)

1   teaspoon salt

¼   teaspoon freshly ground black pepper

2   cups milk

½   cup sour cream

½   cup freshly grated Parmesan cheese

1. Melt the butter in a stockpot over low heat. Add the shallots, garlic, and bay leaf, and sauté until the shallots are translucent. Add the broccoli, stock, salt, and pepper. Cook for 15 minutes over low to medium heat.

2. Remove the soup from the heat and remove the bay leaf. Purée the soup with the milk in small batches in a blender. Return the soup to the pot and heat gently. Whisk in the sour cream and Parmesan, stirring until the cheese has melted. Serve immediately.

A Cook's Café
Anne Arundel County

Sourcing food locally is not an easy feat. At A Cook's Café in Annapolis, owner and executive chef Craig Sewell does it almost exclusively, and "it's a daunting and time-consuming task," he reports. "You have to be completely dedicated to it, and in the years that I've been doing it, it hasn't gotten easier." Sewell ticks off a number of challenges that the average restaurant doesn't have: he can't plan menus months in advance, which is cheaper; getting farmers to deliver is tricky; and the process of interacting directly with the producers is so time-consuming that he really needs a person who is, as he puts it, "divorced from the kitchen" to handle it. Instead, Sewell does it all himself, adding several hours to an already packed schedule that includes running a culinary school, catering, and organizing a new CSA, which he hopes will make his customers more committed to buying locally, as well as buttress the café's earnings in a volatile economy.

But despite the drawbacks, Sewell's commitment to buying locally is absolute. First, it's about food

Craig Sewell

safety. Unlike most chefs, he knows where all of his meat and produce come from, and he has no problems with quality whatsoever. Second, it's about taste. Truly ripe and fresh ingredients simply taste superior to those that may have been picked or packaged many days before they're used, he explains. Third, "It's changed the way I cook. I let the food speak for itself, and use sauces and elaborate techniques less because of the freshness." And finally, there is the sustainability factor. Simply put, he says, "I feel it's my responsibility to help farms grow."

Recipe from A COOK'S CAFÉ

Caramelized Tomato Soup

This is a "cream of . . ." soup that does not need cream, thanks to its velouté sauce: butter and flour are cooked together to form a roux, which thickens the broth into a rich base. Master this soup and the family will have a new comfort food!

6 SERVINGS

3½ pounds fresh tomatoes, or canned plum tomatoes in juice, or a combination

1½ tablespoons brown sugar

4 tablespoons unsalted butter

4 shallots, peeled and minced

3 tablespoons Italian tomato paste (preferably Amore brand in the squeeze tube)

Allspice

2 tablespoons all-purpose flour

2½ cups Chicken Stock (page 26) or Vegetable Stock (page 27)

2 tablespoons dry sherry

Cayenne pepper

1. Preheat the oven to 350°F. Line a rimmed baking sheet with foil. If using fresh tomatoes, cut them into quarters. If using canned tomatoes, reserve the juice. Spread the tomatoes in a single layer on the foil and sprinkle them evenly with the brown sugar. Bake until the tomatoes begin to caramelize, about 30 minutes. Remove from the oven and let them cool slightly.

2. Melt the butter in a large saucepan over medium heat, until foaming. Add the shallots, tomato paste, and a pinch of allspice. Reduce heat to low and cook, stirring occasionally, until the shallots are softened, about 10 minutes. Add the flour and cook, stirring constantly, until thoroughly combined. Gradually add the chicken stock, and then stir in the roasted tomatoes and the reserved tomato juice, if using. Cover and heat to a low simmer until thickened (soup will only thicken when very hot).

3. Blend the soup with an immersion blender, and then strain though a mesh strainer. Stir in the sherry, and cayenne to taste. Serve immediately.

Early Fall Corn Chowder

In Maryland, local corn and bell peppers are available until late September or whenever we have the first frost. This chowder uses the best of summer's local vegetables, but it has fall's colors.

2 tablespoons butter

1 small onion, peeled and diced

2 garlic cloves, peeled and minced

1 small orange or red bell pepper, finely diced

1 large carrot, peeled and thinly sliced

1 teaspoon chopped fresh thyme leaves

6 cups of Chicken Stock (page 26) or Vegetable Stock (page 27)

4 medium potatoes, preferably local Yukon Gold, peeled and diced

½ teaspoon salt

½ teaspoon freshly ground black pepper

4 cups of local bicolor corn kernels

1 cup half-and-half

2 tablespoons chopped fresh parsley

1. Melt the butter in a large stockpot over low heat. Add the onion and garlic and sauté for about 3 minutes, until soft. Add the bell pepper, carrot, and thyme, and sauté for 5 minutes longer. Add the stock, potatoes, salt, and pepper, and turn up the heat to medium. Cook for 25 minutes.

2. Purée 2 cups of the corn with the half-and-half in a blender or food processor. Pour the corn purée into the soup, along with the remaining whole kernels. Reduce the heat and simmer for 4 minutes. Top the soup with the parsley and serve immediately.

Mushroom Bisque with Homemade Croutons

Serve this rich and elegant soup as a first course for a dinner party.

4 tablespoons butter

2 celery stalks, finely chopped

2 medium potatoes, peeled and cut into small cubes

1 large onion, peeled and finely chopped

2 pounds fresh mushrooms, such as shiitakes, chicken of the woods, or cremini, cleaned, dried, woody ends removed, and roughly chopped

3 cups Chicken Stock (page 26) or Vegetable Stock (page 27)

1 teaspoon dried thyme

2 teaspoons salt

½ teaspoon freshly ground black pepper

3 cups milk, scalded

1 cup half-and-half, warmed

3 tablespoons dry sherry

1 teaspoon fresh chives, finely chopped

Garlic Croutons (see below)

1. Melt the butter in a stockpot over low heat. Add the celery, potatoes, and onion, and sauté for 5 minutes, until the onion and celery are translucent. Add the mushrooms, raise the heat to medium-high, and continue to sauté until the mushrooms are soft, about 5 minutes. Add the stock, thyme, salt, and pepper, and simmer, covered, for 20 minutes over medium heat. Remove from the heat and let cool slightly.

2. Blend the soup with a handheld immersion blender or in a blender. Return the soup to low heat and warm gently, carefully whisking in the milk, half-and-half, and sherry. Heat through, but do not allow the soup to boil. Sprinkle with chives and croutons and serve immediately.

GARLIC CROUTONS

3 tablespoons butter

1 garlic clove, peeled and crushed

2 cups stale bread, cut into 1-inch cubes

¼ teaspoon paprika

¼ teaspoon salt

1. Preheat the oven to 325°F. Melt the butter in a medium skillet over low heat. Add the garlic and sauté for 1 to 2 minutes, until fragrant. Add the bread cubes and sprinkle them with paprika and salt. Mix thoroughly. Remove from the heat.

2. Spread the bread cubes onto a baking sheet and toast for 10 to 15 minutes, until the croutons are golden brown.

Curried Pumpkin Soup

Maryland farmers grow 15 million pounds and dozens of varieties of pumpkin every year, from traditional giant to heirloom sugar pumpkins to white pumpkins to my own personal favorite, the Jarrahdale blue pumpkin, a hard-to-find New Zealand heirloom. Its flesh is brilliant orange, sweet and, best of all, fiberless. I find mine at Greenwood Farm in Glen Arm, where Donald Burton's family has farmed since 1840. Greenwood Farms offers unusual varieties of many vegetables and fruits, which is how Donald Burton likes it. In his words, "We need a little variety." I couldn't agree more. This outstanding soup is velvety and slightly spicy with a hint of sweetness. Serve with Two-Cheese Popovers (page 179) or Potato Harvest Yeast Rolls (page 180).

1 (3–4 pound) blue pumpkin or other sweet, creamy pumpkin

3 tablespoons butter

1 medium onion, peeled and finely chopped

1 garlic clove, peeled and finely chopped

4 cups Chicken Stock (page 26) or Vegetable Stock (page 27)

2 tablespoons dark brown sugar

1 teaspoon salt

1 tablespoon curry powder

½ teaspoon ground cardamom

2 cups milk

¼ cup plain yogurt

6–8 SERVINGS

1. Preheat the oven to 350°F. Lightly butter a large, shallow baking pan. Set aside. Cut the pumpkin in half and scoop out the seeds, discarding them, or reserving them to roast separately.

2. Place the pumpkin cut side down in the prepared pan and add 1 cup water. Bake until soft, 45 minutes to 1 hour, depending on the size of the pumpkin. Set aside to cool. When the pumpkin is cool enough, scoop out the flesh and discard the skin. Measure out 4 packed cups of the flesh and set aside.

3. Melt the butter in a stockpot over low heat. Sauté the onion and garlic for 2 minutes, until the onion is translucent. Add the pumpkin, stock, sugar, salt, curry powder, and cardamom, and simmer for 30 minutes over low to medium heat, stirring occasionally. Remove from the heat.

4. Purée the soup using a handheld immersion blender or, working with a food processor, transfer the soup to the food processor in batches and purée until smooth, returning the soup to the stockpot. Add the milk and stir over low heat until the soup is heated through. Ladle the soup into bowls and garnish each with a dollop of yogurt.

NOTE: You can save time by microwaving the pumpkin cut side down in a shallow dish with ½ cup of water for 15 minutes.

Crab Bisque

This special soup is incomparably rich and delicious. My sister-in-law, Eleanor Van Dyke, serves it at her annual Christmas party, where it's always a huge hit. This recipe can easily be doubled or tripled, substituting or mixing lobster, shrimp, oysters, or scallops. You can also substitute backfin crabmeat, which is less expensive because the meat is in smaller pieces.

4–6 Servings

- 1 pound Maryland jumbo lump crabmeat
- 4 tablespoons butter
- 3 celery stalks, diced
- 1 small onion, peeled and finely chopped
- 2 tablespoons all-purpose flour
- 1 tablespoon dry mustard
- 1½ teaspoons salt or seafood seasoning
- ¼ teaspoon freshly ground black pepper
- 2 cups half-and-half
- 2 cups milk
- 2 tablespoons chopped parsley

1. Pick through the crabmeat and remove any shell bits and cartilage. Set aside.

2. Melt the butter in a medium saucepan. Add the celery and the onion and sauté over low heat until they are translucent. Remove the pan from the heat and scoop out the vegetables. Put the vegetables into a cheesecloth bag and tie the bag to the handle of the pan, so that the bag hangs inside the pan, close to the bottom.

3. Return the pan to the heat and add the flour, mustard, salt, and pepper, stirring until blended. Add the half-and-half and the milk and stir constantly until thickened.

4. Add the crabmeat and cook over low heat for 15 to 20 minutes. Remove the vegetable bag and sprinkle the bisque with parsley before serving.

Mushroom Caps Stuffed with Crab and Parmesan

Fall mushrooms pair with the last crabs of the season for this savory appetizer. Almost any grated cheese works well with this recipe, including Broom's Bloom or Chapel's Country Cheddars.

24 fresh medium button mushrooms

1 pound Maryland backfin crabmeat

1⅓ cups mayonnaise

2 eggs

¼ cup milk

¼ cup freshly grated Parmesan cheese

3 teaspoons chopped fresh parsley

1 teaspoon lemon juice

1 teaspoon Worcestershire sauce

1 teaspoon dry mustard

½ teaspoon salt

4 saltine crackers, finely crushed in a blender or food processor

2 dashes hot pepper sauce

⅛ teaspoon paprika

1. Preheat the oven to 375°F. Wash the mushrooms and remove the stems. Scrape and discard some of the flesh from the caps so there is adequate space for the filling. Transfer the mushroom caps to a buttered, foil-lined baking sheet.

2. Clean the crabmeat, removing any cartilage and shells. Transfer the crab to a bowl and set aside.

3. Combine ⅓ cup of the mayonnaise, 1 egg, the milk, Parmesan, parsley, lemon juice, Worcestershire, mustard, and salt in a small bowl. Whisk until the dressing is smooth. Pour the dressing over the crabmeat and toss until mixed. Add the crushed crackers and gently toss to incorporate. Do not overmix.

4. Fill the mushroom caps with the crab mixture. Bake in the oven for 10 to 12 minutes, until the mixture begins to bubble.

5. Mix together the remaining 1 cup mayonnaise, the remaining egg, and the hot pepper sauce in a small bowl. Remove the mushrooms from the oven and top each cap with a spoonful of the topping. Sprinkle with the paprika and return to the oven to cook for an additional 7 to 8 minutes, until golden. Serve immediately.

Smoked Ham and Collard Greens

Prince George's County, the most affluent African American–majority county in America, has a long farming history, much of it rooted in tobacco farming. Many of the members of its dwindling and aging farming community have long ties to the area, some of which go back to Maryland's ugly history of slavery. Collard greens and kale, along with many other typically Southern greens, are common at farm stands throughout Prince George's County and southern Maryland, and collards and smoked ham hocks are standard offerings at church suppers and family gatherings. The key to good collards is to cook them for a long time. I find mine at Miller Farm in Clinton, in southern Prince George's County.

1½ teaspoons salt
1 pound smoked ham hocks
2 pounds collard greens
¼ teaspoon freshly ground black pepper
2 tablespoons cider vinegar
1 teaspoon hot sauce

4 SERVINGS

1. Fill a large stockpot halfway with water. Add 1 teaspoon of the salt and bring the water to a boil. Add the ham hocks. Cook for 1 hour over low to medium heat.

2. Thoroughly wash the collard greens. Cut the stems from the larger, tougher leaves. Stack the leaves and cut them into strips. Add the collards to the pot. Cook over low to medium heat for at least 2 hours.

3. Remove the ham hocks from the pot and pick off the meat. Pour off most of the water, leaving just enough for the collards to be moist. Add the ham pieces back to the greens and season with the remaining ½ teaspoon salt and the pepper, vinegar, and hot sauce, adjusting to taste.

Celery Root and Sweet Potato Gratin

Many root vegetables and winter squashes keep for months, so if you're fortunate enough to have a root cellar or a cool, dry storage area, you can stock up on a medley of vegetables that are the foundation of delicious winter stews and gratins like this one.

4 tablespoons butter

3 shallots, peeled and diced

¼ cup all-purpose flour

3½ cups half-and-half

1 teaspoon salt

½ teaspoon freshly ground black pepper

¼ teaspoon freshly grated nutmeg

1 celery root (about 1 pound)

3 medium sweet potatoes (about 1 pound)

4 ounces Jarlsberg cheese, shredded (1 cup)

4 ounces medium cheddar cheese, shredded (1 cup)

6–8 SERVINGS

1. Preheat the oven to 375°F. Butter a 2-quart baking dish and set aside.

2. Make the sauce: Melt the butter in a small saucepan over low heat. Add the shallots and sauté until translucent, about 2 minutes. Whisk in the flour, cooking and stirring until the mixture is smooth and bubbling. Pour in the half-and-half, whisking constantly until the mixture is smooth. Add the salt, pepper, and nutmeg, and cook until thickened, stirring constantly, about 5 minutes. Remove from the heat and set aside.

3. Peel the celery root and the sweet potatoes with a knife or vegetable peeler. Rinse the vegetables under cold running water and pat them dry. Cut the vegetables into small cubes, about 1 inch across. Mix the vegetables together and put them into the buttered dish.

4. Pour the sauce over the vegetables. Mix the two cheeses together and sprinkle them over the sauce. Bake for 1 hour, until the sauce bubbles and is golden.

Roasted Eggplant with Goat Cheese

Creamy and slightly tart, this is a wonderful appetizer for a fall harvest party, especially with a nice glass of Maryland red wine, like Calvert County's Running Hare Vineyard's award-winning Malbec.

2 large eggplants

3 tablespoons olive oil

3 garlic cloves, peeled
   and minced

3 ounces goat cheese,
   preferably FireFly Farms

¾ teaspoon salt

1 teaspoon chopped
   fresh parsley

4–6 SERVINGS

1. Preheat the oven to 400°F. Cut the eggplants in half, pierce them in several spots, and put them on a parchment-lined baking sheet, flesh side up. Brush the eggplant with 1 tablespoon of the olive oil and sprinkle with the garlic and ¼ teaspoon of the salt. Roast for 45 minutes, until the eggplant flesh is soft.

2. Scoop out the roasted eggplant flesh and discard the skins. Put the eggplant and goat cheese into a food processor and pulse for 5 seconds. Add the remaining 2 tablespoons olive oil and the salt and pulse again to combine. Sprinkle parsley over the dip and serve with vegetables, pita chips, toasted baguette rounds, or crackers.

Recipe from **PEGGY ELLIOTT**

Cornmeal Pudding

Somewhere between pudding and spoon bread, this sweet Indian summer treat is absolutely delicious by itself, with a little maple syrup, or as a side dish to savory offerings.

8 SERVINGS

1½ cups medium-coarse yellow
  or white cornmeal
½ cup (1 stick) butter, melted
½ cup sugar
2 eggs
2 cups milk
½ teaspoon salt

1. Preheat the oven to 400°F. Grease an 8-inch square baking pan and set aside. Bring 2 cups water to a boil. Sift the cornmeal into a large mixing bowl. Add the boiling water and melted butter to the cornmeal and stir. Let the mixture rest for 5 minutes.

2. Add the sugar and the eggs to the cornmeal mixture, beating by hand until well mixed. Add the milk and salt, a little at a time, stirring constantly. Pour into the prepared baking dish. Bake 30 to 40 minutes, until the pudding sets and a knife inserted in the middle comes out clean. Cool slightly and serve warm.

Crispy Potato Pancakes

Crisp and salty, these pancakes are terrific served with fresh applesauce.

6 SERVINGS

4 cups peeled and shredded
  potatoes
1 egg, lightly beaten
3 tablespoons all-purpose flour
1 shallot, peeled and grated
1 teaspoon salt
¼ teaspoon freshly ground
  black pepper
½–1 cup vegetable oil

1. Rinse the potatoes under running water and then drain, squeezing the potatoes to remove excess liquid. Transfer the potatoes to a large bowl. Add the egg, flour, shallot, salt, and pepper, and stir until blended.

2. Preheat the oven to 200°F. Heat ⅓ cup of the oil in a cast iron skillet over medium heat. Drop the batter by ¼ cupfuls into the hot oil. Fry in batches, about 4 minutes on each side, adding more oil as needed. Drain on paper towels and keep warm in the oven until you have fried all of the pancakes. Serve immediately.

Recipe from BAUGHER'S FARM

Baked Corn with Swiss Cheese

I make this in the fall with corn that I've frozen because Maryland's summers are too hot to turn on the oven. It's a wonderful side dish for Thanksgiving.

4–6 SERVINGS

4 cups fresh or frozen corn, thawed

4 ounces Swiss cheese, shredded (1 cup)

⅔ cup evaporated milk

1 egg, beaten

2 tablespoons chopped onion

½ teaspoon salt

½ teaspoon freshly ground black pepper

1 cup soft bread cubes

½ cup (1 stick) butter, melted

1. Preheat the oven to 350°F. Butter a 2-quart baking dish. Combine the corn, ¾ cup of the cheese, the evaporated milk, egg, onion, salt, and pepper in a bowl, and toss until blended. Turn the mixture into the baking dish.

2. Combine the bread cubes with the melted butter and the remaining ¼ cup cheese. Sprinkle the bread mixture over the corn mixture. Bake for 25 to 30 minutes. Serve immediately.

Two-Cheese Popovers

Light as air, but with a slightly custardy taste, these popovers are ideal with soups or stews.

12 POPOVERS

8 eggs

2 cups all-purpose flour

1 teaspoon salt

2 cups milk, warmed

2 ounces Gruyère cheese, shredded (½ cup)

3 ounces cheddar cheese, shredded (⅔ cup)

1. Preheat the oven to 375°F. Grease 12 popover or muffin tins well.

2. Beat the eggs in a large bowl at medium speed until they are light and fluffy, about 2 minutes. Increase the mixer speed and beat the eggs for an additional 3 minutes, until they are thick and pale.

3. Combine the flour and the salt. With the mixer on low, alternate adding the flour mixture and the warmed milk to the eggs. Mix thoroughly. Combine the cheeses in a separate bowl. Divide the batter equally among the popover or muffin tins, filling them two-thirds full. Divide the cheese mixture equally among the tins. Bake for 40 minutes, until golden brown. Prick the popovers and bake for 5 minutes longer. Remove from the oven and serve immediately.

Potato Harvest Yeast Rolls

Buttery and yeasty, with a touch of sweetness, these dinner rolls are a wonderful base for turkey, ham, chicken salad, or just about any sandwich combination. At my house, they complete the Thanksgiving meal.

2 potatoes, peeled and cut into small pieces

2 packages active dry yeast

1 teaspoon sugar

½ cup (1 stick) plus 2 tablespoons butter, melted separately

½ cup unfiltered honey

¼ cup vegetable oil

2 eggs

2 teaspoons salt

5 cups all-purpose flour

2 cups whole-wheat flour

MAKES 30 ROLLS

1. Put the potatoes in a large saucepan and cover with 1½ cups of water. Bring to a boil and then boil for 15 minutes, until soft. Drain the potatoes, reserving 1 cup of the cooking liquid. Set the reserved liquid aside to cool. Mash the potatoes and let them cool until they are very warm, but not hot.

2. When the reserved potato water has cooled to 105–115°F (it should be very warm, but not hot, to the touch), add the yeast and sugar and let stand for 5 minutes, until the mixture is frothy. Add 1½ cups of mashed potatoes, the ½ cup melted butter, honey, oil, eggs, salt, and 1½ cups of the all-purpose flour. Alternating whole-wheat and all-purpose flours, keep adding flour until the mixture forms a soft dough. If the dough is still sticky, add more flour.

3. Turn the dough onto a lightly floured surface or, if you are using a stand mixer, transfer the dough to the mixer's bowl. Knead the dough until it is smooth and elastic, about 6 to 8 minutes by hand, or 2 to 3 minutes with a mixer and dough hook. Transfer the dough to a greased bowl, turning the dough once to oil it, then cover the bowl and let the dough rise in a warm, draft-free place for up to 1 hour, until it has doubled in volume.

4. Preheat the oven to 400°F. Punch down the dough and turn it onto a floured surface. Divide the dough into three long pieces, cutting each piece into ten pieces. Shape the dough into balls and place them in two 9- by 13-inch baking pans. Let the balls rise again for 30 minutes. Bake for 20 to 25 minutes, basting the rolls with the 2 tablespoons of melted butter.

White Potat

Crusty Whole-Wheat Bread

This bread can be left as is, plain, or can be dusted with flour, brushed with milk and sprinkled with cracked wheat or seeds, or brushed with butter. For especially crusty loaves, fill an ovenproof dish with water and place it on the bottom rack of the oven while the bread is baking.

1 package active dry yeast

1 teaspoon sugar

6 cups whole-wheat flour

2 teaspoons salt

2 teaspoons brown sugar

1 tablespoon olive oil

MAKES 1 LARGE LOAF, 2 SMALL LOAVES, OR 18 ROLLS

1. Dissolve the yeast and sugar in 2½ cups warm, not hot, water (105–115°F) in a large bowl. Let it stand for 10 minutes, until the mixture bubbles and is frothy.

2. Mix together the flour, salt, and brown sugar. Gradually add the flour mixture and the oil to the water, mixing to form a firm dough. If your dough is too sticky, add more flour.

3. Turn the dough onto a lightly floured surface or, if you are using a stand mixer, transfer the dough to the mixer's bowl. Knead thoroughly until the dough is smooth and elastic, 5 to 10 minutes by hand, or 3 to 4 minutes with a mixer and dough hook. Shape the dough into a ball and place it inside a large oiled plastic bag. Leave it in a warm, draft-free place to rise until doubled in size, about 1 hour.

4. Punch down the dough and knead it until it's firm, about 2 minutes. Shape into loaves or rolls, using all of the dough for a large round loaf or a 9- by 5- by 3-inch loaf pan, half of the dough each for two smaller loaves, or all of the dough for 18 rolls. Cover the dough and let it rise again.

5. Preheat the oven to 450°F. If extra crustiness is desired, add a pan of water to the bottom rack, below the bread pan. Bake the bread in the center of the oven for about 40 minutes for 1 loaf, 30 to 35 minutes for smaller loaves, or 15 to 20 minutes for rolls. Test for doneness by removing the bread from the pan and tapping the bottom. If it sounds hollow, the bread is done. Turn out the bread onto a rack to cool.

STANTON'S MILL
Garrett County

One of the most notable attractions in the picturesque village of Grantsville in western Garrett County is Stanton's Mill, established in 1797 and now nestled in the Spruce Forest Artisan Village. In the 1950s, a retired biology professor and preservationist, Dr. Alta Schrock, keen to see local crafts and architecture preserved, founded the Spruce Forest Village by bringing together original log cabins from the area, restoring them, and populating them with traditional craftspeople. Artists there today include a world-renowned bird carver, ceramic and fiber artists, quilters, basket weavers, and ironsmiths. The mill stands at the far end of the village and is open on weekends. There, Jason Twig, the miller, gives demonstrations on stone-grinding grains, an ancient process that lives on in Stanton's Mill, which was restored as an authentic 1860s-era grist mill. Twig grinds ten different grains, including locally grown corn and buckwheat. The process, Twig explains, results in superior taste and nutritional value, since the grains are ground at lower temperatures than roller mills, and more of the grain is left intact.

Pizza Margherita

When the nights are cool, but there are still fresh, local tomatoes and herbs available, this pizza is a festive and delicious crowd pleaser. Any number of toppings can be added, including pepperoni, green peppers, olives, or your favorite meats or veggies. Enjoy it with full-bodied local Maryland red wine (page 48).

6–8 SERVINGS

1 package active dry yeast

2 teaspoons sugar

2½ cups bread flour

½ cup semolina flour

2 tablespoons olive oil

1 teaspoon salt

4 cups (1 recipe) Fresh Tomato Sauce with Herbs (page 102)

2 tablespoons concentrated Italian tomato paste (from a squeeze tube)

¼ cup grated Parmesan cheese

2 large tomatoes, sliced

8 ounces Mozzarella cheese, sliced

6 fresh basil leaves, shredded

1. Make the dough: Dissolve the yeast and sugar in 1½ cups warm water (105–115°F) and let stand for 10 minutes, until the mixture is frothy. Stir together the bread and semolina flours. Add the olive oil, salt, and about 2 cups of the flour. Stir well. Add enough of the remaining flour to make a soft dough. If the dough is sticky, add more flour.

2. Turn the dough onto a lightly floured surface or, if you are using a stand mixer, transfer the dough to the mixer's bowl. Knead the dough until smooth and elastic, about 6 to 8 minutes by hand, or 2 to 3 minutes with a mixer and dough hook. Transfer the dough to a greased bowl, turning the dough once to oil it. Cover the dough and let it rise in a warm, draft-free place until doubled, up to 1 hour.

3. Preheat the oven to 500°F. Lightly grease two (12-inch round) pizza pans. Pat and stretch the dough to fill the pans.

4. Stir together the tomato sauce, tomato paste, and Parmesan in a bowl. Distribute the sauce equally between the two pizzas. Top with fresh tomato slices, basil leaves, and mozzarella. Bake for 20 to 25 minutes, until the crust is nicely browned. Serve immediately.

Loïc Jaffres

CAFÉ DES ARTISTES
Leonardtown, St. Mary's County

Washington-based chef Loïc Jaffres wasn't looking to open a French bistro in rural Maryland. But the jovial, mustachioed Frenchman met Karleen, who became his wife, and the rest is culinary history. Today, the cozy Café des Artistes — decorated with shelves of old cameras, cloth napkins at every setting, and a waitstaff with thin ties and aprons — is the heart and soul of Leonardtown, a historic town with a French past of its own. Just down the street, the restless waters of Breton Bay slip into the lower Potomac River.

Fresh, local food is at the heart of Jaffres' cooking, and he changes his menu frequently to offer what's in season. The impeccable ingredients — real cream, farm-fresh eggs, locally sourced chickens, crabs and plump local oysters, roasted pork or beef ribs — primarily come from within a 25-mile radius. What began out of practicality — most food distributors simply wouldn't deliver that far from a metropolitan area — has become a passion and an echo of how food is still procured in Jaffres' native Europe. Jaffres makes it a point to know many of the local farmers and watermen in St. Mary's County and buy from them as often as they can. He maintains a thick, well-thumbed folder of local vendors of everything from arugula to shiitake mushrooms. St. Mary's County includes substantial farming communities of Amish and Mennonites and is still largely rural, which perfectly benefits the restaurant's seasonal menu. In turn, Jaffres helps his suppliers, from watermen to strawberry farmers, and pleases his customers, too.

Crab Imperial Café des Artistes

Make this deliciously rich crab dish as the topping for the oysters on the following page. Or, like John Shields' version (page 62), this imperial can be a stand-alone dish, baked in a 350°F oven for 20 to 25 minutes. Imperial cook-off, anyone?

½ cup (1 stick) plus
    1 tablespoon butter

⅔ cup all-purpose flour

1 cup mussel or clam juice

½ cup heavy cream

1¼ cups grated Parmesan cheese

4 ounces Swiss cheese,
    shredded (1 cup)

6 shallots, peeled and chopped

1 cup dry Maryland white wine

1 teaspoon minced thyme

1 teaspoon minced garlic

1 pound backfin crabmeat,
    cartilage removed

1 cup panko breadcrumbs

½ cup mayonnaise

  Juice from 1 lemon

  Salt and freshly ground
    black pepper

6–8 SERVINGS

1. Melt the ½ cup butter in a small saucepan over medium heat, then whisk in the flour, cooking and stirring until the mixture is smooth, thick, and bubbling. Remove the roux from the heat and set aside.

2. Reduce the mussel juice by half in a medium saucepan over high heat, and then remove the pan from the heat. Return the roux to medium heat and gradually add the mussel juice to the butter mixture, whisking until the sauce thickens. Stirring constantly, slowly add the cream, Parmesan, and Swiss cheese. Remove the cheese sauce from the heat and set aside.

3. Melt the 1 tablespoon butter in a medium skillet. Add the shallots and sauté over medium heat until translucent. Add the wine, thyme, and garlic, and cook until the liquid reduces by half. Add the crabmeat and continue cooking until the moisture has been absorbed. Stir the crab mixture into the cheese sauce and set the mixture aside to cool. When the mixture has cooled, stir in the panko, mayonnaise, lemon juice, and salt and pepper to taste. Refrigerate until ready to use.

Oysters Café des Artistes

Succulent oysters, topped with a rich mixture of crab imperial, spinach, and provolone, come together in this sophisticated, prize-winning appetizer. Jaffres buys his oysters from another St. Mary's establishment, Circle C Oyster Ranch.

12 Circle C Ranch or other Maryland oysters

3 shallots, peeled

½ cup dry white Maryland wine

1 sprig fresh thyme

Cracked black peppercorns

1 tablespoon butter

¼ pound shiitake mushrooms, sliced

1 pound fresh spinach, washed, stemmed, and chopped

Salt and freshly ground black pepper

Crab Imperial Café des Artistes (page 187)

8 ounces Provolone cheese, sliced

MAKES 12 SERVINGS

1. Preheat the oven to 350°F.

2. Steam the oysters: Place 12 oysters in a large baking pan that can be used on the stove. Mince one of the shallots and sprinkle it over the oysters. Add the wine, thyme, and cracked pepper. Cover the pan with aluminum foil and place it on the stove over high heat for 10 minutes. Remove the pan from the heat and allow the oysters to cool. Open the oysters.

3. Make the spinach topping: Slice the remaining two shallots. Melt the butter in a skillet, add the shallots and the mushrooms, and sauté for 2 minutes. Add the spinach and salt and pepper to taste and cook and stir for 2 minutes longer. Remove from the heat.

4. Divide the spinach topping equally among the oysters, top with the crab imperial, and then cover each oyster with a folded slice of Provolone. Transfer the baking dish to the oven and bake for 8 to 10 minutes, until the cheese is bubbling and golden. Serve immediately.

Crab and Gruyère Quiche

Fall "Jimmies" are the best crabs of the year: huge, sweet, and delicious. Paired with the nutty, salty cheese, they create a standout dish for casual entertaining.

4   tablespoons cold butter

4   tablespoons non-hydrogenated vegetable shortening

1½ cups all-purpose flour

6–8 tablespoons ice water

1   pound Maryland jumbo lump crabmeat

⅓   cup onion, peeled and chopped

1   garlic clove, peeled and chopped

4   ounces Gruyère cheese, shredded (1 cup)

4   eggs

1   cup half-and-half

1   teaspoon salt

¼   teaspoon freshly ground black pepper

¼   teaspoon nutmeg

3   tablespoons finely chopped fresh parsley

1. Make the dough: Cut the cold butter and shortening into small pieces. Combine the butter and flour in a mixing bowl, using a pastry cutter until the mixture is crumbly. Add the ice water a tablespoon at a time and mix until the dough holds together nicely but is not wet. Wrap the dough in plastic wrap and refrigerate for 30 minutes.

2. Preheat the oven to 400°F. Pick through the crabmeat, discarding any shells or cartilage. Set aside. Remove the dough from the refrigerator and roll it out to a 10-inch circle on a floured surface. Line a 10-inch tart pan with the dough.

3. Distribute the crabmeat, onion, garlic, and cheese on the crust. Whisk together the eggs, half-and-half, salt, pepper, and nutmeg in a small bowl. Add the parsley and stir to combine. Pour the egg mixture into the shell. Transfer the quiche to the oven and bake for 40 to 45 minutes or until golden brown. Remove from the oven and let cool slightly before serving.

Phil Pyle

FAIR HILL INN
Cecil County

Built in 1764 in rural horse country close to the Delaware border, the historic stone Fair Hill Inn no longer welcomes guests for the night, but it attracts national accolades for its superb farmstead restaurant, which features house-made cheeses, honey from its own beehives, and herbs, lettuce, and fruits from its carefully tended garden. The menu changes monthly and the wine list is outstanding. For all of that — achieved in less than five years — Fairhill's owners, Phil and Venka Pyle and Brian Shaw, won the 2008 Santé award for the Best Sustainable Restaurant in the mid-Atlantic region. Phil Pyle and Brian Shaw are the restaurant's co-chefs, and they have formed strong working relationships with area farmers and watermen to supply the restaurant with key raw ingredients, from local seafood to game, cream, and heirloom poultry. The two chefs butcher all of their own meat, bake all of their own breads and pastries, and produce over a dozen of their own cheeses, so the quality of their raw ingredients is critical. Together, the classically educated Pyle, who trained in Europe under many of France's top chefs, and Shaw, a native of southern Maryland who gained his culinary training through working his way up in a series of restaurants, have several decades of culinary experience, which they bring to bear on seasonally varied menus and elaborate seven-course degustation dinners. Their motto — "Two cooks, one vision: Farmstead Cuisine — Taking the farm-to-table concept literally — We've become the farm" — is unwieldy, but it says a lot about their commitment to a superb, sustainable dining experience.

191

Recipe from FAIR HILL INN

Quail with Oyster Stuffing

Two quintessentially autumnal tastes come together in this elegant dish. If you cannot find a butcher to bone the quail or don't know how to do it yourself, the recipe works equally well with the bones intact, although you will not be able to fit as much stuffing in the cavities.

8–10 SERVINGS

2 day-old baguettes

½ pound smoked bacon, sliced

3–4 tablespoons lard

6–8 shallots, peeled and finely chopped (2 cups)

1½ cups chopped celery

6 garlic cloves, peeled, smashed, and minced

Salt and freshly ground black pepper

3 tablespoons chopped fresh thyme

3 tablespoons chopped fresh French tarragon

3 tablespoons fresh lemon verbena

3 tablespoons fresh chervil

1 tablespoon finely chopped fresh sage

⅔ cup chopped fresh parsley

¾ cup plus 1 tablespoon unsalted butter, melted

24–36 fresh, shucked Maryland oysters or 1 pint preshucked oysters with liquor

2–3 cups Chicken Stock (page 26), or duck or turkey stock (preferably homemade)

1 tablespoon Old Bay Seasoning

10 quail

2 tablespoons olive or vegetable oil

1. Preheat the oven to 400°F. Cut the baguettes into ¾-inch cubes; you should have about 12 cups. Spread the bread cubes in two shallow baking pans or a large sheet tray, and toast until golden, about 20 minutes. Remove the bread cubes from the oven and cool, leaving the oven on.

2. Chop the bacon into ½-inch pieces. Render the fat in a large skillet over medium heat, cooking until the bacon is crisp. Remove the bacon and set aside on a paper towel. Measure the bacon fat remaining in the skillet and add lard until you have ½ cup fat. Put the fat back in the skillet.

3. Add the shallots, celery, garlic, and salt and pepper to taste to the skillet, and sauté over medium heat until the shallots are translucent; transfer the mixture to a large bowl. Add the bread cubes, bacon, thyme, tarragon, lemon verbena, chervil, sage, parsley, melted butter, and oysters and their liquor. Ladle on stock until the stuffing is moist, but not swimming in liquid, and then season with the Old Bay and more salt and pepper to taste; toss well. Taste to ensure proper seasoning.

4. Bone the quail, leaving just the two wing bones and two leg (drum) bones for integrity; remove all thigh, rib, and other bones completely. Season the inside of each quail lightly with salt and pepper. Fill each quail with about ½ cup of the stuffing, making sure that each quail has at least 2 or 3 oysters.

5. Put any remaining oyster stuffing in a well-buttered 8- by 12-inch shallow, ceramic baking dish. Bake, covered with aluminum foil,

in the middle of the oven for about 20 minutes, and then uncover and bake about 20 minutes longer, until the top is browned.

6. Heat the oil and the 1 tablespoon butter in a large skillet, capable of holding at least 5 quail, until the oil and butter dance together quickly in the pan. Season the outside of each quail with a liberal amount of salt and add it to the hot pan, breast side down. When each breast is nicely browned, remove it from the skillet and place it on a baking sheet, breast side up. When all of the quail breasts are seared and browned, transfer the baking sheet to the oven and bake for 20 to 25 minutes.

NOTE: The stuffing can be assembled ahead and held in the refrigerator (unbaked and without oysters) for two to three days. When ready to use, bring the stuffing to room temperature, and then add the oysters.

Fall Beef Stew with Root Vegetables

Hearty and aromatic, this tender stew will fill your house with delectable smells. Make this a totally local meal with Maryland beef, vegetables, and wine.

½ cup all-purpose flour, plus ¼ cup for thickening (optional)

1½ teaspoons salt

½ teaspoon freshly ground black pepper

2½ pounds stewing beef (chuck, short plate, and foreshank cuts work well), cut into 1-inch chunks

¼ cup olive oil

1 medium onion, peeled and finely chopped

4 cups beef broth

1 cup dry Maryland red wine

1 medium onion, peeled and studded with 2 whole cloves

1 bay leaf

4 large potatoes, peeled and cut into 1-inch chunks

1 large sweet potato, peeled and cut into 1-inch chunks

2 medium turnips, peeled and cut into 1-inch chunks

6 carrots, peeled and cut into 1-inch chunks

4 celery stalks, cut into 1-inch chunks

1. Mix together the ½ cup flour, ½ teaspoon of the salt, and the pepper. Dredge the beef chunks in the flour mixture and set aside. Heat the olive oil in a large Dutch oven or stockpot over low heat, add the chopped onion, and sauté until translucent. Increase the heat to high and add the meat, searing for about 4 minutes, until browned on all sides.

2. Add the beef broth, 3 cups of water, the wine, the remaining 1 teaspoon salt, the studded onion, and the bay leaf to the pot and cover. Bring to a boil, and then reduce the heat and simmer for 2½ hours.

3. Add the potatoes, sweet potato, turnips, carrots, and celery to the pot. Simmer for 30 minutes longer, until the vegetables are tender. Remove the studded onion and the bay leaf.

4. If you desire a thicker stew, combine the ¼ cup flour and 1 cup of the hot broth in a small bowl, mixing until smooth. Add back to the stew pot and simmer for about 1 minute, stirring until thickened.

Pork Chops with Goat Cheese and Apple-Cranberry Stuffing

Maryland apples add a note of fruitiness to these hearty and savory farm-fresh pork chops. Source the pork locally at one of Maryland's many farms that sell pork, including Greenbranch Organic Farm in Wicomico County and Whitmore Farm in Frederick County.

6 SERVINGS

6 thick, boneless pork chops, with deep horizontal pockets cut into them

1 teaspoon salt

½ teaspoon freshly ground black pepper

3 tablespoons vegetable shortening

3 tablespoons butter

1 large onion, peeled and finely chopped

2 celery stalks, finely diced

1 Granny Smith, York, Winesap or similar tart apple, peeled, cored, and chopped

6 cups soft bread cubes

2 tablespoons minced fresh sage

1 teaspoon minced fresh rosemary

1 teaspoon minced fresh thyme

1 cup beef broth or Vegetable Stock (page 27)

¼ cup dried cranberries

4 ounces goat cheese, preferably FireFly, cut into six slices

1. Preheat the oven to 350°F. Season the pork chops with ¼ teaspoon of the salt and ¼ teaspoon of the pepper. Heat the shortening in a large cast iron skillet until hot but not smoking. Reduce the heat to medium-low and sear the pork chops for about 2 minutes on each side. Remove the pork chops from the pan and transfer them to a large plate.

2. Reduce the heat to low and add the butter, onion, celery, and apple. Cook about 3 minutes, until the apple is slightly soft. Add the bread cubes, the remaining ¾ teaspoon salt and ¼ teaspoon pepper, the sage, rosemary, and thyme and stir. Add the broth and the cranberries and toss the bread cubes to moisten them. Remove the stuffing from the heat.

3. Stuff each pork chop with a slice of the goat cheese and as much stuffing as will fit into the pocket, about 2 tablespoons. Secure the stuffing with a toothpick poked through either end of the pocket. Transfer the pork chops to a 9- by 13-inch baking dish. Transfer the remaining stuffing to a small, buttered baking dish. Cover the stuffing and slide both dishes in the oven.

4. Bake the stuffing and pork chops for 45 minutes, until the stuffing is golden and the pork chops are cooked through. Remove both dishes from the oven, uncover the stuffing, and serve it immediately with the pork chops.

RUMBLEWAY FARM
Cecil County

Robin Way is a former research scientist at DuPont, not exactly the kind of woman that you picture running an organic farm in the hills above the Susquehanna River. But on an unseasonably warm November day two weeks before Thanksgiving, farmer Way is in her element, presiding over her well-stocked farm store and surveying huge flocks of pastured turkeys — white, broad-breasted birds, as well as dozens of heirlooms, including Red Bourbons and Narragansetts — that she'll soon slaughter right there on the farm to fill holiday orders.

Robin and her husband, Mark, a scientist for the Army, bought the early-eighteenth-century farm after one of Mark's relatives passed away two decades ago. It was in poor shape then, Way says, and they spent the first five years cleaning up the property and raising their three children, Samantha, Melissa, and Mathew. Only gradually did they add cows and pigs, along with a passel of dogs and cats that roam unfettered across the 65 undulating acres. Eventually the Ways took a course with sustainable-foods pioneer Joel Salatin in Virginia and began to adapt his concepts to their farm. They raised most of their own meat, including hens, turkeys, rabbits, and goats. They ate fruits and vegetables straight from the garden and froze or canned the rest. Soon, they began selling some of their meat and gradually evolved to where they are today: selling thousands of chickens and turkeys annually, slaughtering about 3 steer a month, offering ground lamb, pork, and goat for sale, and expanding into a line of jams and jellies, among other things.

Rumbleway Farm today is both a throwback to America's pre–World War II diversified family farms and a glimpse at one view of the future. The farm is

Robin Way

small but self-sufficient, supporting itself through the sales of meat, eggs, and other products. It offers high-quality, certified organic products to a loyal and growing customer base in the area, and it's run without the high cost and adverse environmental and health implications of chemical fertilizers, hormones, and antibiotics. Waste is composted in big piles that are regularly turned; that compost is then spread in the garden, where it's used to raise fruits and vegetables. Robin, as the farm's manager, strives to keep their environmental footprint as light as possible.

The Ways don't plan to grow their business much beyond where it is now. Instead, Robin wants to continue to work on diversification and sustainability, to offer their children "a good lifestyle," and to educate the public. Every September, they host a huge open house: "I like sharing the experience of living on a farm and showing people where their food comes from," Robin says. The scientist and the farmer, it seems, are in perfect alignment.

Roasted Chestnut Stuffing

American chestnut trees, sadly, were almost totally wiped out in a terrible blight that was accidentally introduced around 1900. By 1940, it had killed off virtually all American chestnuts. (Incredibly, a small intact stand of American chestnuts was discovered in 2006 in Georgia, a huge boon to the scientists at the American Chestnut Foundation, who are working to breed a blight-resistant American chestnut.) Most chestnuts that Americans consume are imported from Europe, but it's becoming more common to see Chinese chestnuts at local farmers' markets. I make my stuffing using local chestnuts that I buy from Bobi Crispens at the Anne Arundel County farmers' market in Annapolis. This dish is a natural with roast chicken or turkey, but it also makes a wonderful side dish for other meats, as well.

1½ pounds local chestnuts

½ cup (1 stick) butter

2 onions, peeled and chopped

5 celery stalks, chopped

1 yellow or orange or red bell pepper, chopped

8 cups cubed and toasted day-old bread

3 tablespoons minced fresh parsley

3 tablespoons minced fresh sage

2 tablespoons minced fresh thyme

1 tablespoon minced fresh rosemary

1 teaspoon kosher salt

½ teaspoon freshly ground black pepper

1½ cups Chicken Stock (page 26) or Vegetable Stock (page 27)

10–12 SERVINGS

1. Roast the chestnuts: Carve an X into each chestnut using a sharp paring knife. Soak the chestnuts for 30 minutes in a bowl of water. Preheat the oven to 350°F. Drain the chestnuts and place them on a baking sheet. Bake the chestnuts for 25 to 30 minutes, remove them from the oven, and immediately peel them, using gloves if necessary. If chestnuts are not peeled while they are still hot, you will have a very hard time peeling them. When they are peeled, chop the nutmeats roughly. You should have about 2 cups.

2. Reduce the oven to 325°F. Melt the butter in a large skillet over low to medium heat. Add the onions, celery, and bell pepper, and sauté until the onions are translucent, about 4 minutes. Add the bread, parsley, sage, thyme, rosemary, salt, and pepper, and toss to blend. Add the chestnuts and the broth, tossing until the bread cubes are moist. Remove the skillet from the heat.

3. Transfer the stuffing to a 3-quart buttered casserole dish. Cover with aluminum foil and bake for 1 hour. Serve immediately.

HERITAGE TURKEYS

Heritage turkeys are descended from the original native wild turkeys that Spanish explorers discovered in the Americas in the 1500s. Some of those turkeys were taken back to Spain live (some say by Cortez himself), domesticated, and bred, eventually reaching England around 1520. Ironically, and contrary to what most of us were taught in school, the Pilgrims didn't first encounter turkeys here; rather, they brought the domesticated birds with them from England in the 1600s. Those birds were then bred with the original wild turkeys, resulting in the Narragansett breed, the first of what we now call heritage turkeys. Further breeding resulted in the Bourbon Red, the Jersey Buff, and the Broad-breasted Bronze, from which today's Broad-breasted White turkeys are descended.

Twenty years ago, heritage birds had almost completely disappeared, but they're staging a heartening comeback. Though they make up just a fraction of the fresh turkey market and cost significantly more than their supermarket counterparts, they're worth it if for no other reason than species diversity. But their taste is what will win you over. Heritage turkeys are usually pasture raised and are allowed to roam and live longer, thus developing more fat and flavor. They have a much deeper, richer taste, and they have more dark meat. They're also smaller than the enormous Broad-breasted Whites, which have become so top-heavy that they can no longer reproduce naturally or fly.

Roast Heritage Turkey

At least a dozen farms raise and sell heritage turkeys in Maryland, mostly around Thanksgiving, although you have to put in your order well in advance. Springfield and Rumbleway Farms, where I've bought my heritage birds, both raise several varieties, all of them delicious. Any number of dishes pair beautifully with a roast turkey, including Roasted Chestnut Stuffing (page 198) and Sweet Potato Casserole with Toasted Pecan Topping (page 233).

1 (16–18 pound) Narragansett or other heritage-breed turkey, cavities cleaned, rinsed, and patted dry

6 garlic cloves, peeled

1 tablespoon Dijon mustard

3 tablespoons olive oil

1 teaspoon sea salt

½ teaspoon freshly ground black pepper

1 small onion, peeled

1 teaspoon dried sage

1 teaspoon dried thyme

½ teaspoon dried rosemary

½ teaspoon dried savory

12 SERVINGS

1. Preheat the oven to 325°F. Place the turkey breast side up on a roasting rack in a shallow roasting pan. Make six small incisions in the turkey's skin using a sharp knife. Insert the garlic under the turkey's skin.

2. Spread the mustard over the turkey's skin with a knife, and then drizzle the olive oil all over. Sprinkle the salt and pepper on the turkey's skin and in the cavities, and place the onion in the neck cavity. Sprinkle the sage, thyme, rosemary, and savory over the turkey, and insert a meat thermometer into one of the thigh areas near the breast.

3. Loosely cover the bird with aluminum foil, making a tent over the turkey and lightly tucking the foil around the edges of the pan. Roast for about 4 hours, or 15 minutes per pound. (See Note.) About 30 minutes before the turkey is done, remove the aluminum foil and allow the skin to brown. Continue roasting until the meat thermometer reaches 180°F and the turkey's juices run clear.

4. Remove the turkey from the oven and let it stand, covered, for 20 minutes before carving.

NOTE: If you choose to stuff the turkey, you will need to increase the roasting time. I usually bake my stuffing separately so that vegetarians can eat it, but you can certainly divide the stuffing, putting some in the turkey and baking some separately, if you prefer.

Oyster Stuffing

On the Eastern Shore and down in southern Maryland, turkeys are often stuffed with an oyster dressing.

½ cup (1 stick) butter

3 celery stalks, chopped

1 large onion, peeled and minced

2 garlic cloves, peeled and minced

1 pint Maryland oysters, shucked, with liquor reserved

1 teaspoon lemon juice

1 teaspoon crumbled dry sage

½ teaspoon dried rosemary

1 teaspoon salt

½ teaspoon freshly ground black pepper

4 cups soft bread cubes

1 tablespoon chopped fresh parsley

1 cups Chicken Stock (page 26) or fish stock

1. Preheat the oven to 350°F. Grease a medium baking pan or casserole dish. Melt the butter in a skillet over low to medium heat. Add the celery, onion, and garlic, and sauté until the onion is tender, about 5 minutes. Add the oysters and ½ cup of the liquor and simmer until the edges of the oysters curl up.

2. Mix in the lemon juice, sage, rosemary, salt, and pepper. Add the bread cubes and the parsley and toss until blended. Add the stock and toss again. If the stuffing requires additional moisture, add the remaining oyster liquor. Transfer the stuffing into the prepared pan and bake, covered with aluminum foil, for 30 minutes. Uncover and bake until the stuffing is golden brown, about 15 minutes longer.

BAUGHER'S FARM
Carroll County

Going to Baugher's Farm and Orchards has been a family tradition in Maryland for decades. Set on the outskirts of Westminster in Carroll County, just past where the houses stop, it's a destination that satisfies something in just about everyone. For those who love to pick their own fruit and vegetables, there are ample choices, from strawberries and peas in the spring, to peaches in the summer, to apples and pumpkins in the fall. For those who would rather shop, Baugher's has two stores, one on the farm and another one in Westminster proper, and for those who'd rather just eat, there is a Baugher's restaurant, as well as a bakery that turns out 20 varieties of homestyle pies. Oh, and there's freshly made ice cream, too.

The best thing about Baugher's, though, is that there are still Baughers — several generations, in fact — who own and run the farm. On any given day you might see Allan, who does most of the actual farming; his wife, Marjorie, who works with their daughter, Kay, on the bookkeeping; Nathan, who runs the retail end of the markets; Lorraine, who manages the bakery; and at least one of the dozen or so grandkids who might be helping out in the restaurant or on the farm. Up until 2006, when Allan's mother, Romaine, died at the age of 94, there were four generations of Baughers on the farm. Kay fondly remembers Friday evenings before the big commercial kitchen was built for the bakery in 1981. Everyone in the family helped bake some of the thousands of pies that Romaine produced by herself for decades — all in a single, conventional kitchen oven. Today the farm bakes more than 6,000 pies at Thanksgiving alone — most of which feature Baugher's fruits, including their own canned peaches.

Baugher's is the kind of place that inspires fierce loyalty and deeply ingrained rituals. Among the farm's many repeat customers are a couple who drive up from Florida each year to pick sour cherries, along with a large contingent of Poles, Russians, and Iranians who come from Baltimore and Washington.

Marjorie Baugher

APPLES
SWEET CORN
TOMATOES
PIES & PASTRIES
FARM
PETTING ZOO

PEACHES
MARKET
OPEN 8-7 MON-FRI
      8-6 SAT-SUN
GIFTS

There's even a family who flies in from New York for the Montmorency harvest. And for the roughly two weeks that tart cherries are in season, the orchard is a veritable United Nations, ringing with the sounds of predominantly foreign tongues.

At Baugher's you can linger for hours out among the nearly 1,500 acres of trees and birds. It's a place where children can experience the thrill of picking apples, and where you can choose a pumpkin so big that it requires another person to help you carry it to the car. At Baugher's, despite the three-story cider mill, the modern machinery, and 70,000-bushel controlled-atmosphere storage facility, despite the huge volumes of fruits and vegetables that are grown and sold there, it still feels like a family business, because it is — one where someone is likely to press a ripe pear into your hand and urge you to bite right into it, and where there is always something freshly baked and warm, waiting to be eaten and washed down with a tall glass of fresh milk or sweet cider. The world could use more places like Baugher's.

Fresh Apple Cake with Brown Sugar Icing

This cake should be made with tart apples, because the batter itself is quite sweet. Try combining Granny Smith apples with Staymans, for example, or Mutsus and York Imperials, or Gravensteins with Macouns. I've made it with a number of different apples, and it's turned out delicious every time.

1½ teaspoons cinnamon
1¼ cups vegetable oil
1¾ cups sugar
3 eggs
3 cups diced tart apples (about 4 apples)
½ cup chopped walnuts or pecans
3 cups all-purpose flour
1 teaspoon salt
1 teaspoon baking soda
1 tablespoon plus 1 teaspoon vanilla extract
½ cup (1 stick) butter
½ cup dark brown sugar
¼ cup heavy cream

12 SERVINGS

1. Preheat the oven to 325°F. Grease and flour a 9- by 13-inch baking pan. Dust ½ teaspoon of the cinnamon over the bottom of the pan. Set aside.

2. Beat the vegetable oil and the sugar together in a large mixing bowl with an electric mixer for 2 minutes at a high speed. Add the eggs and beat until smooth. Add the apples and the walnuts. Continue to beat and gradually add the flour, the remaining teaspoon cinnamon, the salt, baking soda, and 1 tablespoon of the vanilla extract. The batter will be very stiff.

3. Pour the batter into the prepared pan, distributing it evenly. Bake for 60 minutes, until a knife blade inserted into the middle of the cake comes out clean. Cool for 1 hour.

4. Make the icing: Melt the butter in a saucepan over a low heat. Stir in the brown sugar and the heavy cream and simmer for 5 to 8 minutes, until thick. Add the remaining 1 teaspoon vanilla and let the icing cool slightly. Pour and spread the icing over the cooled cake.

French Toast with Pan-fried Apples and Maple Syrup

Head up to Milburn Orchards in Cecil County and pick your own Fuji, Honey Crisp, Orange Honey, Royal Gala, or other apple varieties for this perfect fall breakfast. Serve it with crisp bacon and hot coffee.

4 SERVINGS

3 eggs

1 cup half-and-half

1 tablespoon sugar

2 teaspoons vanilla extract

4 1½-inch thick slices challah or French bread

4 tablespoons butter

3 large tart apples, peeled, cored, and sliced

2 tablespoons Maryland maple syrup

Whipped cream (optional)

1. Whisk together the eggs, half-and-half, sugar, and 1 teaspoon of the vanilla until smooth. Line a shallow baking dish with the slices of bread. Pour the egg mixture over the bread and let it soak for 30 minutes, turning the bread several times to maximize the absorption.

2. Melt 2 tablespoons of the butter in a medium skillet over medium heat. Add the apples, maple syrup, and the remaining 1 teaspoon vanilla. Sauté for 5 minutes, until the apples are tender. Remove the apples from the heat. Carefully take the apples out of the pan with a slotted spoon and put them on a plate. Pour any juice from the apples back into the skillet. Return the skillet to the heat and simmer the sauce until it reduces by half. Remove from the heat and set aside.

3. Melt the remaining 2 tablespoons butter in a large skillet. Fry the soaked bread over medium heat for 4 to 5 minutes, turning once, until the French toast is golden brown and puffy. Transfer to a platter or individual plates and top with the apples and the caramelized sauce. Garnish with whipped cream, if desired.

Apple Dumplings with Caramel Sauce

Every fall there are harvest festivals across the state, from the Autumn Glory Festival in Garrett County to the apple festival in Darlington, at the other end of the state, which started out as a local festival more than 20 years ago. It is now one of the state's biggest fall draws, attracting 50,000 people in a single day. Dozens of nonprofit organizations sell apple treats, and along with fresh apples of every variety you'll find apple fritters, candied apples, apple pies, apple cakes of every type, and, my personal favorite, apple dumplings. Each year my husband and I go early to beat the crowds and head right to the Odd Fellows Lodge, where they sell the best apple dumplings you've ever eaten. They're served hot, and they're a meal in and of themselves. Somehow, I always manage to eat two.

¾ cup (1½ sticks) cold butter

⅓ cup sugar

⅓ cup chopped pecans

1½ teaspoons vanilla extract

2 teaspoons cinnamon

2½ cups all-purpose flour

½ teaspoon nutmeg

¼ teaspoon salt

⅔ cup sour cream

6 medium-sized tart apples, peeled and cored

¼ cup milk

½ cup brown sugar, firmly packed

½ cup whipping cream

6 SERVINGS

1. Preheat the oven to 400°F. Grease a 15- by 10-inch rimmed baking sheet and set aside. Soften 2 tablespoons of the butter and combine it in a small bowl with the sugar, pecans, ½ teaspoon of the vanilla, and the cinnamon. Set aside.

2. Stir together the flour, nutmeg, and salt in a medium bowl. Cut in ½ cup (1 stick) of the remaining butter until the mixture forms a crumbly texture. Add the sour cream and mix until the dough can be shaped into a ball.

3. Roll the dough into a 12- by 18-inch rectangle on a lightly floured surface, and cut the dough into six 6-inch squares. Place an apple in the center of each square. Stuff 1½ tablespoons of the butter-pecan mixture into the cored center of each apple. Fold the dough up around the apple and seal the seams well. Place the dumplings on the prepared baking pan, not touching. Brush the dumplings with milk and prick the dough. Bake for 45 minutes to 1 hour, until the dumplings are golden brown.

4. Make the caramel sauce: Heat the brown sugar, the remaining 2 tablespoons butter, the remaining teaspoon vanilla, and the whipping cream in a small saucepan. Cook over medium heat, stirring occasionally, until the mixture comes to a full boil. Remove from the heat and allow to cool for 10 minutes before pouring the mixture over the apples. Serve immediately.

Apple Bread

Quick and delightful, this homey cake tastes even better with a little apple butter on it. Use tart, not sweet, apples for the best results. I love local winesaps or Yorks.

½ cup (1 stick) butter
1 cup sugar
1 egg
2 cups all-purpose flour
1 teaspoon baking powder
1 teaspoon cinnamon
½ teaspoon ground cloves
½ teaspoon salt
2 cups chopped apples
⅔ cup chopped pecans

6–8 SERVINGS

1. Preheat the oven to 350°F. Grease and flour a 9- by 5-inch loaf pan. Cream together the butter and sugar using an electric mixer. Add the egg and beat well.

2. Sift together the flour, baking powder, cinnamon, cloves, and salt, and then add the dry ingredients to the butter mixture. Stir in the apples and pecans. The batter will be extremely thick. Pour the batter into the prepared loaf pan and bake for 1 hour, until a knife blade inserted into the center of the loaf comes out clean. Remove the cake from the oven and cool for 10 minutes in the pan. Remove the cake from the pan and cool on a wire rack.

Italian Prune Plum Tart with Baked Custard and Hazelnuts

Italian prune plums are in season for just two or three weeks in the early fall, and a few of Maryland's orchards feature them, including Ivy Hill Farm in Washington County's picturesque town of Smithsburg. The Martin family, who owns and operates Ivy Hill, came from Switzerland to Pennsylvania in the eighteenth century, eventually settling in Smithsburg in the early nineteenth century, where they've been ever since. The fifth and sixth generations of the Martin family run the farm today, with the seventh already in the wings. This tart is delicious with any stone fruit, especially apricots, as well as with apples and pears.

6	tablespoons unsalted cold butter
1½	cups all-purpose flour
1	teaspoon cider vinegar
¼	teaspoon salt
⅓	cup ground hazelnuts
4	cups Italian prune plums
⅔	cup plus 2 tablespoons sugar
2	eggs
½	cup heavy cream
1	teaspoon vanilla extract

MAKES 1 (9-INCH) TART

1. Make the dough: Cut the butter into very small pieces in a bowl and mix with the flour, using knives or a pastry cutter to get the mixture to the consistency of peas. Add ¼ cup ice water, the vinegar, and the salt, and mix by hand until the dough holds together but is not sticky. Wrap the dough in plastic and chill it in the refrigerator for 30 minutes.

2. Preheat the oven to 375°F. Grease a 9-inch tart pan. On a lightly floured surface, roll out the dough into a circle slightly larger than 9 inches. Line the tart pan with the dough and crimp the edges. Sprinkle the hazelnuts over the dough and return the dough to the refrigerator to chill.

3. Wash and pit the plums lengthwise. Mix the plums with the ⅔ cup sugar in a bowl. Take the tart pan out of the refrigerator. Arrange the plum halves on the dough, pitted side up and overlapping, in concentric circles. Bake for 30 minutes, and then transfer the tart pan to a rack. Reduce the oven temperature to 350°F.

4. While the tart is baking, make the custard: Whisk the eggs, cream, the 2 tablespoons sugar, and the vanilla in a bowl until well blended. Pour the custard mixture over the plums. Return the tart to the oven and bake for 20 minutes longer, until the custard is set and golden. Serve warm with ice cream or whipped cream, if desired.

Pear and Cranberry Crisp

Shaw Orchards, in business since 1909 and the only orchard with one foot in Maryland and the other in Pennsylvania, grows a number of pear varieties, including Red and Yellow Bartlett and Magness. Any of those will result in a luscious and delicately spiced crisp to serve for any occasion.

7 ripe but firm large pears, peeled, cored, and cut into long slices

1 cup fresh cranberries

½ cup sugar

1 cup plus 2 tablespoons all-purpose flour

½ teaspoon ground cinnamon

½ teaspoon ground ginger

⅔ cup light brown sugar, firmly packed

½ cup old-fashioned (not quick) oats

¼ teaspoon salt

½ cup (1 stick) cold butter, cut into pieces

Whipped cream or Vanilla-Bean Ice Cream (page 77) (optional)

1. Preheat the oven to 350°F. Butter an 8-inch square baking dish. Combine the pears, cranberries, sugar, the 2 tablespoons flour, cinnamon, and ginger in a bowl, and toss to combine. Transfer the pear mixture to the baking dish.

2. Combine the 1 cup flour, the brown sugar, oats, and salt in a bowl. Add the butter and cut it in, using a pastry cutter or knife, until the mixture is crumbly. Sprinkle the topping over the filling and transfer the baking dish to the oven.

3. Bake about 1 hour, until the topping is golden and the filling bubbles. Cool for 20 to 25 minutes before serving. Serve with whipped cream or ice cream, if desired.

Nutmeg-Pear Bread with Anise Seed

Fall is the perfect time to bake. The days grow shorter and much cooler, and there are wonderful fruits to use in baking. This nutmeg-infused pear bread also has a hint of anise in it, which gives it a somewhat exotic taste. I prefer Bartlett or Bosc pears for baking, but Comice and Red and Green Anjou also work well, as do some of the harder to find varieties, like Concorde pears.

10 SERVINGS

- 4 tablespoons butter, softened
- 1 cup sugar
- 2 eggs
- 1 teaspoon vanilla extract
- ½ cup plain yogurt
- 2 cups all-purpose flour
- 2 teaspoons baking powder
- 1 teaspoon anise seed, crushed
- ½ teaspoon baking soda
- ½ teaspoon salt
- ½ teaspoon nutmeg
- 1 cup chopped pears
- ½ cup chopped walnuts

1. Preheat the oven to 350°F. Grease and flour a 9- by 5-inch loaf pan. Cream together the butter and sugar in a large mixing bowl with an electric mixer until the mixture is light and fluffy. Add the eggs, one at a time, and beat until well blended. Add the vanilla extract and the yogurt.

2. In a separate bowl, combine the flour, baking powder, anise seed, baking soda, salt, and nutmeg. Gradually add the dry ingredients to the batter, mixing to incorporate. Stir in the pears and nuts and mix until blended.

3. Pour the batter into the prepared pan and bake for 50 minutes to 1 hour, or until a toothpick inserted into the middle of the cake comes out clean. Cool the cake in the pan for 15 minutes, then remove it and let it cool completely on a wire rack.

Carrot Cake with Black Walnuts

This moist cake is packed with the sweetness of fall carrots and local black walnuts. I use black walnuts that I gather on our farm, waiting for the green husk to dissolve and the black ink to dry. As hard as they are to crack, the nut is sweet and delicious. If you can't find local walnuts, regular nuts are delicious, too.

12 SERVINGS

4 eggs

1½ cups (3 sticks) butter, softened

2 cups granulated sugar

3 teaspoons vanilla extract

2 cups all-purpose flour

2 teaspoons baking soda

2 teaspoons baking powder

2 teaspoons ground cinnamon

½ teaspoon salt

3 cups grated carrots

2 cups chopped Maryland black walnuts

1 (8-ounce) package cream cheese

2 cups confectioners' sugar

1. Preheat the oven to 350°F. Grease and flour a 9- by 13-inch pan or two 8-inch round cake pans. Beat together the eggs, 2 sticks of the butter, the granulated sugar, and 2 teaspoons of the vanilla. Mix in the flour, baking soda, baking powder, cinnamon, and salt. Fold in the carrots and stir. Fold in 1 cup of the walnuts and stir.

2. Pour the batter into the prepared pan(s). Bake for 40 to 50 minutes for the 9- by 13-inch pan or 30 to 35 minutes for the 8-inch round layers, until a knife inserted into the middle of a cake comes out clean. Cool for 15 minutes and then remove the cake(s) and transfer to a wire rack to cool completely.

3. Make the frosting: Combine the remaining 1 stick butter in a medium bowl with the cream cheese, confectioners' sugar, and the remaining 1 teaspoon vanilla. Beat with an electric mixer until the frosting is smooth and creamy. Stir in the remaining 1 cup walnuts. Frost the cooled cake.

BUTLER'S ORCHARD
Montgomery County

Susan Butler calls her family's 60-year-old orchard in Germantown "an oasis," which is an understatement. Set in the middle of one of America's most expensive and developed counties, 300 acres of farmland seems nothing short of a miracle. And George and Shirley Butler, the farm's founders, and Susan, Todd, and Wade, their three grown children who work with them, understand that. The farm is open 8 months of the year — complete with pick-your-own fruits and vegetables, tractor rides, "Blossom Week" educational tours to teach kids about pollination, summer camp sessions where children can plant and harvest crops, a strawberry festival, and, at year's end, cut-your-own Christmas trees. The Butlers know that people don't pick the volume of food they once did, but that they still want to come out and have the experience and take home some fresh berries or the peas they picked that morning.

"Agritourism" or "agritainment," where families like the Butlers combine traditional agriculture with inviting the public onto their farms, is a trend that benefits everyone. It helps save family farms by bringing in additional revenue. And watching the many families enjoying themselves at Butler's every weekend, it's obvious that the connections they're making to the farm will last much longer than the produce they take home.

Spiced Pumpkin Bread

Baby Bear, Amish Pie, Small Sugar, Cheese, and Baby Pam pumpkin varieties, several of which you'll find at Butler's, all make excellent, moist pumpkin breads. Queen Anne Farm in Prince George's County also features numerous pumpkin varieties, including several heirlooms.

¾ cup (1½ sticks) butter, softened

2 cups sugar

4 eggs

2 cups pumpkin purée

⅔ cup orange juice

2 tablespoons molasses

3⅓ cups all-purpose flour

1¼ teaspoons salt

1 teaspoon baking powder

1 teaspoon baking soda

1 teaspoon ground cinnamon

1 teaspoon ground cloves

1 cup raisins

1 cup chopped pecans

1½ teaspoon vanilla extract

MAKES 4 SMALL OR 2 LARGE LOAVES

1. Preheat the oven to 350°F. Grease and flour two 9- by 5-inch loaf pans or four 7- by 3½- by 2-inch loaf pans, and set aside. Beat the butter in a large bowl with an electric mixer at medium speed. Gradually add the sugar. Add the eggs, one at a time, and mix to incorporate. Blend in the pumpkin, orange juice, and molasses.

2. In a separate bowl, combine the flour, salt, baking powder, baking soda, cinnamon, and cloves. Add the dry ingredients to the creamed mixture. Stir in the raisins, pecans, and vanilla.

3. Spoon the batter into the prepared baking pans. Bake for 50 to 55 minutes in larger loaf pans or 25 to 30 minutes in the smaller pans; a wooden toothpick inserted into the center of one of the loaves should come out clean. Cool in pans 10 minutes; remove from pans and let cool completely on a wire rack.

Raspberry-filled Chocolate Cake with Chocolate–Cream Cheese Icing

When the raspberry bushes in my yard are bare, I go down to Larriland Farm in Howard County, one of my favorite pick-your-own places in Maryland. Larry and Polly Moore own Larriland, and they and three of their four children run the place, offering, among other crops, 14 acres each of strawberries and peaches, and 5 acres each of blueberries and raspberries, including purple, black, and red raspberries. What is especially appealing about Larriland is that the Moores use integrated-pest management, which dramatically minimizes the use of pesticides, and they employ other management practices to ensure that the land will remain productive for generations to come. I try to pick extra for freezing and then use them all winter for shakes, jam, and fruit coulis. This is a very decadent chocolate cake with a beautiful and delicious surprise in the middle.

3½ cups all-purpose flour

2 cups unsweetened cocoa powder

2½ teaspoons baking soda

¼ teaspoon salt

1½ cups (3 sticks) butter, softened

1⅓ plus ½ cup granulated sugar

1⅓ cup brown sugar

4 eggs

6 teaspoons vanilla extract

3 cups buttermilk

3 pints fresh raspberries

3 tablespoons cornstarch

1 (8-ounce) package cream cheese

¾ cup confectioners' sugar

3 ounces bittersweet chocolate, melted and cooled

Shaved chocolate for garnish

12 SERVINGS

1. Preheat the oven to 350°F. Line the bottoms of two 9-inch round cake pans with waxed paper. Grease and flour the paper and sides of the pans.

2. Mix the flour, cocoa, baking soda, and salt together in a large bowl. Combine the butter, the 1⅓ cups granulated sugar, and the brown sugar in a separate large bowl, and cream together with an electric mixer until light and fluffy. Beat in the eggs, one at a time, and then beat in 4 teaspoons of the vanilla extract.

3. On low speed, alternate adding the buttermilk and the dry ingredients into the creamed butter and sugar. Mix just until blended; do not overmix. Divide the batter equally between the pans. Bake the cake for 40 to 45 minutes, until a toothpick inserted into the middle of one of the cakes comes out clean. Remove the cakes from the oven and cool for 10 minutes on a wire rack. Take the layers out of the pans, remove the waxed paper, and cool completely.

4. Meanwhile, make the raspberry filling: Combine 2 pints of the raspberries and the ½ cup granulated sugar in a small saucepan. Dissolve the cornstarch in ¼ cup hot water and add the slurry to the raspberries. Bring the mixture to a boil and simmer for 3 minutes, until the mixture thickens. Remove the filling from the heat and set the saucepan in a bowl of ice water to cool completely.

5. Make the frosting: Beat the cream cheese, confectioners' sugar, melted chocolate, and the remaining 2 teaspoons vanilla in a bowl until the mixture is light and fluffy.

6. Assemble the cake: Cut each cake layer in half horizontally. Place one cake layer on a serving plate; spread with raspberry filling. Repeat the process with all but the top of the remaining layers. Spread the frosting on the top and sides of the cake. Garnish the cake with a circle of raspberries around the edge of the cake and shaved chocolate in the middle.

4 Winter

Winter brings the cold and much-hoped-for snow in western Maryland. Stiff winds whip off the ocean and the Bay, sending us indoors for oyster stew and fritters. It's time for holiday craft festivals and tree-lighting ceremonies, sledding and skiing, skating on Rash Field in Baltimore, and candlelight tours in Annapolis. There is holiday baking and slow-cooked roasts, southern Maryland stuffed ham and cut-your-own Christmas trees, and hotcakes on the woodstove with lots of fresh maple syrup from Maryland's own sugar maples.

Cabbage Stir-fry with Caraway Seeds

Caraway imparts a wonderful flavor to this quick and easy side dish.

- 4 tablespoons butter
- 1 small onion, peeled and minced
- 1 small green cabbage, cored and thinly sliced
- 1 cup Chicken Stock (page 26) or Vegetable Stock (page 27)
- 1 tablespoon caraway seeds
- 1 teaspoon salt
- ¼ teaspoon freshly ground black pepper

Melt the butter over low heat in a skillet. Add the onion and sauté for 3 to 5 minutes, until the onion is translucent. Add the cabbage and sauté for 5 minutes longer, then add the stock and turn the heat up to medium-high. Cover and cook for 10 minutes. Uncover and continue cooking until the stock is absorbed. Add the caraway seeds, salt, and pepper, and toss well. Remove the cabbage from the heat and serve immediately.

Red Cabbage with Cider and Apples

Rotkohl or *Rotkabbis*, as the Swiss call red cabbage, was a staple Sunday vegetable in our household during the fall and winter months. In Maryland you'll find it out in the garden as late as December. It is the perfect accompaniment to a pork roast, turkey, or meatloaf.

6 SERVINGS

- 2 tablespoons butter
- 1 large onion, peeled and diced
- 2 medium tart apples, peeled, cored, and chopped
- 1 large head of red cabbage, very finely sliced
- ½ cup apple cider
- ½ cup Chicken Stock (page 26) or Vegetable Stock (page 27)
- ¼ cup red wine vinegar
- 1 bay leaf
- ½ teaspoon salt
- ¼ teaspoon freshly ground black pepper

Melt the butter over low heat in a large saucepan and add the onion and the apples. Sauté for about 3 minutes, until the apples are soft and the onion is translucent. Add the red cabbage and continue to sauté for 2 minutes longer. Add the apple cider, stock, vinegar, bay leaf, salt, and pepper, and cook for about 1 hour, until the cabbage is thoroughly soft and most of the liquid is gone. Remove the bay leaf before serving.

Brett Grohsgal

Even' Star Organic Farm
St. Mary's County

Walk the typical Maryland farm in February, and you won't see much growing outside. But follow Brett Grohsgal around Even' Star Organic Farm, and you'll quickly sense that this is no ordinary farm and Grohsgal no ordinary farmer. In the dead of winter, as far as the eye can see, green asserts itself, not in covered houses or cold frames, but out in the fields: Brussels sprouts, arugula, bok choy, mustard greens, turnip tops, and more — all alive and growing.

It takes an optimistic person to think that he can successfully beat the winter by growing crops in the fields year-round, and a gifted man to make that happen. Grohsgal is both. Trained in soil science and plant genetics at Berkley and North Carolina State University before spending 18 years as a chef, Grohsgal has been successfully growing and breeding cold-hardy strains of vegetables, especially Asian cabbages and greens, since 1997 on his 100-plus-acre farm. It's a challenge he obviously loves. Developing hardier, more disease-resistant strains of vegetables is Grohsgal's old-age insurance policy he says, his way to keep the farm in the black long after he's no longer able to do the heavy work of farming himself.

For now, though, the farm is very profitable, due in no small part to Grohsgal's ability to sell field-grown local produce during a season of high demand and low availability. Grohsgal's winter CSA customers and wholesale clients, including American University in Washington DC, happily receive their salad and stir-fry greens every other week throughout the winter. His certified organic mizuna, choy sum, pak choy, and tat soy show up on menus in some of Washington's hottest restaurants and on dinner plates across St. Mary's County.

Roasted Turnips and Rutabagas

The mellow complexity of these roasted roots complements meat and vegetarian dishes alike.

3–4 cups trimmed, unpeeled
    baby turnips, rutabagas,
    or a mixture

3 tablespoons olive oil

1 teaspoon salt

½ teaspoon freshly ground
    black pepper

2 tablespoons chopped onion

1 tablespoon minced garlic

2 teaspoons chopped fresh
    thyme or rosemary, or 1
    teaspoon dried rosemary

4 SERVINGS

1. Preheat the oven to 375°F. Cut any larger roots into pieces about 1½ inches long; leave smaller ones whole. Place the roots in a roasting pan, and add the olive oil, salt, and pepper, and toss. Bake for 30 minutes, stirring occasionally, until only the very centers of the larger roots are still hard.

2. Add the onion, garlic, and herbs, and continue roasting for 15 minutes longer, until all the roots are just soft. Many roots will have begun to caramelize (turn brown, shriveled, and sweet). Serve immediately.

Shredded Brussels Sprouts

At Rumbleway Farms in the cold-weather months, Robin Way and her husband host multicourse dinners that are open to the public to supplement their farm income. This is one of Robin's recipes from those winter dinners.

¼ cup olive oil

¼ cup chopped onions

½ cup sliced fresh mushrooms

1 cup butternut squash, peeled and diced into small pieces

2 pounds fresh Brussels sprouts, trimmed and thinly sliced

2 tablespoons butter

½ teaspoon salt

½ freshly ground black pepper

6 SERVINGS

1. Heat the olive oil in a large skillet over medium heat until hot. Add the onions, mushrooms, and squash, and cook for 5 minutes.

2. Add the Brussels sprouts and sauté for about 3 minutes. Add ½ cup water, the butter, salt, and pepper, and cook for 5 minutes longer, until most of the liquid is gone and the sprouts are tender, but have not lost their color.

Chapel's Country Zucchini and Squash Casserole

Premium cheeses made by hand with fresh-from-the-cow milk are flavorful accents to a recipe that has been handed down for generations in Holly Foster's family. You can substitute different vegetables and cheeses, or add lean, browned ground beef to the layers to have a complete meal.

2–3 small green zucchini cut into thin round slices

2–3 small yellow squash cut into thin round slices

1 large onion, peeled and cut in half, then sliced thin

2 large tomatoes, thinly sliced

2 ounces Chapel's Colby-Dill Cheese, or other Colby cheese, shredded (½ cup)

2 ounces Chapel's Herbal Jack Cheese, or other Jack cheese, shredded (½ cup)

2 ounces Chapel's Cheddar Cheese, or other cheddar cheese, shredded (½ cup)

1 teaspoon salt

½ teaspoon freshly ground black pepper

2–4 SERVINGS

1. Preheat the oven to 350°F. Grease a large baking or casserole dish.

2. Layer the ingredients in the casserole dish, alternating two vegetables with a different cheese for each layer. For example, begin with zucchini and tomato, topped with the Colby, followed by the squash and onion, topped with the Herbal Jack. Sprinkle some of the salt and pepper on each layer. Continue layering until all the ingredients have been used. Bake for 45 to 60 minutes, until golden and bubbly. Serve immediately.

Chapel's
Country Creamery

Garlic & Chive Cheddar

Made from fresh Milk, All natural ingredients,
Aged over 60 days.

Ingredients: Raw Whole Milk, Salt, Vegetable Rennet,
Garlic, Chives, and Cheese Culture.

Keep refrigerated.

Distributed by Chapel's Country Creamery, LLC
Billy and Holly Thomas, Easton, Maryland
410-820-6647   www.chapelscountrycreamery.com

CHAPEL'S COUNTRY CREAMERY
Talbot County

Holly Foster

Holly Foster, a tiny woman who doesn't look old enough to be the mother of four, was afraid of cows before her husband, Eric, gave her one for Christmas a number of years ago. He urged her to go out to the barn on her own, try to milk Rainey, as they named the cream-colored Jersey, and "learn from her," as Eric put it. Filled with trepidation, she did.

What happened next surprised her. "I just connected with her," Holly says. "It was so cool milking her." Until then it had been Eric, a lifelong farmer, who had wanted a herd of cows to make cheese. But it was Holly who became passionate about the idea and gave it life. She took cheesemaking courses, traveling to California and other places on her own — something else she'd been afraid of — and she tried her hand at producing cheeses from the milk of their cows, and she loved it. Eventually she found an Amish cheesemaker in Lancaster County, Pennsylvania, who agreed to work with her to make and cave-age the cheeses. After what amounted to an apprenticeship, Holly launched Chapel's Country Cheeses to great acclaim at the 2005 Waterfowl Festival in nearby Easton. From there, she began marketing her cheeses online, to chefs, and in retail stores and markets in Maryland, Virginia, and Washington DC.

The Fosters' herd has expanded to 110 head of Jersey and Holstein dairy cows, which Holly and Eric milk twice a day, a job she has come to love, despite the long hours that go with it. Because of Maryland's health department restrictions on making raw milk cheeses, until recently, Holly traveled with the milk to Pennsylvania for cheesemaking. In her repertoire are a specially aged cheddar with a bloomy white rind, assorted Jack and Colby cheeses, and a raw milk variety called Chapelle. Holly also crafts specialty cheddars with crab spice seasoning, chives, and sundried tomatoes. Much to her surprise, Holly is at the forefront of Maryland's nascent artisanal cheesemaking industry, which lags far behind states like Vermont and California. Legislation passed by Maryland's General Assembly designated Chapel's Country Creamery one of a handful of Maryland dairies eligible to take part in a pilot program to make raw milk cheeses on site for the first time.

In 2009, the Fosters opened their on-farm processing plant and caves and have begun making their signature cheeses just a few hundred yards from where they collect the milk. Now Holly is making 600 to 900 pounds of cheese at home, trying to keep up with a demand that already exceeds her yearly output of 20,000 pounds of handmade, high-quality gourmet cheeses.

Gratin Dauphinois
(Scalloped Potatoes with Gruyère Cheese)

No one can resist this particular combination of potatoes and cheese, particularly with locally grown organic potatoes, which will store well all winter in a cool, dark location.

2½ pounds boiling potatoes, such as Red Bliss or Yukon Gold

4 tablespoons butter

2 garlic cloves, peeled and minced

¼ cup all-purpose flour

3½ cups half-and-half

1 teaspoon salt

¼ teaspoon freshly ground black pepper

6 ounces Gruyère cheese, shredded (1½ cups)

¼ cup breadcrumbs

8 SERVINGS

1. Peel the potatoes and cut them into ¹⁄₁₆-inch-thick rounds. Layer them in a 3-quart or similar shallow baking dish.

2. Preheat the oven to 400°F. Melt the butter in a medium saucepan over medium heat. Add the garlic and sauté for 2 minutes, until pale golden. Whisk in the flour, cooking and stirring until the mixture is smooth and bubbling. Gradually add the half-and-half, salt, and pepper, whisking constantly. Bring to a gentle boil and simmer until the sauce thickens, continuing to whisk constantly. Remove the sauce from the heat and pour over the potatoes. Sprinkle the Gruyère over the casserole and sprinkle the breadcrumbs over the cheese. Bake for 1 hour. If the top gets too brown, cover with aluminum foil and continue to bake until the potatoes are tender.

Vegetarian Stuffed Cabbage Rolls with Rice

Maryland farm stands and farmers' markets carry local cabbage throughout the winter. These meatless stuffed cabbage rolls are cold-weather fare, hearty, savory, and rib-sticking. You can always freeze and reheat any leftovers.

1 large head green cabbage

3 tablespoons butter

1 medium onion, peeled and diced

1 large carrot, peeled and finely minced

2 cups cooked white or brown rice

2 cups breadcrumbs

1 teaspoon dried sage

½ teaspoon salt

½ teaspoon freshly ground black pepper

1⅓ cups Vegetable Stock (page 27) or beef broth

¾ cup dry white wine

¾ cup heavy cream

1 teaspoon thyme

¼ teaspoon nutmeg

MAKES 12 CABBAGE ROLLS

1. Cut the core out of the head of cabbage with a large knife, leaving a hole in the middle. Place the whole head of cabbage in a large saucepan filled with water. Turn the heat to high and bring the water to a boil. When the water has reached a boil, turn off the heat and leave the cabbage in the water for 5 minutes. Remove the cabbage from the water and allow to cool. When the cabbage is cool enough to handle, peel off the leaves. You will need 12 large leaves. Set those off to one side. Coarsely chop any remaining cabbage.

2. Melt the butter in a large skillet over medium heat and sauté the onion and carrot until they are soft, about 5 minutes. Reduce the heat to low and add the rice, breadcrumbs, sage, salt, pepper, and stock. Toss the mixture thoroughly to moisten the breadcrumbs and the rice. Remove the skillet from the heat and set aside.

3. Preheat the oven to 350°F. Lay the cabbage leaves flat on a work surface. Remove the toughest part of each leaf by cutting a V-shaped, ½-inch incision into the stem. Place about 3 tablespoons of the stuffing mixture in the center of each cabbage leaf. Tuck the sides of each cabbage leaf into the center, and then roll the stuffed cabbage leaf to make a small packet. Place each stuffed cabbage roll seam side down in a 9- by 13-inch glass baking dish. Scatter the leftover chopped cabbage over the cabbage rolls. Pour the wine and cream over the cabbage rolls and sprinkle with the thyme and nutmeg. Cover with aluminum foil and bake for 1 hour. Remove the foil and bake uncovered for 15 minutes longer.

RICHARD WATTERS
Harford County

At 78 years old, Richard Watters would like nothing better than to work fewer hours and cut back on the arduous manual labor involved in vegetable farming. Farm labor, though, is hard to find these days, and the profit margins on Watters' modest 15-acre farm are slim, so the slight, stooped man with heavily calloused hands and light, almost translucent eyes, continues to till and tend his fields alone. In doing so, Watters remains in the dwindling ranks of African American farmers in Maryland — around a hundred, according to the last agricultural census — who are not leaving farming for other professions. Watters, whose sole child, a daughter, earned a PhD in English, and teaches, doesn't have anyone who will farm his land once he is gone, but if it bothers him, he doesn't dwell on it. Instead, he says he keeps farming because he loves to grow things, and the rich loamy soil he tends is like a trusted partner and ally. Over the years Watters has grown a variety of flowers and vegetables to sell at regional farmers' markets, but it's his crimson-, orange-, and white-fleshed sweet potatoes that customers return for year after year. Watters is one of only a handful of farmers who grow a variety of sweet potatoes, including Hayman, Beauregard, Jewel, and Georgia Jet. Holding up a single, huge sweet potato that weighs well over eight pounds and could easily feed a family, Watters shakes his head in amazement, still astonished at what he pulls from the soil with a little luck and a lot of hard work.

Sweet Potato Casserole with Toasted Pecan Topping

Simply one of the most delicious casseroles ever, this is a slight variation on a recipe that my sister-in-law, Eleanor Van Dyke, gave me years ago.

6–8 large sweet potatoes
1 cup (2 sticks) butter
¾ cup milk, heated
1 tablespoon vanilla
½ teaspoon salt
2 cups pecan halves
1 cup brown sugar
½ cup all-purpose flour

12 SERVINGS

1. Preheat the oven to 400°F. Prick the sweet potatoes and place them on a foil-lined baking sheet. Bake in the oven for 1 hour or until soft. Remove the sweet potatoes from the oven and allow to cool for 15 minutes. Reduce the oven temperature to 350°F.

2. Cut the sweet potatoes open, scoop out all the flesh, and spoon it into a large mixing bowl. Add 1 stick of the butter, the warm milk, vanilla, and salt. Beat the sweet potato mixture with an electric mixer on low speed until the butter is melted and the mixture is smooth and creamy. Butter a large baking dish and spoon the sweet potato mixture into it. Cover with aluminum foil and place it in the oven. Bake for 25 minutes.

3. While the casserole is baking, make the topping: Melt the remaining 1 stick butter in the microwave and let it cool for 5 minutes. Mix the pecans, brown sugar, and flour together with the melted butter.

4. Remove the casserole from the oven and uncover it. Spoon the topping over the casserole and return it to the oven, uncovered. Bake 15 minutes longer. Serve immediately.

Sweet Potato Biscuits

Quick and delicious, these biscuits go well with just about anything, from local honey and preserves to ham. They're especially good with soups and stews on a cold winter's night.

1½ cups all-purpose flour
 3 teaspoons baking powder
 ½ teaspoon salt
 1 cup boiled, strained, and mashed sweet potato
 4 tablespoons butter, melted
 1 teaspoon orange zest
 ½ cup milk

MAKES 12 BISCUITS

1. Preheat the oven to 400°F. Combine the flour, baking powder, and salt in a bowl.

2. Mix the mashed sweet potato with the melted butter and the orange zest, and then gradually stir in the milk. Add the sweet potato mixture to the dry ingredients, incorporating it and kneading the dough until it becomes pliable. Roll out the dough to a thickness of 1 inch on a floured surface and cut out rounds with a biscuit cutter. Bake the biscuits on an ungreased baking sheet for 15 minutes, until golden brown. Serve the biscuits hot.

Country Sausage Breakfast Bake

This recipe comes from Kate Dallam, who makes her own pork sausage and sells it at her Broom's Bloom Dairy store. It's perfect for a Sunday brunch, served with Crispy Potato Pancakes (page 178) made from local potatoes, and some pan-fried apples.

1 cup milk

2 eggs, slightly beaten

1 cup all-purpose flour

¾ teaspoon salt

1 pound well-seasoned ground pork or country sausage

4 SERVINGS

1. Whisk the milk and eggs in a medium bowl until well combined. Sift in the flour and salt and mix until incorporated. Beat the batter with an electric mixer until smooth and bubbly, about 5 minutes. Let the batter rest for about 1 hour.

2. Preheat the oven to 450°F. Shape the pork into patties and cook in a skillet over medium heat until the patties are evenly browned and cooked through. Save 2 tablespoons of the pork fat.

3. Arrange the cooked sausage in a shallow baking dish with the reserved pork fat. Put the baking dish in the oven just until the dish is very hot, 3 to 4 minutes. Pour the batter over the sausages and bake 20 to 25 minutes longer, until the casserole is golden brown. Serve immediately.

David Smith

SPRINGFIELD FARM
Baltimore County

The gently rolling, stone-pocked land that is Springfield Farm in Sparks is home to one of the oldest farms in Maryland. David Smith's family acquired it in the seventeenth century. He is the 16th generation on the land, and he doesn't have to look far to see the 17th and 18th, as two of his three daughters and their families live and work there, too, making it a true family farm. And so even though Smith traveled the world, first in his

23-year military career and then as a marketer in the defense industry, his chickens literally came home to roost when he moved back in 1995. Although he says that at the time he had "no inclination to farm," Smith, like many other healthy retirees, decided that he was too young not to do something meaningful to fill his time. First he acquired laying chickens — "for the grandchildren," as his wife, Lilly, says — and some rabbits. In 2000 they added broiler chickens and turkeys, and, not much later, pigs and sheep. Geese and other exotic fowl, including guinea hens, quail, and pheasants, also began roaming the electrified enclosures that Smith rotates around his pastures. He took some courses in slow food and sustainability and was convinced he could make his farm self-sustaining and profitable by selling his eggs and meat to consumers who wanted to know where their food was raised. A local restaurateur who saw Smith's hand-lettered sign for eggs was among his first customers, convincing him to supply his restaurant with fresh eggs on a weekly basis.

Today, the bearded, fit-looking Smith sells to some of Baltimore's and Washington's top chefs and restaurants, charging nearly three times for his eggs what commercially raised ones bring. His daughters run a thriving on-farm store that carries everything they raise, as well as some products from Pennsylvania Amish farms. While fall is his busiest time, with turkey and goose orders for Thanksgiving and Christmas, Smith's biggest year-round sellers are his chickens and the farm-fresh eggs — 45,000 dozen of them — that his flock of Rhode Island Red/Sex-link cross laying hens produces.

The eggs, with sunflower yellow yolks that transform plain scrambled eggs into gustatory delights and cake batters into seas of saffron, are the result of what Smith deems "Allowing chickens to have their chickenness." This means allowing them to roam at will in their moveable pastures, scratching for seeds and insects, because no matter where you look on Smith's farm, that's what they're doing, sometimes a few thousand of them at a time, depending on the time of year. It's working, too: In a 2007 study commissioned by *Mother Earth News* in which Smith's and 13 other farms' eggs were tested,

the pastured eggs had one-third less cholesterol, one-quarter less saturated fat, two-thirds more vitamin A, seven times more beta-carotene, and 21 times the omega-3 fatty acids than regular commercial eggs. And among all the eggs tested, Springfield Farms' were the lowest in cholesterol and saturated fat per 100 grams. With numbers like that, it's hard to imagine disputing Smith's claim that his eggs are the "very best tasting around."

Chicken and Dumplings

This comfort-food recipe is a variation on one that has been in David Smith's family for generations.

1 (3–4 pound) free-range chicken, preferably organic

1 small onion, peeled

3 garlic cloves

1 bay leaf

½ teaspoon dried thyme

2 teaspoons salt

½ teaspoon freshly ground black pepper

4 large carrots

4 celery stalks

2 large potatoes

2 cups all-purpose flour

2 teaspoons baking powder

2 tablespoons butter, melted

3 tablespoons chopped fresh parsley

1 tablespoon chopped fresh tarragon

⅔ cup milk

6 SERVINGS

1. Make the soup: Wash the chicken thoroughly and pat it dry. Place it in a large stockpot and cover with 6 cups of water. Bring the water to a boil and add the onion, garlic, bay leaf, thyme, 1 teaspoon of the salt, and the pepper.

2. Peel the carrots; put one whole carrot into the pot. Cut the remaining carrots into 1-inch chunks and set them aside. Put one celery stalk into the pot. Slice the rest of the celery into 1-inch chunks and set them aside. Cover the stockpot with a lid. Peel the potatoes and cut them into 1-inch chunks. Place them in a small bowl and cover with cold water.

3. Simmer the chicken, covered, for 3 hours. The liquid will be reduced by about one-third. Remove the carcass of the bird and put it into a bowl to cool. Strain the chicken stock, discarding the vegetables and any bones. Return the stock to the pot.

4. Make the dumplings: Combine the flour, baking powder, and the remaining 1 teaspoon salt in a food processor and pulse briefly to combine the ingredients. Add the butter, parsley, and tarragon through the food processor feeding tube and pulse for 5 seconds. Gradually add the milk, pulsing, until the mixture forms a ball. Remove the dough from the food processor and allow it to rest for 15 minutes.

5. Pick off all the chicken meat from the carcass and return the meat to the stockpot, along with the reserved chopped carrots, celery, and potatoes. Cover, and bring the soup to a simmer. Roll out the dumpling dough onto a lightly floured surface, making an 8- by 10-inch rectangle. Cut four long strips out of the dough and cut the strips into 24 dumplings. Lift the lid of the pot and gently lower all the dumplings into the liquid. Cover tightly and steam the dumplings for 18 minutes without stirring them or lifting the lid off the pot. Ladle the hot soup and dumplings into warmed soup plates. Serve immediately.

Oyster Fritters Southern Maryland Style

Golden and delicious, these puffy fritters are unforgettable.

1 cup all-purpose flour
2 teaspoons baking powder
½ teaspoon salt
½ teaspoon paprika
2 eggs
1 cup milk
1 quart shucked
 oysters, drained
1 cup vegetable oil

4 SERVINGS

1. Mix together the flour, baking powder, salt, and paprika in a medium bowl. Stir the eggs and milk together and pour into the flour mixture. Mix well, until the batter is smooth. Stir the oysters into the batter.

2. Pour the oil into a large cast iron skillet. Heat the oil until it is very hot but not smoking. Drop the batter by tablespoonfuls into the hot oil and fry the fritters until golden on both sides. Continue frying in batches until all the batter is used, adding more oil if needed. Serve immediately.

Spicy Oysters with Bacon and Cheese

This is how Michele Hayden likes to fix her oysters on a cold winter day.

1 dozen fresh oysters
 in the shell
6 strips bacon
6 slices Colby cheese
 Worcestershire sauce
 Hot sauce
 Old Bay or other seafood
 seasoning
 Lemon slices

4–6 SERVINGS

1. Preheat the oven to 450°F. Shuck the oysters, reserving the shells. Rinse and drain the oyster meat and clean and dry the shells.

2. Put the oyster shells on a baking sheet. Place 1 oyster in each shell. Add 2 to 3 drops Worcestershire to each. Top each oyster with ½ strip of uncooked bacon. Add 3 to 4 drops of hot sauce to each. Cover each oyster with ½ slice of the cheese.

3. Bake the oysters for 20 minutes, until the cheese is golden and bubbly. Remove the baking sheet from the oven and sprinkle lightly with seafood seasoning. Serve immediately with lemon wedges as a garnish.

OYSTERS

Long before crabs became synonymous with Maryland, the oyster was king in the Chesapeake region. Ever since the first Americans settled by the waters of the Chesapeake and her tributaries, the oyster has been a staple of their diet, providing not just an important source of protein but also key vitamins and minerals, including iodine, iron, magnesium, calcium, and zinc. Proof of the oyster's longstanding abundance and popularity can still be found in the mountains of oyster shells, some of them ancient and known as middens, piled up across the region. Oyster shells were also commonly used to pave roads and fill in reclaimed land in seafood towns like Crisfield on the Eastern Shore. By the midnineteenth century, Maryland's oyster industry had reached its apex, with a September 18, 1880, *Baltimore Sun* article reporting that Maryland watermen harvested 10,569,012 bushels of oysters in the 1879–1880 season. Back then, Maryland was the world's oyster capital, with thousands of mostly African American men and immigrant women employed in hundreds of shucking and packing houses in Baltimore, southern Maryland, and on the Eastern Shore. In fact, so dominant was the oyster to Maryland's maritime economy that in the 1880 census, a majority of males on the lower Shore listed "oystering" as their vocation.

The oyster industry in Maryland today is a mere shadow of what it was once. Overharvesting, pollution, and two diseases, MSX and Dermo, have dethroned the seafood king. Only in the past few years has there been any reason for optimism, the result of more stringent harvesting regulations, a state-sponsored effort to restore and restock the oyster beds, and environmental policies and scientific efforts aimed at bringing the Bay ecosystem back to health. And in fact, watermen who are still oystering say that the quality of the oysters harvested in the 2008–2009 season was the best they'd seen in decades, a cause for celebration and at least cautious optimism.

Oysters are enjoyed many ways: fried, steamed, sautéed, baked, barbequed, and stewed. Purists, however, insist that the only way to eat oysters is raw, with a splash of fresh lemon juice, a sliver of freshly shaved horseradish, or maybe a dash of hot sauce. Raw bars are very popular in Maryland, whether in Ocean City, Tilghman Island, Annapolis, or Baltimore. Maybe it's the reputed aphrodisiac qualities of the bivalves, but men seem especially fond of oysters, and slurping down a dozen or two is a time-honored tradition, especially at popular places like Faidley's Seafood in Baltimore's Lexington Market, where they've been selling all manner of fresh seafood, including what many consider to be the finest crab cake in Maryland, since 1886.

Oysters are harvested using a variety of methods: hand or hydraulic tonging, dredging, and even diving. They're sold fresh in the shell, freshly shucked, canned, or frozen. Shucked oysters come in three sizes — counts, selects, and standards — and are sold by the pint, quart, half-gallon, or gallon. Counts are the biggest oysters and are typically used for stews and entrées. Selects are smaller and are suited to frying and hors d'oeuvres. Standards are the smallest oyster size and are typically used for oyster fritters. Because bivalves take their flavor from the water they live in, oysters from saltier waters are generally used for raw consumption, because they have the briniest, most distinctive flavor. Oysters taken from waters with a lower salt content are generally milder in flavor and are used for cooking.

When buying shell oysters, make sure they are tightly closed or pull close when touched. If they are open and don't close, the oyster is dead and should be discarded. Fresh shell oysters must be kept in a cold refrigerator or on ice, ideally with a damp cloth over them. The shelf life of shell oysters is roughly 2 weeks in the refrigerator; the shelf life of shucked, refrigerated oysters is 7 to 10 days. When buying shucked oysters, make sure they are plump and have a light color, with clear oyster liquor.

As anyone who has ever waited in a raw bar line can attest, proficiency at oyster shucking is a highly prized skill. In Maryland, oyster shucking is taken so seriously that we hold a national oyster-shucking contest and cook-off every November in Leonardtown. While you may never achieve the dazzling speed of competitive shuckers, it's actually fairly easy to shuck your own oysters, although

it takes practice and some safety precautions. First, rinse the oysters thoroughly in cold water, scrubbing them vigorously. Next, don a thick rubber glove or mitt or hold a towel and position the oyster in your palm with the cupped side down and the flat shell up. Insert a paring or oyster knife between the shells, at or near the hinge of the oyster. Then twist the knife so that the hinge pops and the oyster's muscles — top and lower ends — are cut and detached. Remove the top shell and scrape the meat from the top into the bottom shell if eating the oysters raw on the half shell. If not, cut the oyster loose from both shells and put it into a container, reserving its liquor for cooking. Before using, make sure that there is no shell fragment clinging to the muscle, which is common.

CIRCLE C OYSTER RANCH
St. Mary's County

Richard Pelz isn't a waterman in the traditional sense, nor is he your typical scientist, although what he does combines elements of both. Pelz is a crusader, and a stubborn and very smart one at that. His energy is focused on two fronts: cleaning up the Chesapeake Bay and ensuring that the world's food supply contains adequate sources of protein. His weapon of choice: the Eastern oyster, *Crassostrea virginica*, which for thousands of years has been the lifeblood of the Chesapeake — not just economically, but also environmentally. Oysters are living filters, cleaning about 50 gallons of water a day apiece, removing the algae and phytoplankton that block sunlight and oxygen from reaching the bottom of the Chesapeake Bay. A hundred years ago, there were so many oysters in the Bay that it took just a few days for them to filter all of the water in the Chesapeake. But the native oyster has suffered a disastrous decline due to a near-fatal mix of overharvesting, pollution, and virulent diseases.

Pelz and a growing number of scientists and public policy makers believe that if the Bay is ever to recover and oysters make a comeback, then aquaculture — commercially farming oysters on raised platforms — will play a critical role. And if in the process aquaculture is producing the best-tasting oyster that many people have ever eaten, well, that's just fine with Pelz, too.

Pelz developed artificial floating reefs to grow his oysters. He seeds those reefs with oyster spats from a genetic line that he and a scientist in Virginia have been collaborating on for years. But unlike wild oysters that grow on reefs in the Bay and on river bottoms, Pelz's grow in just inches of water, tied to a dock. "You have to put the oysters where the food and the oxygen are," Pelz explains. "Oysters eat algae that grow in Bay waters and the lion's share of fresh algae, and the oxygen it produces, is found in the first 12 to 18 inches of water."

Pelz would like to see oyster farms fanned out across the Chesapeake Bay region, and he is doing all he can to make that possible, including selling his floating reefs — complete with 600 oyster spats — to anyone who is interested and has the requisite waterfront. And, despite fierce resistance from traditional watermen who see Pelz as a competitor, Circle C Ranch Oysters are thriving, with more than a million grown and eaten to date. Pelz's bivalves have gained an impressive reputation with chefs and home cooks throughout the region.

On a beautiful winter day on St. Jerome's Creek, a small tributary of the Chesapeake, Pelz points to the crystal clear water, the abundance of sea grasses, and the schools of fish that are readily visible from his dock, where tens of thousands of oysters are growing and cleaning the water. "Ten years ago," he says, "this water was all but dead, and the authorities were ready to close it to any fishing. Look at it today. My oysters have saved this creek."

Recipe from CIRCLE C OYSTER RANCH

Creamy Oyster Casserole

Creamy and briny at the same time, this casserole is a Maryland winter favorite. The recipe is from Richard Pelz, adapted from a recipe his grandmother used to make.

6 SERVINGS

- 24 oysters, shucked, liquor reserved
- 1 cup (2 sticks) butter, cut into tiny pieces
- ½ teaspoon salt
- 1 teaspoon Old Bay or other seafood seasoning (optional)
- 2 cups crushed saltine crackers
- 2 cups heavy cream

1. Preheat the oven to 350°F. Line the bottom of a 9- by 13-inch glass casserole dish with half of the oysters. Dot the oysters with half of the butter, and then sprinkle on ¼ teaspoon of the salt and ½ teaspoon of the Old Bay, if desired. Add half of the crushed crackers. Repeat with the second layers.

2. Pour the oyster liquor over the layers. Add the heavy cream. Bake uncovered for 45 minutes and serve immediately.

Fried Perch with Cornmeal Crust

Maryland has abundant stocks of white and yellow perch, which are fished in and around the Bay year-round. Though perch is a smallish fish that some complain has too many bones, I think the sweet taste is well worth it, especially filleted and pan-fried with a little lemon. Served with tartar sauce as a tangy complement, it's a little taste of summer in the middle of winter.

4 SERVINGS

- 2 pounds perch fillets
- 2 eggs
- ¾ cup yellow cornmeal
- ½ cup all-purpose flour
- ½ teaspoon salt
- ½ teaspoon freshly ground black pepper
- ⅓ cup vegetable oil for frying
  Tartar Sauce with Dill and Capers (page 123)
  Lemon slices

1. Rinse and dry the perch fillets. Whisk the egg with 2 teaspoons water in a shallow bowl. Mix together the cornmeal, flour, salt, and pepper in a separate bowl.

2. Heat the oil to 350°F in a cast iron skillet. Dip the fillets in the egg mixture and then dredge them in the flour mixture. Fry the fish for 3 to 4 minutes on each side, until the crust is golden brown. Serve the perch immediately with tartar sauce and a garnish of lemon slices.

ROCKFISH

Among the many fish species that populate Maryland waters, including perch, flounder, bluefish, carp, catfish, cod, croaker, hake, porgy, seabass, spot, drum, shad, and mackerel, the rockfish holds a special place. The distinctively striped silvery fish — which elsewhere goes by the names striped bass, striper, greenhead, squidhound, and lineside — is so beloved that it's been Maryland's official state fish since 1965. Lore has it that "rock," as it's known in local shorthand, got its name from Rock Hall, a quaint town on the Chesapeake with waters that used to be so packed with *Morone saxatilis* that the

fish jumped right into fishermen's boats. While it's more likely that the moniker came from its earlier classification as *Roccus saxatilis,* what isn't in dispute is that Marylanders are crazy about the rockfish's firm, white, mild flesh.

Nearly fished out of existence several decades ago, the rockfish has made a dramatic comeback in the Chesapeake Bay after a state-imposed fishing moratorium allowed it a chance to rebound. The rockfish is an anadromous fish, meaning that it lives in saltwater but spawns in freshwater, and the Chesapeake is the rockfish's preferred spawning grounds. Hatchlings stay in the Chesapeake Bay for 3 to 5 years before heading out to the Atlantic Ocean. With a life span of 25 to 30 years, rockfish can grow up to 5 feet long and can weigh more than 75 pounds, although they are typically much smaller.

Rockfish is most often baked, usually whole, and is frequently stuffed with crabmeat, which allows the two mild flavors to complement each other. Rockfish is sold fresh and frozen, wild-caught and farm-raised. When buying fresh fish, look for firm flesh, bright and clear eyes, red gills, and shiny skin; the fish should also not have a pronounced smell. Fresh fish should be used or frozen within 1 to 2 days.

To clean and dress a rockfish, rinse the fish in cold water and then remove the scales, scraping them with a knife from tail to head. Cut the fish the whole length of its belly from vent to the head, and remove its entrails. Then, cut off the head and pectoral fins and remove the dorsal, or back, fin by cutting the flesh on the sides. Rinse the fish thoroughly again. The rockfish is now dressed. Depending on the size of your fish and your preference, you may want to cut the rockfish into steaks or fillets; otherwise, the fish can be baked whole or frozen. Properly wrapped, rockfish will keep 6 months in the freezer.

Rockfish in Tomato Saffron Cream Sauce over Rice

In January, February, and March, especially, the rockfish in Maryland is just unbeatable. Rock Hall, on the Eastern Shore almost directly across the Bay from Annapolis, claims the title of "Rockfish Capital" of Maryland, and they do serve some awfully tasty rockfish at their annual festival.

3 tablespoons butter

½ cup finely chopped shallots

1 celery stalk, cut in half

1 (12-ounce) can whole tomatoes

⅓ cup dry white wine, preferably a Maryland wine

1 teaspoon saffron threads

2 sprigs fresh thyme, or ½ teaspoon dried thyme

¾ teaspoon salt

¾ cup water or fish stock

1½ pounds fresh rockfish fillet

1 cup white rice

2 cups Chicken Stock (page 26) or Vegetable Stock (page 27)

1 cup heavy cream

2 tablespoons chopped fresh parsley

4 SERVINGS

1. Melt 2 tablespoons of the butter in a skillet. Add all but 1 teaspoon of the shallots and sauté over medium heat. Add the celery, tomatoes, wine, saffron, thyme, ½ teaspoon of the salt, and the water or fish stock. Cook for 10 minutes, stirring occasionally.

2. Add the rockfish to the skillet and reduce the heat to medium-low; maintain the liquid at a gentle simmer. Cook until the fish is just cooked through, about 8 minutes. Remove the fish from the sauce and transfer it to a plate; cover with aluminum foil to keep the fish warm. Continue cooking the sauce for about 10 minutes, until it is reduced by half.

3. Melt the remaining 1 tablespoon butter in a medium saucepan over low heat. And the remaining 1 teaspoon shallot and sauté for 2 minutes, until softened. Add the rice, stock, and the remaining ¼ teaspoon salt. Simmer, covered, for 15 to 20 minutes, until all the broth has been absorbed. Remove from the heat, fluff the rice with a fork, and keep covered until ready to serve.

4. Purée the saffron sauce with a handheld immersion blender. Remove the skin from the rockfish and cut the rockfish into 1-inch pieces. Add the fish and the heavy cream to the sauce in the skillet and simmer gently for 5 minutes. Transfer the fish in its sauce to a serving dish and sprinkle with the parsley. Serve immediately with the rice.

BROOM'S BLOOM DAIRY
Harford County

In suburban Harford County, just past the vinyl-clad subdivisions that pock the Bel Air suburbs, a simple building with poplar siding stands on the edge of a 210-acre farm. Broom's Bloom, as the farm was christened in 1726, belongs to Kate Dallam and her husband, David, a dairy farmer and the eighth generation of his family to live and work there. Off in the distance is the new dairy barn — rebuilt after a terrible fire — where David is back to milking his Holstein cows twice a day. A fancy computer that milked the cows robotically, an innovation that came with the rebuilt barn and that David hated, has been banished, sold to a less sentimental dairy farmer. School groups regularly come through on tours, affording students the increasingly rare experience of seeing firsthand where milk really comes from.

For years now, however, it's been the small building, not the milking barn, that has attracted the most people. Walk inside and you'll find yourself in the middle of a packed, sweet-smelling, old-fashioned ice cream parlor and country store sporting home-sewn curtains, a horseshoe-shaped counter built from local woods, and old county maps. Scattered around are mismatched chairs and a dozen or so glass-top tables that were once doors on Kate's parents' farm. Kate has even slipped her grandmother's collection of colorful postcards under the glass, so patrons can admire them as they eat.

But the most important feature is the chalkboard that everyone consults to find the ice cream and sorbet flavors of the day. Kate used to make the ice cream herself in a back room, usually on Mondays when the store was closed. Now, demand is so high that Kate has a woman who helps with the ice cream, making several batches a day, carefully measuring and pouring ingredients into a disconcertingly modern machine with a voracious appetite for fruit, nuts, and spices. Kate varies the flavors from week to week and even day to day, depending on demand, the availability of local produce, customer's requests, and Kate's own inspiration. She tries to have at least a dozen flavors to choose from, including a velvety vanilla and a rich, full-bodied chocolate. In summer she adds strawberry, peach, and red and black raspberry ice creams to the menu, along with lighter treats like cantaloupe or green tea sorbet.

Ironically, Kate never imagined herself an ice cream maker. It was something that evolved out of the Dallams' realization that rising feed and energy costs and volatile milk prices left them no choice but to diversify beyond raw milk to survive. One day after visiting an ice cream operation on a dairy farm in Delaware, she decided to take a course in making ice cream and then came home to see if she was any good at making it herself. If the perpetually packed parking lot and happy customers are any indication, the answer, obviously, is yes.

David and Kate Dallam

Lamb Stew

As is often the case, farmers marry into other farm families. Kate Dallam, who with her husband, David, owns Broom's Bloom Dairy, is the sister of Worley Umbarger, who with his wife, Cindi, owns Woolsey Farm, where they raise delicious lamb, among other products. Kate features Woolsey Farm products at her dairy store, and Cindi sells Kate's products at the farmers' markets. Kate developed this recipe using Woolsey Farm lamb.

2 pounds lamb, cut into cubes, preferably Woolsey Farm's

¼ teaspoon salt

¼ teaspoon freshly ground black pepper

2 tablespoons vegetable oil

¼ cup of all-purpose flour

3½ cups Vegetable Stock (page 27)

1 (12-ounce) can apricot or mango nectar or juice

1 (2-inch) cinnamon stick or ¼ teaspoon ground cinnamon

3 garlic cloves, peeled and finely minced

½ teaspoon ground cumin

½ teaspoon cardamom

½ teaspoon saffron threads, crushed

3 medium carrots, peeled and cut into 1-inch slices

1½ cups fresh or frozen pearl onions

1 cup dried apricots

1 cup prunes

Mashed Sweet Potatoes (page 249) (optional)

Fresh sage leaves (optional)

6 SERVINGS

1. Season the lamb well with the salt and pepper. Heat the oil in a large Dutch oven over medium-high heat. Brown the lamb on all sides, about 5 minutes. When the lamb is well browned, remove it to a plate and drain the excess oil from the pot. Sprinkle the flour over the lamb, coating it evenly.

2. Return the stockpot to the heat. Stir in the stock, nectar, cinnamon, garlic, cumin, cardamom, and saffron. Return the lamb to the pot, along with any accumulated juices. Bring the mixture to a boil, reduce the heat, and simmer for 1 hour, until the meat is nearly tender.

3. Add the carrots, onions, apricots, and prunes to the pot, and return the stew to a boil. Reduce the heat and simmer, covered, for 30 minutes, until the vegetables are tender. Remove the cinnamon stick. Serve immediately with mashed sweet potatoes, if desired. Garnish the stew with sage leaves, if desired.

Cindi and Worley Umberger

Recipe from **Broom's Bloom Dairy**

MASHED SWEET POTATOES

6 SERVINGS

2 pounds sweet potatoes, peeled and cut into 1-inch chunks

4 tablespoons butter

¼ cup plain yogurt

½ teaspoon salt

¼ cup milk

Cook the sweet potatoes in a large pot of boiling water for 20 minutes, until tender. Drain the sweet potatoes, transfer them to a large mixing bowl, and roughly smash the potatoes. Add the butter, yogurt, and salt to the bowl. Mash the mixture by hand or with an electric mixer. Add the milk gradually until you achieve the desired consistency.

THE SAVAGE RIVER LODGE
Garrett County

It isn't easy finding the Savage River Lodge, which is part of its charm. Visitors have to wend their way a mile and a half down and up an unpaved road, past a barrier, over a bridge, and through a state park before they pull up to the handsome wood and stone lodge that Jan Russell and her husband, Mike Dreisbach, own and operate. With 13 miles of hiking trails surrounded by 700 acres of state forest, visitors who love relaxation, quiet, and the outdoors have been coming to western Maryland's most elegant getaway since it opened in 1999.

Mike Dreisbach and Jan Russell

The 42-acre property offers cross-country skiing, birding, fly fishing, and hiking, to name a few activities. Or, if guests prefer, they can just sit on the porch of their elegantly appointed private cabins — there are 18 in all, each equipped with a gas fireplace — and do nothing but work up an appetite for the excellent cuisine and wine list the lodge prides itself on. Dreisbach, having grown up in western Maryland, places a special emphasis on sourcing things locally, whether that means the artisans who built and outfitted the main lodge and cabins, or the local farmers who supply the lodge's kitchen. From serving its own maple syrup (which winter guests can help Dreisbach tap and boil) to buying local bison, venison, pork, lamb, beef, and poultry, along with seasonal local vegetables including morel mushrooms and wild ramps, the restaurant has become a favored special dining destination for local residents of western Maryland, in addition to the lodge's overnight guests. No doubt due in part to the years of combined hospitality industry the gracious couple accrued separately and jointly, the lodge is consistently singled out for its elegant yet relaxed and inviting atmosphere. It has also garnered favorable reviews in numerous food and wine publications, including *Wine Spectator*, which has given the lodge an "Award of Excellence" every year since 2003.

Maple-Bison Meatloaf

Local bison, supplied by the Garrett Country Market, and the lodge's own maple syrup make this meatloaf the hands-down favorite at the Savage River Lodge. At home, any combination of meats — bison, elk, antelope, veal, pork, and beef — may be used. Ask the butcher to grind the bacon for you.

2½ pounds ground beef

1 pound ground bison

½ pound ground veal or turkey

¾ pound ground bacon

3 eggs, beaten

¾ cup Maryland maple syrup, plus extra for topping

3 tablespoons molasses

3 tablespoons honey

⅓ cup ketchup

3 tablespoons Dijon mustard

3 tablespoons minced fresh sage

3 tablespoons minced fresh parsley

5 teaspoons minced fresh thyme

5 teaspoons hot sauce

1 tablespoon salt

2 teaspoons freshly ground black pepper

1 teaspoon cider vinegar

Fresh breadcrumbs

14–16 slices bacon

16 SERVINGS

1. Combine the ground beef, bison, veal, and bacon in a large mixing bowl. Add the eggs, the ¾ cup maple syrup, the molasses, honey, ketchup, mustard, sage, parsley, thyme, hot sauce, salt, pepper, and vinegar. Mix everything together very well, being careful not to let the mixture get too warm or overmixed.

2. Cook a small portion of the mixed meatloaf in a hot skillet and taste. Adjust seasoning as necessary with more sweetness, saltiness, or vinegar. Repeat if necessary. Once a desired flavor is reached, sprinkle the mixture with breadcrumbs a little at a time. You are looking for an almost dry consistency.

3. Lay out the bacon strips on plastic wrap so they are overlapping horizontally. Lightly coat the bacon with the extra maple syrup. Evenly spread the meatloaf mixture down the center of the maple-coated bacon. Wrap the bacon around the meatloaf mixture so that the bacon ends meet. Wrap the meatloaf tightly in plastic wrap. Store the meatloaf in the refrigerator until firm, at least 1 hour.

4. Preheat the oven to 350°F. Put the meatloaf on a baking sheet and return to room temperature. Transfer the sheet to the oven and bake until a meat thermometer inserted in the meatloaf indicates an internal temperature of 155°F. Slice the meatloaf between pieces of bacon and serve.

BISON MEAT

Bison meat has grown in popularity around the country, and Maryland is no exception, with 14 registered bison farms spread across the state, from the mountains of Garrett County to the flat lands of the Eastern Shore and southern Maryland. The "healthy red meat," as bison is touted, can be substituted in virtually all cases for beef, and it makes especially flavorful burgers for summertime grilling. It's also a fine stand-in for beef, pork, and lamb roasts, as well as ground meat for meatloafs, stuffed tomatoes, etc. Nutritionally, bison meat is much lower in fat and cholesterol than chicken, beef, pork, or lamb, and it contains significantly more iron and vitamin B12 than any of those meats, as well. Gunpowder Bison Trading Company in Baltimore County grazes its herd on 70 acres sloping down to the Gunpowder River, administering no hormones or antibiotics and dry aging its meat, which it sells online, at the farm, and at farmers' markets. Twin Springs Bison Farm and Market in Carroll County has been in operation for 10 years and the meat raised on its 300-acre farm is on the menu at popular restaurants across Maryland, while at the Garrett Country Market in Garrett County bison offerings include hot dogs and jerky, both of which are very popular. Having been nearly hunted to extinction in the 1880s, bison are making a slow but impressive comeback, and no one is surprised anymore to see bison grazing in pastures throughout rural Maryland, where our relatively long growing seasons allow herds to pasture graze most months of the year. With demand outstripping the supply of bison meat (from an all-time low of 80–90 bison in the 1880s, their numbers have climbed back to around 500,000), farmers like Bill

Edwards of SB Farms in Hurlock (which also sells buffalo wool yarn) and Dick Wildes and Sandra Woolard of Land O' Lakes Farm in Hollywood, anticipate a steady supply of customers for years to come.

Rabbit Stew

Simmered until the rabbit is meltingly tender, this hearty winter stew will keep the cold at bay. A number of Maryland farms, including Rumbleway and Whitmore Farms, sell their own rabbits.

1–2 tablespoons vegetable oil

¾ pound bacon, diced

1 cup onions, peeled and diced

1 cup carrots, peeled and diced

1 cup diced celery

1 (3–5 pound) rabbit, cleaned and cut into pieces

1 (28-ounce) can whole tomatoes

2 cups frozen or fresh corn kernels

3–5 large potatoes, peeled and cut into 1-inch chunks

Salt and freshly ground black pepper

4 SERVINGS

1. Heat the oil in a large stockpot over medium heat and cook the bacon, onions, carrots, and celery until tender. Remove the bacon and vegetables from the pot and set aside.

2. Brown the rabbit pieces in the stockpot over medium heat until golden on all sides. Remove the pot from the heat. Drain any remaining oil from the stockpot. Add 1 cup of water to the pot and stir. Return the bacon and vegetables to the pot and add the tomatoes. If needed, add additional water to cover the rabbit meat. Cook on low heat, covered, for 1½ hours.

3. Add the corn and potatoes and simmer for an additional 45 minutes. Remove the rabbit meat and cut it up. Return the meat to the pot. Season with salt and pepper to taste.

Southern Maryland Stuffed Ham

This is the Raley family's recipe, which adds the kale "just for a little color." Stuffed ham is traditionally served cold, with white bread, alongside the rest of the Thanksgiving or Christmas accompaniments: turkey, mashed potatoes, and so on.

3 heads green cabbage
1 pound kale
3 pounds onions, peeled
¼ cup crushed red pepper flakes
1 (20-pound) corned ham, deboned

1. Shred the cabbage, kale, and onions together in a food processor. Transfer the cabbage mixture to a large bowl and stir in the pepper flakes

2. Place the ham on a large piece of multilayer cheesecloth. Stuff the cavity of the ham with as much filling as possible. Drape the rest of the stuffing over the top of the ham. Pull the cheesecloth over the ham and tie a knot in both ends of the cheesecloth. Transfer the ham to a large stockpot and add enough water to cover. Bring the water to a boil, and cook the ham for 5 hours.

3. Remove the pot from the heat and take the ham out of the water. Untie the cheesecloth and transfer the ham to a platter to cool. Slice and serve hot or at room temperature.

SOUTHERN MARYLAND STUFFED HAM

Residents of St. Mary's County are proud of their unique tradition of stuffed ham. But to put it mildly, people harbor divergent opinions about how their stuffed ham should be fixed. Although everyone agrees that Christmas wouldn't be Christmas without Maryland's first European-influenced culinary tradition, what goes into it is the subject of what some locals lightheartedly call "the stuffed-ham wars."

First, a bit of history: "The theory is that when the colonists were first here, they had winter vegetables – basically cabbage and onions and some kale and maybe watercress – they had salt and pepper, and they had brined hams," says Ann Raley, whose own family, the Jarboes, arrived in St. Mary's City in 1639. The hams would have been put into vats with salt and water around September and brined for several months, Raley explains. By Christmas, the hams were ready and the colonists wanted to stuff the hams with the greens to make a festive holiday dish. Since the hams had bones in them, the only way to actually stuff them was to make slits all over and wedge the greens into those slits. Thus the stuffed ham was created.

The disputes arose over the proportion of cabbage to kale. Ann Raley's husband, Dan, a St. Mary's County Commissioner whose family settled in the area in 1634, the same year as the original colonists, explains: "The further south you go in the county, the less greens are used, and the more cabbage. But in the northern end of the county they do all kale and almost no cabbage." And then, in an uncharacteristically honest statement for a politician, he pronounces, "It tastes better with the cabbage and the onions. The kale is mushy and bitter."

There are other differences as well: some prefer their corned hams boned, that is, with the bone out and the stuffing inserted into the cavity and over the top of the ham. The Raleys, who for years ran the market that Dan's family started in 1934, made their stuffed ham that way and sold them by the hundreds each fall and winter. It was so popular that it was featured on the Food Network as one of the best local foods in America. (The Chinese family who bought the store from the Raleys continues to sell the stuffed ham that way – alongside their own fusion stuffed-ham spring roll.)

Traditionalists prefer the bone in and the stuffing in the slits, saying it imparts more flavor that way. Unfortunately, bone-in ham is increasingly hard to find. If you are able to procure one and want to go to the extra effort of preparing it that way, you will need to make a series of 3-inch incisions around the entire ham, in rows from top to bottom, using a sharp knife. You should cut at least 2 dozen pocket incisions. Because the ham does not have a large pocket like the boneless hams, you will be stuffing a portion of the greens into the pockets. Using your fingers or a teaspoon, stuff about 1 tablespoon of the greens mixture into each pocket. As in the boneless version, the remaining stuffing will be draped over the top of the ham, and you will wrap and cook it just as you would the boneless version.

The stuffed ham wars will undoubtedly continue. But however you stuff it, once it's boiled for 5 hours, cooled, and cut up, it's simply delicious and uniquely southern Maryland.

VOLT
Frederick County

Bryan Voltaggio, Frederick County's acclaimed chef and native son, doesn't appear entirely comfortable in the chic lounge of his celebrated and hip restaurant, Volt, which is housed in a restored Victorian mansion in downtown Frederick. One senses he'd rather be in the kitchen than out of it, cooking, rather than talking. Interviews, which he has been giving on a regular basis since his acclaimed appearance against fellow chefs, including his brother, Michael, on Bravo Channel's *Top Chef*, are obviously an unwelcome distraction he has learned to live with. Emerging from his high-tech stainless steel kitchen (complete with the now obligatory chef's table where diners sit in the middle of the action), sleeves rolled up to reveal colorfully tattooed forearms, Voltaggio frowns in greeting. It's only when the topic eventually turns to farmers and sourcing local food that the young chef's renowned passion flickers in his eyes.

Good food isn't just about taste and presentation, he insists. "It starts with a sensibility of sustainability and responsibility and looks at supporting local people."

Indeed, Voltaggio does more than his share of buying top-quality, locally grown and harvested ingredients. He frequents farmers' markets and nearby farms, searching for everything from beef, goat, and heirloom tomatoes, to fava beans, farm-fresh speckled eggs, and as many other fruits, meats, cheeses, and vegetables as he can find. Favorite suppliers include Whitmore Farm in Emmittsburg

Bryan Voltaggio

(for lamb, pork and eggs), Summer Creek Farm in Thurmont (for organic fruits and vegetables), and Cherry Glen Farm in Boyds. A local man who supplies Volt with freshly foraged mushrooms, including chanterelles, remains nameless.

Voltaggio's love of local foods started at home — literally. His parents had a garden, and he and his siblings were known to go out and pick whatever they wanted from it, whenever they wanted.

Surrounded by farms in Frederick County, Voltaggio, who credits his grandfather with giving him his first cooking lessons, learned as a child that flavor starts with freshness, and freshness means proximity to the source. But it was when he became a father himself, Voltaggio says, that he truly appreciated how critical it was to support local farmers. Otherwise, he asked, how could his own son grow up and experience the same truly fresh, locally grown food he had eaten as a boy? The new American cuisine today is global, the 33-year-old says, precisely because it has started going back to local ingredients, something that most other countries never went away from.

And so it is fitting that the man who traveled as far as France to perfect his cooking style in the end chose to come home to open his first restaurant. And coming home, for Voltaggio and his wife and young son, meant supporting local farmers who play a central role in sustaining Frederick County's rural landscape.

To make that point, Voltaggio has become well known for staging elaborate seasonal dinners on local farms and vineyards, including a multicourse feast at historic Whitmore Farm. There, well-dressed guests eat in a renovated barn, overlooking pastures filled with animals eventually destined for the dinner plate.

The diners who eat his creations may appreciate his dazzling culinary artistry more than they admire his commitment to local agriculture, but Voltaggio loses no opportunity to show them the connection. "I want to strengthen the relationship between chef and grower," the rising culinary star says. "Through our choices of ingredients we become engaged in creating a great dining experience, as well as supporting local agriculture."

Pork with Mixed Beans,
see page 260

Recipe from **BRYAN VOLTAGGIO**

Iberico–Red Wattle Pork with Mixed-Bean Ragout

A signature dish at Volt, Bryan Voltaggio's award-winning restaurant in Frederick, this is the ultimate winter comfort food, made with pork from sustainably raised Iberico–Red Wattle pigs. Chef Voltaggio suggests serving this dish with a 2007 Crumbling Rock red wine from Black Ankle Vineyards.

½ pork belly (approximately 5 pounds), fat trimmed to yield the meatier part of the belly

3 cloves garlic, peeled and minced

2½ teaspoons pink salt*

3 tablespoons kosher salt

1 tablespoon brown sugar

2½ tablespoons coarsely ground tellicherry or other black peppercorns*

1½ teaspoons coarsely ground long pepper*

1½ teaspoons juniper berries, crushed

5 fresh bay leaves, stacked and cut into ribbons

1 teaspoon freshly grated nutmeg

6 sprigs fresh lemon thyme

1 cup lard, previously rendered from trimmed fat or store-bought

1 cup finely chopped onion

½ cup finely chopped celery

½ cup finely chopped carrot

3 cups beef or pork stock

1 cup extra virgin olive oil

¼ cup diced fennel

¼ cup diced red onion

¼ cup diced parsnips

2 tablespoons honey

2 tablespoons yellow mustard seeds

2 teaspoons sherry vinegar

1 cup vegetable stock

1 teaspoon sugar

½ cup pork demi-glace*

Mixed-Bean Ragout (page 261)

4 SERVINGS

1. Trim the pork belly so it is squared off and the edges are neat. Combine the garlic, salts, brown sugar, peppers, juniper berries, bay leaves, nutmeg, and thyme in a bowl and mix well. Rub the cure over the entire belly.

2. Store the pork belly in a sealed container and refrigerate it for 3 days. After it has cured, rinse the pork belly in cool water to remove the curing salt. Pat it dry with paper towels.

3. Preheat the oven to 300°F. Cut the belly into 3-ounce portions and melt the lard in a medium Dutch oven over high heat. Brown the meat in the lard on all sides and then remove to a plate. Sauté the onion, celery, and carrot in the lard until caramelized, 8 to 10 minutes. Add the beef stock and the pork belly to the pan and bring to a simmer. Cover the pan and braise in the oven for 3 hours, or until fork tender.

4. Make the soffritto: Heat the olive oil in a medium skillet, and then add the fennel and red onion, slowly toasting to a light brown caramelization, about 8 minutes. Add the parsnips halfway through the cooking, as the sugars in the parsnips will caramelize more quickly than the fennel and onion sugars.

5. Add the honey to the vegetable mixture, and then bring to a simmer. Remove from the heat and let cool.

6. In a small skillet, bring the mustard seeds, vinegar, vegetable stock, and sugar to a simmer over medium heat. Stew the mustard seeds very slowly until the stock is almost completely absorbed, about 30 minutes. Add the seed mixture to the vegetable mixture. Stir in the pork demi-glace and set aside. Before plating, bring the soffritto back to a simmer.

Available at specialty food stores

MIXED-BEAN RAGOUT

3½ tablespoons canola oil

¾ cup medium-diced onion

¼ cup plus 2 tablespoons medium-diced carrots

¼ cup plus 2 tablespoons medium-diced celery

2 sachets d'epice (small piece of cheesecloth filled with dried thyme, parsley stems, bay leaf, peppercorns, and cloves, and tied closed)

1 cup dried cranberry beans, cleaned and rinsed

8¼ cups light pork stock*

2 sheets parchment paper, cut to the size of your medium saucepan

1 cup dried cannellini beans, cleaned and rinsed

16 baby haricots verts (Carmellini beans)

3 tablespoons unsalted butter

4 tablespoons extra-virgin olive oil

Salt and freshly ground pepper

48 arugula leaves

1. Heat 2 tablespoons of the canola oil in a medium saucepan over medium heat. When the oil shimmers, add ½ cup of the onion, the ¼ cup carrots, and the ¼ cup celery, and sweat until translucent.

2. Add one sachet and the cranberry beans and cover with 4 cups of the stock. Lay one sheet of parchment paper on the surface of the bean mixture; this will prevent a skin layer from forming. Cook the beans for 45 minutes at a lazy simmer. Check periodically and stir to ensure even cooking.

3. Heat the remaining 1½ tablespoons canola oil in another medium saucepan over medium heat. When the oil shimmers, add the remaining ¼ cup onion, the 2 tablespoons carrots, and the 2 tablespoons celery, and sweat until translucent.

4. Add the remaining sachet and the cannellini beans and cover with 4 cups of the stock. Lay the remaining sheet of parchment paper on the surface of the bean mixture. Cook the beans for 45 minutes at a lazy simmer. Check periodically and stir to ensure even cooking.

5. Remove the parchment paper from both pans of beans and drain the beans, one pan at a time, reserving the cooking liquid. Discard the sachets. Combine the cranberry and cannellini beans and return the mixture to the cooking liquid; let cool until ready to use.

6. Bring a medium saucepan of salted water to a boil and blanch the green beans for 5 minutes. Drain the beans, and then shock them in an ice bath.

7. Assemble the pork and beans: Add 1 tablespoon of the butter and 2 tablespoons of the olive oil to the cranberry bean mixture and reheat in the cooking liquid. Simmer until the liquid reduces to glaze the beans.

8. Heat the remaining 2 tablespoons butter and the remaining ¼ cup stock in a medium saucepan over medium heat. Add the green beans to warm and season with salt and pepper.

9. Spoon a straight line of soffritto onto each plate. Spoon a portion of the bean ragout onto each plate. Scatter the green beans on the plates. Stand the pork belly upright. Dress the arugula leaves with the remaining 2 tablespoons olive oil and place them around the pork belly. Finish with the remaining soffritto.

SOUTH MOUNTAIN CREAMERY
Frederick County

South Mountain Creamery, tucked in the piedmont of Frederick County, is a modern dairy with old-fashioned values. When Abby and Tony Brusco, both in their early thirties, contemplated taking over Abby's parents' dairy farm and building a creamery on site, they knew they had to do something unusual to distinguish themselves from their competitors and cheaper supermarket products. Perhaps surprisingly for a young couple, they chose not to concentrate on quantity, but on quality dairy products and stellar customer service. "If you get the quality to where it should be, then the volume will follow," Tony, a former corporate executive turned creamery manager, says.

Today, the Bruscos' decision to offer home delivery of their own delectably rich heavy cream, half-and-half, milk, yogurt, and butter seems like a stroke of marketing genius, capitalizing on the wave of nostalgia that many people are feeling today, recalling a simpler time when the milkman was a regular in many neighborhoods. At the time, however, it was a huge gamble. And quality notwithstanding, their marketing efforts proved woefully inadequate to the task of bringing in a sufficient customer base. "Four years ago we were one phone call away from closing," Tony recalls with a rueful smile. "The banks were looking at us and weren't seeing what they wanted to see. We had a real struggle."

A piece in the *Washington Post* about their unique delivery service helped turn things around, sparking widespread interest and bringing in a flood of new customers. In a single year, the Bruscos nearly doubled their customer base — from 2,100 to 3,800 — and it's still growing. And while growth brought its own problems, such as inadequate computer software to handle the new volume of online orders, the Bruscos were well on their way to success. Today they are constantly strategizing about adding new routes and products. In addition to their own line of dairy products, customers can order locally and sustainably produced meats and cheeses, freshly baked breads, and a number of seasonal specialties, like Thanksgiving turkeys and Christmas hams. South Mountain Creamery is also looking at adding vegetables to their product line, using a CSA model that will result in dropping a weekly bag of

Abby and Tony Brusco

vegetables on customers' doorsteps at the same time they get their milk.

While both Bruscos lament 80-hour work weeks — a far cry from Tony's corporate job and perks that he enjoyed before taking over the creamery's management — it's clear that these two love what they're doing and the satisfaction that comes with helping to keep farming alive. As part of their mission to educate the public, South Mountain is open to customers seven days a week, not just through their farm market, which sells ice cream in addition to everything else they deliver, but with farm tours. They encourage families and school groups to come out and try their hand at feeding calves or watching the cows get milked, because by doing so both Bruscos recognize that they're exposing their customers to a way of life that has vanished for most Americans. And even though it occasionally frustrates her that people don't understand, for example, why the cows aren't out grazing in the middle of winter, Abby understands that they're ensuring the farm's own survival by introducing the public to their 200 well-kept Holstein–Brown Swiss crosses and the hormone- and antibiotic-free dairy products they're producing. "We don't want to be an extra," says Abby. "We want our customers to see us as a necessity." Apparently, many of them already do.

Country Pot Roast and Gravy with Potatoes and Root Vegetables

Few meals evoke as much nostalgia as pot roast, and with good reason. Serve with Sweet Potato Biscuits (page 234) or Potato Harvest Yeast Rolls (page 180).

½ cup all-purpose flour

1½ tablespoons plus ½ teaspoon salt

1½ teaspoons freshly ground black pepper

1 (4–pound) beef chuck roast

2 tablespoons vegetable shortening

2 teaspoons Dijon mustard

1 large onion, peeled and chopped

8 small potatoes, peeled and halved

4 carrots, peeled and quartered

1 rutabaga, peeled and cut into 2-inch chunks

1 medium sweet potato, peeled and cut into 2-inch chunks

1 cup half-and-half

8 SERVINGS

1. Preheat the oven to 325°F. Mix together ¼ cup of the flour, the 1½ tablespoons salt, and the pepper. Rub the mixture all over the roast until it is thoroughly covered. Heat the shortening in a large Dutch oven; add the roast and brown it over medium-high heat for 10 minutes, turning the roast to brown all sides evenly.

2. Remove the pot from the heat and spread the mustard on the roast. Add 1½ cups hot water and the onion and cover the pot. Transfer the roast to the oven and cook for 3 hours. Pull the pan out of the oven and add the potatoes, carrots, rutabaga, and sweet potato. Return the pan to the oven and roast for 1 hour longer. Remove the roast from the oven and place the roast and vegetables on a serving platter, reserving the pan drippings. Cover the platter to keep it warm until you're ready to serve.

3. Make the gravy: Pour the pan drippings into a bowl and let the fat rise to the top. Skim the fat off and discard. Measure out 1 cup of liquid, adding water if needed. Pour the drippings back into the Dutch oven and stir in the remaining ¼ cup flour. Cook the mixture over low heat, adding the remaining ½ teaspoon salt and half-and-half. Keep stirring until the gravy boils and thickens; serve the gravy with the roast.

Golden Hazelnut Biscotti

The orange yolks of farm-fresh eggs (I use eggs from Andy's Eggs in Fallston; they sell their eggs year-round at the Waverly Market in Baltimore) and the deep yellow of good butter lend a golden hue to these orange-scented treats. I make these biscotti every year for Christmas and give them away as presents; they are hugely popular.

4¼ cups all-purpose flour

1½ teaspoons baking powder

½ teaspoon salt

1 cup plus 6 tablespoons turbinado (raw) sugar

½ cup granulated sugar

¼ cup grated orange zest (preferably from organic oranges)

2 teaspoons crushed anise seed

1 cup (2 sticks) cold butter, preferably South Mountain Creamery, cut into pieces

6 farm-fresh eggs

¼ cup strained fresh orange juice

2 teaspoons vanilla extract

2 cups chopped hazelnuts

50–60 BISCOTTI

1. Combine the flour, baking powder, and salt in a large bowl. Whisk together the 1 cup turbinado sugar, the granulated sugar, orange zest, and anise seed in a separate bowl until well mixed. Add the sugar mixture to the flour mixture and stir to combine.

2. Use an electric mixer set on low to blend the butter into the dry ingredients, mixing until the pieces of butter are the size of peas. Whisk 4 of the eggs, the orange juice, and the vanilla in a small bowl, and then add the egg mixture to the dough, mixing just until combined. Add the hazelnuts and stir until incorporated. The dough will be sticky. Let the dough rest for 30 minutes.

3. Meanwhile, make the glaze: Separate the remaining 2 eggs, reserving the yolks for another use. Beat the egg whites with a whisk or electric mixer until foamy. Set aside.

4. Preheat the oven to 350°F. Line two baking sheets with parchment paper. Cut the dough into quarters and roll each quarter into a log, roughly 13- by 1½-inches. Place the logs on the lined baking sheets, about 3 inches apart. Brush the tops with some of the egg glaze and sprinkle turbinado sugar over the cookies. Bake for 35 minutes, rotating the sheets for even baking. Remove from the oven and let cool for 35 minutes.

5. Reduce the oven temperature to 300°F. Saw the logs crosswise with a serrated knife, cutting ½-inch-thick slices. Lay the biscotti flat on the baking sheets, brush with the remaining glaze and sprinkle with turbinado sugar; bake for 15 minutes. Turn the biscotti over and bake for another 10 to 15 minutes, until they're evenly golden. Remove from the oven and cool before storing.

Stove-Top Rice Pudding with Maple Syrup

This is a variation of a recipe that Peggy Elliott provided. Maple syrup gives it a wonderfully sweet flavor.

¾ cup white rice
¼ teaspoon salt
2 tablespoons butter
3 cups milk
½ cup raisins
3 eggs
½ cup sugar
¼ cup Maryland maple syrup
2 teaspoons vanilla extract
Whipped cream (optional)
Cinnamon (optional)

6 SERVINGS

1. Bring 3 cups of water to a boil in a large saucepan. Add the rice, salt, and butter, and simmer, covered, for 15 minutes.

2. Bring the milk just to the boiling point in a separate small saucepan, and then remove it from the heat. Add the scalded milk and raisins to the rice and stir. Simmer an additional 15 minutes, covered.

3. Beat together the eggs, sugar, maple syrup, and vanilla, and add to the rice mixture, stirring well. Simmer for an additional 5 minutes. Remove the rice pudding from the heat and cool. Serve with a garnish of whipped cream and a sprinkle of cinnamon, if desired.

S AND S MAPLE CAMP
Corriganville, Allegany County

Leo Shinholt is a man who found his calling early in life. One warm winter day when he was just eight years old, his grandfather showed him how to make a hollow wooden spout to tap the rising sap of a nearby maple tree. "It was just over there," Shinholt says on another warm winter morning 53 years later, pointing to a stand of tall maples with metal buckets hanging from spouts — remnants of the old way of collecting sap. That day, he and his grandfather collected the sap from the tree, built a fire, and boiled the sugar "water" for hours over an open fire until, much reduced, it yielded delicious, amber-colored syrup. "That was my first time maple sugaring," says the kindly man with a gentle demeanor and blue coveralls. "And I've loved it ever since."

Apart from a stint in the service, Shinholt has never stopped making maple syrup, first as an avocation and then, once he returned from the Army, as his business. Behind us is Shinholt's sugaring operation, S and S Maple Camp, a modest building that puffs out sweet clouds like an atomizer spraying perfume and which houses the entire syrup-making process. Shinholt's dog, Hugo, his constant companion, lifts his nose in frequent appreciation, while inside two men work at grading and bottling the finished syrup. Shinholt sells the syrup right there in Corriganville and in other markets, even as far away as Asia, where the maple syrup is used in a popular diet. Shinholt smiles at the thought. "Back when I started sugaring, you couldn't give it away," he recalls.

Shinholt's maple syrup all comes from tapping maple trees within a 12-mile radius with an intricate system of plastic tubing that replaced metal buckets, and which leads to central collection spots. In addition to the property his grandfather left him, where the sugaring operation is housed, Shinholt owns 360 acres on Mt. Savage and other land as well, with more than 4,000 taps in all. He also buys sugar water from his nephew. Those multiple sources make S and S Maple Camp Maryland's largest sugaring operation and usually yield enough to keep his loyal customers in syrup year-round.

Shinholt doesn't like the fact that maple syrup has grown to be so expensive. So, despite offers to sell his syrup for much higher prices, he chooses to keep his maple syrup affordable at $33 per gallon, well below what others charge. "These people who have been coming through my doors for decades, they're going to get my syrup," he insists emphatically. "It is not a rich man's food." And then he takes a small bottle of the still-warm syrup from the stockpile, unscrews the lid, and hands it to a visitor. "Take a sip," he says. "Isn't that the best thing you've ever tasted?" And he smiles broadly, not even waiting to hear the answer, which he knows will always be "Yes."

Leo Shinholt

Maple Crème Brulee

Fresh cream and real maple syrup make this the ultimate in smooth and satisfying desserts. It's exquisitely rich, so small portions suffice.

1 quart heavy cream, preferably South Mountain Creamery
1 cup milk, preferably South Mountain Creamery
1 vanilla bean
½ cup Maryland maple syrup
6 egg yolks
Maple sugar

6 SERVINGS

1. Preheat the oven to 325°F. Pour the heavy cream and milk into a medium saucepan. Split the vanilla bean open, scrape the seeds into the pan, and add the vanilla bean pod. Heat the cream mixture and bring just to the boiling point. Remove from the heat. Remove the vanilla bean.

2. Whisk together the maple syrup and egg yolks in a medium bowl. Gradually whisk the hot cream mixture into the yolk mixture. Divide the custard among 6 ramekins. Set the ramekins into a roasting pan and fill the pan with hot water halfway up the sides of the ramekins. Cover the pan with foil. Bake the custards until set in the center, about 1 hour. Refrigerate the custards, uncovered, until cold. Before serving, top the custards with maple sugar and burnish with a blowtorch or put under a broiler until the sugar melts and forms a crust. Cool slightly and then serve.

Smith Island Cake

Maryland's official dessert, this 9- or 10-layer cake is the pride of the Smith Island women. It takes some practice to get this right, especially because the layers are more like crepes than actual cake layers.

2 cups granulated sugar

2 cups (4 sticks) unsalted butter

5 eggs

3 cups all-purpose flour

1 heaping teaspoon baking powder

¼ teaspoon salt

4 cups evaporated milk

2 teaspoons vanilla

½ cup plus 1 tablespoon unsweetened cocoa powder

2 pounds confectioners' sugar

12 SERVINGS

1. Preheat the oven to 350°F. Cream together the sugar and 2 sticks of the butter in a large bowl with an electric mixer. Add the eggs one at a time and beat until smooth. Sift together the flour, baking powder, and salt. Mix the dry ingredients into the egg mixture one cup at a time. With the mixer running slowly, pour in 1 cup of the evaporated milk, then the vanilla and ½ cup water. Mix just until blended.

2. Lightly grease ten 9-inch round cake pans (if you don't own ten cake pans, rotate among three). Put about ¼ cup of the cake batter in each pan, using the back of the spoon to spread evenly. Distribute any excess batter equally among the pans. Bake three layers at a time on the middle rack of the oven for 7 to 8 minutes. (A layer is done when it starts to separate from the side of the pan.) Let the layers cool in the pans or turn the pan over in your hand and flip the layer out onto a clean, waxed paper–covered counter.

3. Make the icing: Melt the remaining 2 sticks butter in a saucepan. Remove the pan from the heat and stir in the remaining 3 cups evaporated milk. Whisk in the cocoa until smooth. Return the pan to the heat and cook for about 10 minutes over low heat. Do not allow the icing to boil or it will scorch. Remove the icing from the heat and whisk in the confectioners' sugar slowly. Return to the heat and cook the icing over low heat until it starts to thicken; it should stick to back of a spoon or to the whisk. Cool the icing for 30 minutes.

4. Assemble and frost the cake when the layers have cooled completely. Spread icing lightly on each layer, leaving the sides and top of the cake for last. (Remember, it takes practice, and each time you make one it will get easier.) Cut into slices and serve.

SUSAN'S
Smith Island

A potential guest's first hint that Susan's on Smith Island is not your average bed-and-breakfast is the fact that innkeeper Susan Evans is rarely home during the work week. In fact, she leaves the house at around 7:20 every morning to go to work, whether or not her guests are up. That's because Evans, a 13th-generation Smith Islander, has a longer and more unusual commute than most of us: a 45-minute, 12-mile ferry ride from Ewell to the mainland town of Crisfield, where she works at a local hospital. She isn't typically home until 6:15 or so, when, after traveling back to the island on the 5:30 ferry, she'll make a quick stop at her parents' house, about 100 feet from the dock, to pick up whatever her waterman father has caught for dinner.

And if she does have guests, they're usually with her, since the ferry is the only way to get to Smith Island, other than by private boat, and guests will have had ample time to chat with Evans or any of the six or so other women who work off-island. Once the seafood is carried back to Evans' three-bedroom cottage, guests can settle in and relax before dinner, taking in the stunning views from the glassed-in porch that looks right out to the water, or they can explore the island by foot or on bikes.

Welcome to Smith Island, one of Maryland's most special places. Set smack in the middle of the Chesapeake Bay, surrounded by marshes teeming with waterfowl, it's actually a series of small islands with three villages. More important, it's the only inhabited offshore island left in Maryland. Separated from the mainland by 12 miles of the Tangier Sound, it was first discovered by Captain John Smith in 1606 (the island isn't named for him, however) and settled by Welsh and Englishmen between 1650 and 1680 The three families that dominate the island today — the Evans, Tyler, and Bradshaw families — are the same families that settled there 350 years ago, and traces of the old English accent linger, too. On Smith Island, as in few places in this country, it's common to hear that someone is the 13th or 14th generation there. And now as then, the men take to the water for their work. The women, on the other hand, travel off-island if they have jobs. They have no choice. With just about 300 inhabitants, no police force, no bank, no movie theater, and no local government, jobs are nonexistent except for working as watermen or in tourism, which is seasonal and sporadic. The good news, though, is that there's no crime whatsoever, everyone knows everyone and helps each other, and if a stranger does come to visit, every single person on the island will wave or say hello.

When the warm, outgoing Evans decided to remodel her home so that paying guests could have a bathroom of their own, she never intended it to be a full-time endeavor. Rather, she thought it was a good way of getting more people to visit and care about Smith Island, whose land is slowly vanishing in the Bay and whose population is gradually dwindling to precarious numbers. Evans hopes that some of the visitors might consider, as some already have, buying a home there and becoming a part of this extraordinary place where pomegranate and fig trees flourish everywhere and the color of the water shifts every 15 minutes. And Evans is at her most persuasive when she's feeding guests the freshest seafood they've ever eaten, topped off with her rendition of the Smith Island Cake — 10 crêpe-thin cake layers held together with a cooked chocolate icing — formally designated Maryland's official dessert.

No one is certain who baked the first Smith Island cake. Lore has it that the original families baked it, although it only had four layers at the time. Over the years the height of the cake grew as the women competed against each other to see who could make the most layers. Today, Smith Island Cakes most commonly vary from eight to eleven layers, depending on who's making it. And these days, with the added recognition it's received from its official status, a lot of the island women are baking it and selling it on the mainland, or through the mail. The batter is a straightforward yellow cake batter, but it's apportioned in minuscule amounts among a number of pans, and each layer is baked for just five or six minutes and then cooled on waxed paper. Assembling and icing the cake can be tricky and takes years of practice, Evans says. She learned to make the cake from her mother, who learned from her mother, and so on. "It's an island thing," Evans says, shrugging. "They've always been made, and every woman knows how to make one." Asked if she'd be willing to teach a visitor the secrets of the cake, Evans grins and says yes, adding, "But you'll have to come back for that."

Recipes by Category (with page number)

Food, Farms, and Families

The following information listed here for the contributors was accurate as of the first printing of this book (2010).

A Cook's Café
Craig Sewell
911 Commerce Road
Annapolis, MD 21401
410-266-1511
www.acookscafe.com
Caramelized Tomato
  Soup, 166

American Chestnut Foundation
50 North Merrimon Avenue,
Suite 115
Asheville, NC 28801
828-281-0047
www.acf.org

Andy's Eggs
Andy Bachman
2601 Harford Road
Fallston, MD 21047
410-877-7452

Baugher's
Marjorie Baugher & Kay Baugher Ripley
1236 Baugher Road
Westminster, MD 21158
410-848-5541
www.baughers.com
Baked Corn with Swiss
  Cheese, 179
Fresh Apple Cake with
  Brown Sugar Icing, 204

Bietschehof Farm
Jean Durst
175 Hetrick Road
Grantsville, MD 21536
301-746-7049

Black Ankle Vineyards
Sarah O'Herron & Ed Boyce
14463 Black Ankle Road
Mt. Airy, MD 21771
240-464-3280 or 301-829-3338
www.blackankle.com
Risotto with Fresh Greens
  and Basil, 51

The Black Olive Restaurant
Pauline & Stelios Spiliadis
814 S. Bond Street
Baltimore, MD 21231
410-522-7292 or
443-891-3209
www.theblackolive.com
Rockfish Kabobs in Classic
  Greek Marinade, 128

Boordy Vineyards, Inc.
12820 Long Green Pike
Hydes, MD 21082
410-592-5015
www.boordy.com

Brome Howard Inn
Lisa & Michael Kelley
18281 Rosecroft Road
St. Mary's City, MD 20686
301-866-0656
info@bromehowardinn.com
www.bromhowardinn.com
Eggs Florentine, 42
Grilled Confetti Rockfish, 66

Broom's Bloom
Kate & David Dallum
1700 S. Fountain Green Road
Bel Air, MD 21015
410-399-2697
www.bbdairy.com
Country Sausage Breakfast
  Bake, 235
Lamb Stew, 248
Mashed Sweet Potatoes, 249

Butler's Orchard
Susan Butler
22200 Davis Mill Road
Germantown, MD 20876
301-972-3299
www.butlersorchard.com
Spiced Pumpkin Bread, 217

Café des Artistes
Karleen & Loïc Jaffres
41655 Fenwick Street
Leonardtown, MD 20650
301-997-0500
www.cafedesartistes.ws
Crab Imperial Café des
  Artistes, 187
Oysters Café des Artistes, 188

Calvert's Gift Farm
Jack & Becky Gurley
16813 Yeoho Rd
Sparks, MD 21152
410-472-6764
giftcal@aol.com
Spring Greens Nests with
  Fontina Cheese, 33
Creamy Kohlrabi Slaw, 162

Cantler's Riverside Inn
Daniel Donnelly
458 Forest Beach Road
Annapolis, MD 21409
410-757-1311
www.cantlers.com
Pan-fried Maryland Soft-shell
  Crabs with Lemon, Capers,
  and Herbs, 58

Captain's Table
2 15th Street
Ocean City, MD 21842
410-289-7192
http://massarosrestaurants.
com/captainstable

Catoctin Mountain Orchard
Harry Black
15036 North Franklinville Rd
Thurmont, MD 21788
301-271-2737
http://catoctinmountain
orchard.com

Chapel's Country Creamery
Eric & Holly Foster
10380 Chapel Rd
Easton, MD 21601
410-820-6647
www.chapelscreamery.com
Chapel's Country Zucchini
  and Squash Casserole, 227

Circle C Oyster Ranchers Association
Richard Pelz
49944 Airedele Road
Ridge, MD 20680
301-243-8324
rich@oysterranching.com
www.oysterranching.com
Creamy Oyster Casserole, 243

Colora Orchards
Stephen Balderston
1265 Colora Road
Colora, MD 21917
410-658-4622
coloraorchards@zoom
internet.net
www.coloraorchards.com
Apple Bread, 209
Mrs. Balderston's Streusel
  Cream Peach Pie, 146

Crispens Farms and Greenhouses
Bobi Crispens
820 Generals Highway
Millersville, MD 21108
410-987-6034

Deep Creek Cellars
177 Frazee Ridge Road
Friendsville, MD 21531
301-746-4349
www.deepcreekcellars.com

Dragonfly Farms Vinegary
Claudia Nami & Susan Lewis
P.O. Box 10
Mount Airy, MD 21771
240-353-8408
www.dragonflyvinegary.com
Dragonfly Gazpacho, 98
Blue Cheese Dressing, 163

Even' Star Organic Farm
Brett Grohsgal
48322 Far Cry Road
Lexington Park, MD 20653
301-866-1412
Cucumber Salad with Asian
 Dressing, 83
Pesto Sauce with White
 Wine, 99
Roasted Turnips and
 Rutabagas, 225

Faidley Seafood
World Famous
Lexington Market
203 North Paca Street
Baltimore, MD 21201
410-727-4898
www.faidleyscrabcakes.com

Fair Hill Inn
Phil Pyle Jr.
3370 Singerly Road
Elkton, MD 21921
410-398-4187
www.fairhillinn.com
Quail with Oyster
 Stuffing, 192

Fiore Winery
Mike & Rose Fiore
3026 Whiteford Road
Pylesville, MD 21132
410-879-4007
www.fiorewinery.com

FireFly Farms
Andrea Cedro
1363 Brenneman Road
Bittinger, MD 21522
301-245-4630
andrea@fireflyfarms.us
www.fireflyfarms.com
Chèvre Croquettes on Spring
 Field Greens, 23
Wild Mushroom Tartlettes
 with Goat Cheese and
 Bacon, 34

Gardener's Gourmet
Cinda Sebastian
3201 Uniontown Road
Westminster, MD 21158
410-876-7940

Gertrude's
John Shields
10 Art Museum Drive
Baltimore, MD 21218
410-366-5512
www.gertrudesbaltimore.com
Rockfish Imperial, 62
Chesapeake Oyster Stew, 60

Godfrey's Farm
Tom & Lisa Godfrey
302 Leager Road
Sudlersville, MD
410-438-3509
www.godfreysfarm.com
Oven-roasted Asparagus
 with Toasted Almonds, 32

Greenbranch Organic Farm
Ted Wycall
5075 Nutters Cross Road
Salisbury, MD 21804
443-783-3495
www.greenbranchfarm.com

Greene's Lamb Farm
David and Nancy Greene
2014 White Hall Road
White Hall, MD 21161
410-329-6241

Greenwood Farm
Donald Burton
11224 Harford Road
Glen Arm, MD 21057
410-592-6095

Gunpowder Bison and Trading Company
Trey & Angie Lewis
1270 Monkton Road
Monkton, MD 21111
410-343-2277
www.gunpowderbison.com

Hales Farms, Inc.
Will Hales
1320 Robins Avenue
Salisbury, MD 21804
 410-749-6188

Harris Orchard
Bill Harris
1221 Lower Pindell Road
Lothian, MD 20711
301-627-0977

Michele & Jimmy Hayden
2703 Toddville Road
Toddville, MD 21672
410-397-8196
Fried Oysters, 38
Spicy Oysters with Bacon
 and Cheese, 239

Inn at Perry Cabin
Chef Mark Salter
308 Watkins Lane
St. Michaels, MD 21663
410-745-2200
www.perrycabin.com
Crab Spring Roll with Pink
 Grapefruit, Avocado, and
 Toasted Almonds, 116

Ivy Hill Farm
John Martin
13840 Smithsburg Pike
Smithsburg, MD 21783
301-824-4658
www.ivy-hill-farm.com

Jehovah-Jireh Farm
Myron & Cathy Horst
7033 Ed Sears Road
Dickerson, MD 20842
301-874-6181
www.jehovahjirehfarm.com

Larriland Farm
Larry & Polly Moore
2415 Woodbine Road
Woodbine, MD 21797
301-854-6110
www.pickyourown.com

Lohr's Orchard
3212 Snake Lane
Churchville, MD 21028
410-836-2783
www.lohrsorchard.com

Marvesta Shrimp Farms
Scott Fritze
P.O. Box J
Hurlock, MD 21643
410-943-1733
www.marvesta.com

Maryland Department of Agriculture
50 Harry S. Truman Parkway
Annapolis, MD 21401
Mark Powell
Maryland's Best
410-841-5770
www.marylandsbest.net
Noreen Eberly
Maryland Seafood
and Aquaculture
410-841-5820
www.marylandseafood.org
Solomons Island Clam
   Chowder, 30
Clams Mornay in Puff
   Pastry, 132

Maryland Wineries Association
Kevin Atticks
22 W. Padonia Road, #C236
Lutherville, MD 21093
410-252-9463
www.marylandwine.com

Meadow Brook Farm
Rebecca Thompson
5650 Hilltop Road
La Plata, MD 20646
301-934-3835

Milburn Orchards
The Milburn Family
1495 Appleton Road
Elkton, MD 21921
800-684-3000
www.milburnorchards.com

Miller Farms
The Miller Family
10140 Piscataway Road
Clinton, MD 20735
301-297-9370

Musachio Produce Farm
Michael & Anne Musachio
12522 Ridgely Road
Ridgely, MD 21660
410-634-2044

One Straw Farm
Joan & Drew Norman
19718 Kirkwood Shop Road
White Hall, MD 21161
410-343-1828
joan@onestrawfarm.com
www.onestrawfarm.com
Arugula and Nectarine
   Salad, 91
Arugula Pesto, 32
Fattoush Salad, 92
Sweet and Savory Beet
   Soup with Orange Juice
   and Yogurt, 28

Queen Anne Farm
The Brady Family
18102 Central Avenue
Mitchellville, MD 20716
301-249-2427
www.queenannefarm.com

Quigley Farm
Todd & Amy Hanna Steiner
2614 Whiteford Road
Whiteford, MD 21160
410-452-5568

Raley's Town and Country Market
13270 Point Lookout Road
Ridge, MD 20680
301-872-5121
Southern Maryland
   Stuffed Ham, 256

Rinehart Orchards
JD Rinehart
14511 Rinehart Road
Smithsburg, MD 21783
301-824-2045
www.rinehartorchards.com

Roseda Beef
Mike Brannon
15620 Carroll Road
Monkton, MD 21111
410-962-5530
mike@roseda.com
www.rosedabeef.com

Flank Steak Salad with Mixed
   Spring Greens and Ranch
   Dressing, 70
Grilled Sirloin Tip Roast
   with Coffee Spice Rub, 135

Rumbleway Farm
Robin Way
592 McCauley Road
Conowingo, MD 21918
410-658-9731
www.rumblewayfarm.com
Rabbit Stew, 225
Shredded Brussels
   Sprouts, 226

Running Hare Vineyard
Mike & Barb Scarborough
150 Adelina Road
Prince Frederick, MD 20678
410-414-8486
runningharevineyard.com

S and S Maple Camp
Leo Shinholt
P.O. Box 138
Corriganville, MD 21524
301-724-1433

Sand Hill Farm
Charlene Dilworth
13095 Greensboro Road
Greensboro, MD 21639
410-482-6123

Savage River Lodge
Jan Russell & Mike Dreisbach
1600 Mt. Aetna Road
Frostburg, MD 21532
301-689-3200
jan@savageriverlodge.com
www.savageriverlodge.com
Maple-Bison Meatloaf, 252

SB Farms, Inc.
Bill Edwards
7010 Hynson Road
Hurlock, MD 21643
410-754-5821
www.sbfarmsinc.com

Seeds Savers Exchange
3094 North Winn Road
Decorah, IA 52101
563-382-5990
www.seedsavers.org

Shaw Orchards
The Shaw Family
5594 Norrisville Road
White Hall, MD 21161
410-692-2429 or 717-993-2974
www.shaworchards.com

Shlagel Farms
Russ and Eileen Shlagel
12850 Shlagel Road
Waldorf, MD 20601
301-645-4554
www.shlagelfarms.com

Spring Valley Farm
Dan & Elizabeth Derr
724 Conowingo Road
Conowingo, MD 21918
410-378-3280
www.springvalleyfarm.com

South Mountain Creamery
Abby & Tony Brusco
8305 Bolivar Road
Middletown, MD 21769
301-371-8565
www.southmountain creamery.com

Springfield Farm
David Smith
16701 Yeoho Rd
Sparks, MD 21152
410-472-0738
mail@ourspringfieldfarm.com
www.ourspringfieldfarm.com
Chicken and Dumplings, 238

Stanton's Mill
Jason Twigg
84 Casselman Road
Grantsville, MD 21536
301-895-3332

Stoney's
3939 Oyster House Road
Broomes Island, MD 20615
410-586-1888
www.stoneysseafood.com
Several locations; see website for details

Susan's on Smith Island
Susan Evans
20759 Caleb Jones Road
Ewell, MD 21824
410-425-2403
Smith Island Cake, 271

Swann Farms
J. Allen Swann
7740 Swann Lane
Owings, MD 20736
443-904-2687

Sweet Aire Farm
Art Johnson
2324 Castleton Road
Darlington, MD 21034
410-457-5683

Traders Seafood, Steak & Ale
8132 Bayside Road
Chesapeake Beach, MD 20732
301-855-0766

Twin Springs Bison Farm
5203 N. Church Street
Lineboro, MD 21102
410-239-4103

Van Dyke's Seafood
Eleanor & Roger Van Dyke
212 Franklin Street
Cambridge, MD 21613
410-228-9000
www.vandykesseafood.com
Crab Bisque, 173
Eleanor Van Dyke's Crab Cakes, 120

Victory Farm
Sarah Ruckelshaus
24420 Chestertown Road
Chestertown, MD 21620
410-778-4669

Volt Restaurant
Bryan Voltaggio
228 N. Market Street
Frederick, MD 21701
301-696-VOLT
www.voltrestaurant.com
Iberico-Red Wattle Pork with Mixed-Bean Ragout, 260

Whitmore Farm
William Morrow
10720 Dern Road
Emmitsburg, MD 21727
www.whitmorefarm.com

Woolsey Farm
Cindi & Worley Umbarger
630 Glenville Road
Churchville, MD 21028
443-807-0655

Zekiah Farm
Cindy & David Thorne
P.O. Box 784
Bryantown, MD 20617
240-216-4065
www.zekiahfarms.com

Index

Page numbers in *italics* indicate photographs.

DISHING UP®
More Delicious State Flavors from Storey

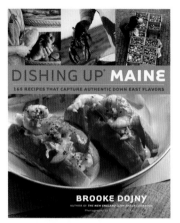

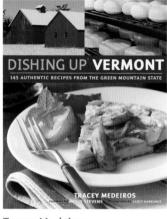

Brooke Dojny
Journey through the foodways of the Pine Tree State — from fresh seafood to blueberries and maple syrup.

Tracey Medeiros
Get an insider's view of Vermont dishes made with natural meats, fresh produce, and rich dairy products.

Dave DeWitt
Taste what fuels the Land of Enchantment, from Chipotle-Pumpkin Seed Pesto to Blue Corn Chicken Taquitos.

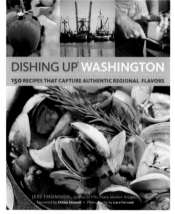

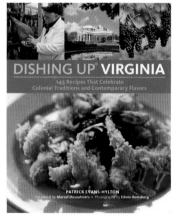

Ashley Gartland
Farm-to-table flavors shine in this collection highlighting Oregon's prized fruits, seafood, cheeses, wines, and more.

Jess Thomson
Celebrate the Evergreen State's bounty, both wild and cultivated, with recipes from many of Washington's world-class chefs.

Patrick Evans-Hylton
Colonial traditions mingle with contemporary flavors in this gastro celebration of the Old Dominion state.

Join the conversation. Share your experience with this book, learn more about Storey Publishing's authors, and read original essays and book excerpts at storey.com.
Look for our books wherever quality books are sold or by calling 800-441-5700.